Memorable Quotations of

John F. Kennedy

Memorable Quotations of
John F. Kennedy

Compiled by

Maxwell Meyersohn

Thomas Y. Crowell Company

New York / Established 1834

To the memory of my mother and father

Preface

The purpose of this volume is to serve as a guide to the views of John F. Kennedy on a wide variety of matters, foreign and domestic, expressed during the presidential election of 1960 and in the course of his duties and functions in the White House.

The quotations were selected from the late President's remarks at meetings, ceremonies, and press conferences; his official statements and messages; and his public addresses, including his acceptance speech at the Democratic National Convention of 1960, his campaign speeches, the inaugural address, and the speech he was to have delivered in Dallas on November 22, 1963.

The chief sources of the selections are *The Speeches of Senator John F. Kennedy—Presidential Campaign of 1960*, Part 1 of Senate Report 994, the final report of the Committee on Commerce on Freedom of Communications, U.S. Government Printing Office, 1961; *Public Papers of the Presidents of the United States: John F. Kennedy* (3 vols., 1961, 1962, 1963), U.S. Government Printing Office, 1962, 1963, 1964; and White House press releases and presidential messages and reports to the Congress. Informal and extemporaneous remarks were also collected from news accounts, principally those in *The New York Times* and the *Washington Post*.

I am grateful to the staff of the Thomas Y. Crowell Company, especially Mr. Edward Tripp and Mr. Patrick Barrett, for their help in the preparation of this book.

Contents

Part II
The Affairs of the Nation

Let us carry forward the plans and programs of John Fitzgerald Kennedy, not because of our sorrow or sympathy, but because they are right.

With his memory and spirit to inspire us, with his words and works to guide us, we shall live up to his trust. We shall finish his fight.

PRESIDENT LYNDON B. JOHNSON

Memorable Quotations of

John F. Kennedy

Part I

The World
in Crisis

I

Freedom vs.
Totalitarianism

Mortal Struggle

1 / A CRUCIAL JUNCTURE

Our world is near the climax of an historic convulsion. A tidal wave of national independence has nearly finished its sweep through lands which contain one out of every three people in the world. The industrial and scientific revolution is spreading to the far corners of the earth. And two irreconcilable views of the value, the rights and the role of the individual human being confront the peoples of the world.

Message to Congress on foreign aid, April 2, 1963

2 / CONVULSIVE ERA

Abroad, the balance of power is shifting. There are new and more terrible weapons—new and uncertain nations—new pressures of population and deprivation.

Acceptance speech, Democratic National Convention, Los Angeles, July 15, 1960

3 / WORLD STRUGGLE

Across the face of the globe freedom and communism are locked in a deadly embrace.

Campaign address, Zembo Mosque Temple, Harrisburg, Pa., Sept. 15, 1960

4 / NATURE OF THE CONTEST

This is a contest of nerve and will. The next 10, 15, or 20 years may determine the outcome. The Soviet system and our system are on trial. The question will be, which system has the longest staying power? Which can maintain itself in good times and bad? Which can serve as an inspiration to people around the world? Do they want to move with them or with us? Khrushchev and the President of the United States only personify the two sides. The real question is, which system and which people have the power, the will, the determination and the conviction? I think we do.

Campaign remarks, North Tonawanda, N.Y., Sept. 28, 1960

5 / "ONLY THE STRONG"

The complacent, the self-indulgent, the soft societies are about to be swept away with the debris of history. Only the strong, only the industrious, only the determined, only the courageous, only the visionary who determine the real nature of our struggle can possibly survive.

Address, American Society of Newspaper Editors, Washington, D.C., April 20, 1961

6 / FREEDOM'S WEAPON: SELF-DISCIPLINE

If the self-discipline of the free cannot match the iron discipline of the mailed fist, in economic, political, scientific and all the other kinds of struggles as well as the military, then the peril to freedom will continue to rise.

Ibid.

7 / A LONG HARD FIGHT

Basically they [the Communists] believe that the United States lacks the nerve, the will, and the determination for a long, long hard fight. It is one thing to stand up to a military invasion, it is one thing to go to war and defeat the Japanese and Hitler. It is quite another thing, year after year, decade after decade, to be engaged in struggles all around the world, in countries which we did not know anything about 10 years ago.

Campaign address, American Legion Convention, Miami Beach, Oct. 18, 1960

8 / LESS OBVIOUS WARFARE

The struggle today is less obvious, less immediate, than it was in World War II or in the days of the Korean war. But, nevertheless, the struggle

goes on—a great worldwide battle as to whether the Communist or the
free world is ultimately going to prevail, whether we are going to succeed or whether our enemy is going to succeed.

> Campaign address via telephone to AMVET Convention, Miami Beach, Aug. 26,
> 1960

9 / COLD WAR

The mere absence of war is not peace.

> State of the Union Message, Jan. 14, 1963

10 / COMMUNIST EMPIRE

Today . . . the Kremlin rules a ruthless empire stretching in a great half
circle from East Berlin to the Vietminh.

> Campaign address, Mormon Tabernacle, Salt Lake City, Sept. 23, 1960

11 / ASIA

In Asia, the relentless pressures of the Chinese Communists menace the
security of the entire area—from the borders of India and South Vietnam
to the jungles of Laos, struggling to protect its newly won independence.

> State of the Union Message, Jan. 30, 1961

12 / THE DANGER

The reality of danger is that all free men and nations live under the constant threat of the Communist advance. Although presently in some disarray, the Communist apparatus controls more than one billion people, and
it daily confronts Europe and the United States with hundreds of missiles,
scores of divisions and the purposes of domination.

> News conference, Washington, D.C., Jan. 24, 1963

13 / TOUGH QUESTION

The hard, tough question for the next decade . . . is whether a free society with its freedom of choice, its breadth of opportunity, its range of
alternatives, can meet the single-minded advance of the Communists. Can
a nation organized and governed such as ours endure? Can we carry
through at an age where never before we will witness not only new development of weapons not only of destruction, but also a race for mas-
tery of the sky and the rain, the ocean and the tides, the far side of space,
and the inside of men's minds.

> Campaign remarks, Memphis, Sept. 21, 1960

14 / AMERICAN SPIRITUAL SUPREMACY

In one area the Communists can never overcome us—unless we fall back to their level—and that is the area of spiritual values—moral strength— the strength of our will and our purpose—the qualities and traditions that make this nation a shining example to all who yearn to be free.

This is our single greatest advantage. For this is not a struggle for supremacy of arms alone—it is also a struggle for supremacy between two conflicting ideologies: freedom under God versus ruthless, godless tyranny. The contest, moreover, is not merely to gain the material wealth of other nations—it is a contest for their hearts and minds. And the challenge to all Americans now is not merely the extent of our material contribution as taxpayers—but the extent to which we can find greater strength for the long pull in our traditions of religious liberty than the masters of the Kremlin can ever exact from disciplines of servitude.

Campaign address, Mormon Tabernacle, Salt Lake City, Sept. 23, 1960

15 / THE BASIC CLASH

Since the close of the Second World War, a global civil war has divided and tormented mankind. But it is not our military might, or our higher standard of living, that has most distinguished us from our adversaries. It is our belief that the state is the servant of the citizen and not its master. This basic clash of ideas and wills is but one of the forces reshaping our globe—swept as it is by the tides of hope and fear, by crises in the headlines today that become mere footnotes tomorrow.

State of the Union Message, Jan. 11, 1962

16 / THE ISSUE

The central issue is between those who believe in self-determination and those in the East who would impose upon others the harsh and repressive Communist system.

Address to Irish Parliament, Dublin, June 28, 1963

17 / COERCION VS. FREEDOM

As the older colonialism recedes, and the neocolonialism of the Communist Powers stands out more starkly than ever, they [the developing and nonaligned nations] realize more clearly that the issue in the world struggle is not communism versus capitalism, but coercion versus free choice.

State of the Union Message, Jan. 14, 1963

18 / THE DIVISIVE ISSUE

If there is a single issue in the world that divides the world it is independence—the independence of Berlin, or Laos, or Vietnam; the longing for independence behind the Iron Curtain, the peaceful transition to independence in those newly emerging areas whose troubles some hope to exploit.

Address, Independence Hall, Philadelphia, July 4, 1962

19 / MOUNTING CRISES

Each day the crises multiply. Each day their solution grows more difficult. Each day we draw nearer the hour of maximum danger, as weapons spread and hostile forces grow stronger. . . . Our analyses . . . make it clear that—in each of these principal areas of crisis—the tide of events has been running out and time has not been our friend.

State of the Union Message, Jan. 30, 1961

20 / COMMUNISM'S CHALLENGE TO FREEDOM

The challenge is not to us alone. It is a challenge to every nation which asserts its sovereignty under a system of liberty. It is a challenge to all those who want a world of free choice. It is a special challenge to the Atlantic community—the heartland of human freedom.

Address to the nation on the Berlin crisis, Washington, D.C., July 25, 1961

21 / "THE GREAT THREAT TO PEACE"

Where we feel the difficulty comes is the effort by the Soviet Union to communize, in a sense, the entire world. If the Soviet Union were merely seeking to protect its own national interests, to protect its own national security, and would permit other countries to live as they wish—to live in peace—then I believe that the problems which now cause so much tension would fade away.

We want the people of the Soviet Union to live in peace—we want the same for our own people. It is this effort to push outward the Communist system, on to country after country, that represents, I think, the great threat to peace.

Interview by Aleksei I. Adzhubei, Washington, D.C., Nov. 25, 1961

22 / COMMUNIST AMBITIONS

Our greatest challenge is still the world that lies beyond the cold war—but the first great obstacle is still our relations with the Soviet Union and

Communist China. We must never be lulled into believing that either power has yielded its ambitions for world domination—ambitions which they forcefully restated only a short time ago.

State of the Union Message, Jan. 30, 1961

23 / MR. KHRUSHCHEV

Mr. Khrushchev is not a fool. . . . He is shrewd, he is vigorous, he is informed, and he is competent. He is not putting on an act when he talks about the inevitable triumph of the Communist system, for this is what he believes, and this is what he is determined to achieve, and this is what we in this nation are equally determined to prevent.

Campaign address, Pikesville, Md., Sept. 16, 1960

24 / COMMUNISM A TOUGH ENEMY

This is no ordinary enemy and this is no ordinary struggle. Extraordinary efforts are called for by every American who knows the value of freedom and who believes that this country still has its greatest contributions to make to that cause.

Campaign address, Washington, D.C., Sept. 20, 1960

25 / NO SHORTCUTS

We must recognize there are no shortcuts, no easy way, no overnight, weekend meetings, which will bring a change in the balance of power in the world.

Campaign remarks, Providence, Nov. 7, 1960

26 / THE SAME PRICE

It is . . . possible to lose a war, especially a cold war, without firing a single shot on either side. But defeat in the cold war would be just as catastrophic as if it were suffered on the battlefields, for the price of defeat in both contests is slavery.

Campaign message to the nation's new voters, Washington, D.C., Oct. 5, 1960

27 / LONG DAYS AHEAD

I know that sometimes we get impatient, we wish for some immediate action that would end our perils. But I must tell you that there is no quick and easy solution. The Communists control over a billion people, and they recognize that if we should falter, their success would be imminent.

We must look to long days ahead, which if we are courageous and persevering can bring us what we all desire.

> Address to the nation on the Berlin crisis, Washington, D.C., July 25, 1961

28 / THE COMMUNIST DANGER CONTINUES

At many points around the globe, the Communists are continuing their effort to exploit weakness and poverty. Their concentration of nuclear and conventional arms must still be deterred. The familiar contest between choice and coercion, the familiar places of danger and conflict are all still there—in Cuba, in Southeast Asia, in Berlin, and all around the globe, still requiring all the strength and the vigilance that we can muster.

> Address to the nation on the Nuclear Test Ban Treaty, Washington, D.C., July 26, 1963

Freedom: Foundation of the Western Ethic

29 / FREEDOM

Freedom is not merely a word or an abstract theory, but the most effective instrument for advancing the welfare of man.

> Message to the Inter-American Economic and Social Conference, Punta del Este, Uruguay, Aug. 5, 1961

30 / FREEDOM INDIVISIBLE

If men and women are in chains, anywhere in the world, then freedom is endangered everywhere.

> Campaign statement, Washington, D.C., Pulaski Day, Oct. 2, 1960

31 / UNIVERSAL CONCERN

Unless liberty flourishes in all lands, it cannot flourish in one.

> Address, Paulskirche, Frankfurt, West Germany, June 25, 1963

32 / POWERFUL IDEA

We can proudly say that no secular idea has taken such a powerful hold on man's imagination as the idea of democracy which has gone forth from this hemisphere.

> Address, El Bosque housing project, San José, Costa Rica, March 19, 1963

33 / PEOPLE FIRST

We hold the view that the people come first, not the government.

Campaign remarks, Greensboro, N.C., Sept. 17, 1960

34 / NEVER A WALL

Freedom has many difficulties and democracy is not perfect. But we have never had to put a wall up to keep our people in, to prevent them from leaving us.

Address, City Hall, West Berlin, June 26, 1963

35 / AMERICAN GENESIS

It was the American Revolution—not the Russian—which began man's struggle for national independence and individual liberty.

Campaign address, National Council of Women, New York City, Oct. 12, 1960

36 / SAME REVOLUTIONARY BELIEFS AT ISSUE

The world is very different now. For man holds in his mortal hands the power to abolish all forms of human poverty and all forms of human life. And yet the same revolutionary beliefs for which our forebears fought are still at issue around the globe—the belief that the rights of man come not from the generosity of the state but from the hand of God.

Inaugural address, Jan. 20, 1961

37 / THE CHIEF WEAPONS OF FREEDOM

In a world which continues to face unprecedented difficulties, the values of the American Revolution are an incalculable asset to our country. Your forefathers fought for the principles embodied in the Declaration of Independence—the right of a people to revolt against tyranny. At a time when great ideological systems lock in combat for the minds and hearts of mankind, these weapons remain the chief weapons in our arsenal.

Message to the 72nd Continental Congress of the Daughters of the American Revolution, Washington, D.C., April 15, 1963

38 / INDESTRUCTIBLE YEARNING

Dictatorship can suppress but cannot destroy the aspirations of a people to live in freedom, dignity and peace.

Statement on political situation in the Dominican Republic, Palm Beach, Fla., Dec. 20, 1961

39 / IRREVERSIBLE TREND

The one great irreversible trend in the history of the world is on the side of liberty—and we, for all time to come, are on the same side.

Address, Democratic Party dinner, Los Angeles, Nov. 18, 1961

40 / MAJORITY FOR FREEDOM

I hold the view that the tide and history can move with us, that those people who desire to be free outnumber those who are willing to sell their lives to the Communist system.

Campaign remarks, Fairborn, Ohio, Oct. 17, 1960

41 / UNIVERSALLY INFECTIOUS

Even in areas behind the curtain, that which Jefferson called "the disease of liberty" still appears to be infectious.

Address, Independence Hall, Philadelphia, July 4, 1962

42 / FREEDOM NON-NEGOTIABLE

While we shall negotiate freely, we will never negotiate freedom. Our answer to the classic question of Patrick Henry is still no. Life is not so dear and peace is not so precious "as to be purchased at the price of chains and slavery." And that is our answer, even though, for the first time since the ancient battles between Greek city-states, war entails the threat of total annihilation, of everything we know, of society itself. For to save mankind's future freedom, we must face up to any risk that is necessary. We will always seek peace—but we will never surrender.

Address, University of Washington, Seattle, Nov. 16, 1961

43 / ETERNALLY NEW

It is freedom that is new, and despotism and tyranny that is as old as civilization is—and it is freedom that will win—not because of any law of history—but because we will have the strength and the determination that will bring the victory.

Campaign address, Raleigh, N.C., Sept. 17, 1960

44 / INTERNATIONAL DEMOCRACY

My country favors a world of free and equal states.

Address, U.N. General Assembly, Sept. 25, 1961

45 / IRRESISTIBLE FORCE

The desire to be free of foreign rule—the desire for self-determination—is the most powerful force in the modern world. It has destroyed old empires—created scores of new nations—and redrawn the maps of Asia, the Middle East, and Africa. America must be on the side of man's right to govern himself, because these are our historic principles—because the ultimate triumph of nationalism is inevitable—and because nationalism is the one force with the strength and endurance to threaten the integrity of the Communist empire itself.

> Campaign address, National Council of Women, New York City, Oct. 12, 1960

46 / INFINITE CAPACITY

No area of the world has ever had an overabundance of democracy and freedom.

> Campaign address, Zionists of America Convention, New York City, Aug. 26, 1960

47 / FREE CHOICE FOR ALL

Let us . . . apply the principle of free choice and the practice of free plebiscites in every part of the globe.

> Address, U.N. General Assembly, Sept. 25, 1961

48 / FREEDOM TO DISSENT

The unity of freedom has never relied on uniformity of opinion.

> State of the Union Message, Jan. 14, 1963

49 / FREEDOM TO KNOW AND TO JUDGE

We seek a free flow of information across national boundaries and oceans, across iron curtains and stone walls. We are not afraid to entrust the American people with unpleasant facts, foreign ideas, alien philosophies and competitive values. For a nation that is afraid to let its people judge the truth and falsehood in an open market is a nation that is afraid of its people.

> Remarks to Voice of America employees on the Voice's 20th anniversary, Washington, D.C., Feb. 26, 1962

50 / FREEDOM TO LEARN MAKES A FREE WORLD

The pursuit of knowledge itself implies a world where men are free to follow out the logic of their own ideas. It implies a world where nations are free to solve their own problems and to realize their own ideals. It implies, in short, a world where collaboration emerges from the voluntary decisions of nations strong in their own independence and in their own self-respect. It implies, I believe, the kind of world which is emerging before our eyes—the world produced by the revolution of national independence which is today, and has been since 1945, sweeping across the world.

Address, Berkeley Division of the University of California, March 23, 1962

51 / TIDE TOWARD FREEDOM

There used to be so much talk a few years ago about the inevitable triumph of communism. We hear such talk much less now. No one who examines the modern world can doubt that the great currents of history are carrying the world away from the monolithic idea toward the pluralistic idea—away from communism and toward national independence and freedom. No one can doubt that the wave of the future is not the conquest of the world by a single dogmatic creed but the liberation of the diverse energies of free nations and free men.

Ibid.

52 / INITIATIVE

We must . . . act to spread freedom as well as to react against the spread of communism.

Campaign address, Raleigh, N.C., Sept. 17, 1960

Communism: Instrument of Tyranny

53 / ALL-POWERFUL COMMUNIST STATE

We face an adversary who moblizes all of the resources of the state for the service of the state.

Campaign remarks, Norristown, Pa., Oct. 29, 1960

54 / COMMUNIST DEVICES

What we find to be objectionable and a threat to the peace, is when a system is imposed by a small militant group by subversion, infiltration, and all the rest.

Interview by Aleksei I. Adzhubei, Washington, D.C., Nov. 25, 1961

55 / TYRANNY'S WEAPONS

We possess weapons of tremendous power, but they are least effective in combating the weapons most often used by freedom's foes: subversion, infiltration and civil disorder.

Address, University of Washington, Seattle, Nov. 16, 1961

56 / SCAVENGER

Communism has sometimes succeeded as a scavenger, but never as a leader. It has never come to power in any country that was not disrupted by war or internal repression or both.

Address, North Atlantic Treaty Organization headquarters, Naples, July 3, 1963

57 / OUTMODED SYSTEM

Rejecting reform and diversity in freedom, the Communists cannot reconcile their ambitions for domination with other men's ambition for freedom. It is clear that this system is outmoded and doomed to failure.

Ibid.

58 / GOAL: MONOLITHIC WORLD

The Communists rest everything on the idea of a monolithic world—a world where all knowledge has a single pattern, all societies move toward a single model, all problems and roads have a single solution, and a single destination.

Address, Berkeley Division of the University of California, March 23, 1962

59 / CHURCH AND STATE

Here in our land church and state are separate and free—in their lands neither is free, and the church lives in constant fear of the state.

Campaign address, Mormon Tabernacle, Salt Lake City, Sept. 23, 1960

60 / DISCREDITED DOCTRINE

There are those who tell us that the only road to economic progress is violent Communist revolution, followed by the complete subjection of man to the will of the state. They come with banners proclaiming that they have new doctrines, that history is on their side. But in reality, they bring a doctrine which is as old as the Pharaohs of Egypt and as the Pharaohs of Egypt is doomed by history.

Address at state dinner, San Carlos Palace, Bogotá, Colombia, Dec. 17, 1961

61 / THE COMMUNIST WAY

What you get is a denial of liberty, the class struggle, the rifle squads, and it seems to me you get no commensurate economic progress.

Exchange with Brazilian university students, Washington, D.C., July 31, 1962

62 / INHERENT WEAKNESS

A police state finds it cannot command the grain to grow.

State of the Union Message, Jan. 14, 1963

63 / REGIMENTATION OF LABOR

Nothing more exactly identifies the totalitarian or closed society than the rigid and, more often than not, brutish direction of labor at all levels.

Manpower report to Congress, March 11, 1963

64 / LABOR UNDER COMMUNISM

It's no accident that there has not been a strike in the Soviet Union for thirty, or thirty-five, or forty years. And Communists who in Latin America, or Africa, or Asia, say that they represent the people cannot possibly, under any rule of reason or debate, say that a labor movement is free when it is not able to express its rights, not only in relationship to the employer but also to speak out and recognize the limitations of governmental power.

Address, AFL-CIO Convention, Miami, Dec. 7, 1961

65 / COMMUNIST PROMISES

They promise free elections and free speech and freedom of religion. But once power is achieved, elections are eliminated, speech is stifled and the worship of God is prohibited. They pledge economic progress and increased human welfare. But they are unable to fulfill these pledges and their failure is etched in the dramatic contrast between a free, powerful and prosperous Western Europe and the grim, drab poverty of Communist Eastern Europe. Whenever such doctrines have had to face the united will of free men they have been defeated, and they will be defeated again in our time.

Address at state dinner, San Carlos Palace, Bogotá, Colombia, Dec. 17, 1961

66 / COMMUNIST WALLS

It is our adversaries who must build walls to contain their people.

Address, University of Costa Rica, San José, March 20, 1963

67 / THE BERLIN WALL

All the world knows that no successful system builds a wall to keep its people in and freedom out—and that the wall of shame dividing Berlin is a symbol of Communist failure.

State of the Union Message, Jan. 14, 1963

68 / COMMUNIST COLONIALISM

Colonialism in its harshest forms is not only the exploitation of new nations by old, of dark skins by light, or the subjugation of the poor by the rich. My nation was once a colony, and we know what colonialism means: the exploitation and subjugation of the weak by the powerful, of the many by the few, of the governed who have given no consent to be governed, whatever their discontent, their class or their color. And that is why there is no ignoring the fact that the tide of self-determination has not yet reached the Communist empire where a population far larger than that officially termed "dependent" lives under governments installed by foreign troops instead of free institutions, under a system which knows only one party and one belief, which suppresses free debate and free elections, and free newspapers, and free books, and free trade unions and which builds a wall to keep truth a stranger and its own citizens prisoners.

Address, U.N. General Assembly, Sept. 25, 1961

69 / THE ENEMY

Mr. Khrushchev—while he may symbolize and personify our danger—is not the enemy. Defeating Mr. Khrushchev in debate does not defeat the enemy. For the enemy is the Communist system itself—implacable, insatiable, unceasing in its drive for world domination.

Campaign address, Mormon Tabernacle, Salt Lake City, Sept. 23, 1960

70 / COMMUNIST INTRANSIGENCE

I foresee no spectacular reversal in Communist methods or goals.

State of the Union Message, Jan. 14, 1963

71 / COMMUNIST UNANIMITY ON ULTIMATE GOAL

What comfort can we take from the increasing strains and tensions within the Communist bloc? Here hope must be tempered with caution. For the Soviet-Chinese disagreement is over means, not ends. A dispute over how to bury the West is no ground for Western rejoicing.

Ibid.

72 / COMMUNIST CHINA: POTENTIAL THREAT

We assess its power at 700,000,000 people increasing at 14,000,000 or 15,000,000 a year, surrounded by countries which are in every case but one much smaller, which are faced with very difficult geographic and social problems, which do not have a strong national history, so that we find a great powerful force in China organized and directed by the Government along Stalinist lines surrounded by weaker countries. So this we regard as a menacing situation. In addition . . . that Government is not only Stalinist in internal actions but also has called for war, international war, in order to advance the final success of the Communist cause. We regard that as a menacing factor.

And then, you introduce into that mix nuclear weapons and . . . it may take some years, maybe a decade before they become a full-fledged nuclear power, but . . . we're going to be around in the Nineteen Seventies and we would like to take some steps now which would lessen that prospect that a future President might have to deal with.

I would regard that combination, if it is still in existence in the Nineteen Seventies, of weak countries around it, 700,000,000 people, Stalinist Government and a nuclear power and a Government determined on war as a means of bringing about its ultimate success, as potentially a more dangerous situation than any we've faced since the end of the second war.

News conference, Washington, D.C., Aug. 1, 1963

73 / COMMUNIST CHINA'S AGGRESSIVE POLICIES

When the Red Chinese indicate a desire to live at peace with the United States, with other countries surrounding it, then quite obviously the

United States would reappraise its policies. We are not wedded to a policy of hostility to Red China. It seems to me Red China's policies are what create the tension between not only the United States and Red China but between Red China and India, between Red China and her immediate neighbors to the South, and even between Red China and other Communist countries.

News conference, Washington, D.C., Nov. 14, 1963

America: Chief Defender of Freedom

74 / BEST DOCTRINE

We preach the best doctrine ever known, the equality of man, the Government gets consent from the governed, and that everyone is entitled to life, liberty, and the pursuit of happiness, and we will maintain that position.

Campaign address, Syria Mosque, Pittsburgh, Oct. 10, 1960

75 / IMAGE OF LIBERTY

We want to make sure that the United States, which has always stood for freedom, continues to be identified . . . as a revolutionary country, believing in the most drastic doctrine that mankind has ever known, government by the consent of the governed.

Campaign remarks, Battle Creek, Mich., Oct. 14, 1960

76 / TRULY REVOLUTIONARY

. . . we fight for . . . the most revolutionary of all doctrines, the right of people to be free.

Campaign address, Tampa, Oct. 18, 1960

77 / DEMOCRACY'S BUSINESS

The unfinished business of this society is the maintenance of freedom here and around the world.

Campaign remarks, Minneapolis, Oct. 1, 1960

78 / AMERICAN TASK

Our task is to pursue a policy of patiently encouraging freedom and carefully pressuring tyranny—a policy that looks toward evolution, not revolution—a policy that depends on peace, not war.

Campaign remarks, Polish-American Congress, Chicago, Oct. 1, 1960

79 / DEVOTION TO HUMAN RIGHTS

Let the word go forth from this time and place, to friend and foe alike, that the torch has been passed to a new generation of Americans—born in this century, tempered by war, disciplined by a hard and bitter peace, proud of our ancient heritage—and unwilling to witness or permit the slow undoing of those human rights to which this nation has always been committed, and to which we are committed today at home and around the world.

    Inaugural address, Jan. 20, 1961

80 / OUR GOAL

Our basic goal remains the same: a peaceful world community of free and independent states—free to choose their own future and their own system so long as it does not threaten the freedom of others.

    Some may choose forms and ways that we would not choose for ourselves, but it is not for us that they are choosing. We can welcome diversity—the Communists cannot. For we offer a world of choice, and they offer a world of coercion. And the way of the past shows clearly that freedom, not coercion, is the wave of the future.

    State of the Union Message, Jan. 11, 1962

81 / FREE CHOICE

The United States supports the idea that every people shall have the right to make a free choice as to the kind of government they want.

    Interview by Aleksei I. Adzhubei, Washington, D.C., Nov. 25, 1961

82 / SELF-RULE

This nation is committed to the principle of self-determination and will continue to support and encourage responsible self-rule throughout the world and particularly in those territories under the jurisdiction of the United States.

    Letter to Congress on proposed legislation granting greater self-rule to the Virgin Islands, April 6, 1962

83 / NATIONAL SELF-INTEREST

We must recognize that every nation determines its policies in terms of its own interests.

    Address, Mormon Tabernacle, Salt Lake City, Sept. 26, 1963

84 / EXPORT OF FREEDOM

The future peace of the world depends upon our carrying abroad this concept of freedom and of equality, which we know will prevail over all the doctrines of dictatorship and totalitarianism, wherever the two are free to compete in the marketplace of public opinion.

Campaign statement on Citizenship Day, Washington, D.C., Sept. 17, 1960

85 / FREEDOM'S SUSTAINER

As long as the United States lives, so freedom lives. As long as we build our strength, as long as we are on the move, as long as we are a progressive society, then the future belongs to us and not to Mr. Khrushchev.

Campaign remarks, Hamtramck, Mich., Oct. 26, 1960

86 / PREDICTION FOR FREEDOM

Mr. Khrushchev says with confidence that our children and grandchildren will be Communists. I think we should say with the same confidence that his children will be free.

Campaign address, Michigan State Fair, Detroit, Oct. 26, 1960

87 / "WE SHALL PAY ANY PRICE"

Let every nation know, whether it wishes us well or ill, that we shall pay any price, bear any burden, meet any hardship, support any friend, oppose any foe, in order to assure the survival and the success of liberty.

Inaugural address, Jan. 20, 1961

88 / FREEDOM'S LEADER

Our strength as well as our convictions have imposed upon this nation the role of leader in freedom's cause. No role in history could be more difficult or more important. We stand for freedom. That is our conviction for ourselves—that is our only commitment to others. No friend, no neutral and no adversary should think otherwise. We are not against any man—or any nation—or any system—except as it is hostile to freedom.

Message to Congress on urgent national needs, May 25, 1961

89 / "BORN OF REVOLUTION"

We stand, as we have always stood from our earliest beginnings, for the independence and equality of all nations. This nation was born of revolu-

tion and raised in freedom. And we do not intend to leave an open road
for despotism.

Ibid.

90 / PRIVILEGED GENERATION

In the long history of the world, only a few generations have been
granted the role of defending freedom in its hour of maxium danger. I
do not shrink from this responsibility—I welcome it. I do not believe that
any of us would exchange places with any other people or any other generation. The energy, the faith, the devotion which we bring to this endeavor will light our country and all who serve it—and the glow from
that fire can truly light the world.

Inaugural address, Jan. 20, 1961

91 / THIS GENERATION'S RESPONSIBILITY

Our generation of Americans must meet its responsibility, not only to
ourselves, but to all those who wish to trod on freedom's road.

Campaign address, Columbia, S.C., Oct. 10, 1960

92 / COMMITMENT TO LEADERSHIP

Today this nation, conceived in a revolution, nurtured in liberty, matur-
ing in independence, has no intention of abdicating its leadership in that
worldwide movement for independence to any nation or society committed to systematic human oppression.

Address, Independence Hall, Philadelphia, July 4, 1962

93 / PACESETTER FOR THE FREE WORLD

This, for the American people, is a time for vision, for patience, for work
and for wisdom. For better or worse, we are the pacesetters. Freedom's
leader cannot flag or falter, or another runner will set the pace.

Message to Congress on foreign aid, April 2, 1963

94 / LIGHTS FOR LEADERSHIP

In a world full of frustrations and irritations, America's leadership must
be guided by the lights of learning and reason.

Text of undelivered Dallas address, Nov. 22, 1963

95 / "THE BURDEN AND THE GLORY"

It is the fate of this generation . . . to live with a struggle we did not start, in a world we did not make. But the pressures of life are not always distributed by choice. And while no nation has ever faced such a challenge, no nation has ever been so ready to seize the burden and the glory of freedom.

State of the Union Message, Jan. 11, 1962

96 / HISTORY'S CHARGE

Our nation is commissioned by history to be either an observer of freedom's failure or the cause of its success.

Ibid.

97 / DEFENDER OF FREEDOM

Only the United States stands between the Communists and world domination. Therefore, we must be prepared to bear our burdens.

Campaign address, Charlotte, N.C., Sept. 17, 1960

98 / OUR PRIVILEGE

It is our obligation and our privilege to be the defenders of the gate in a time of maximum danger, to be the only hope for freedom. . . . Has any people since the time of ancient Athens ever had a comparable opportunity, a comparable responsibility?

Campaign address, Houston, Sept. 12, 1960

99 / WELCOME CHALLENGE

I welcome the chance for the United States to be the great defender of freedom at a time when freedom is meeting its most serious test.

Campaign remarks, Philadelphia, Oct. 29, 1960

100 / CENTRAL THEME OF AMERICAN POLICY

. . . we have one simple central theme of American foreign policy which all of us must recognize, because it is a policy which we must continue to follow, and that is to support the independence of nations so that one bloc cannot gain sufficient power to finally overcome us.

Address, Mormon Tabernacle, Salt Lake City, Sept. 26, 1963

101 / AMERICA'S SELF-INTEREST

The United States has rightly determined, in the years since 1945 under three different administrations, that our interest, our national security, the interest of the United States of America, is best served by preserving and protecting a world of diversity in which no one power or no one combination of powers can threaten the security of the United States. . . . That is what we have been engaged in for 18 years, to prevent that happening, to prevent any one monolithic power having sufficient force to destroy the United States.

Ibid.

102 / KEY TO WORLD FREEDOM

For the next ten or twenty years, the burdens will be placed completely upon our country for the preservation of freedom. We stand in the center and we are associated with allies, we are associated with those who are neutral, but who are friendly to us, we are associated with those who have a latent hostility to us, but all depends upon the keystone, which is the United States, and that is a sober responsibility for a country which twenty years ago prided itself on its long isolationist and neutralist tradition.

Talk to college students, White House lawn, Aug. 28, 1962

103 / STRENGTH FOR WORLD RESPONSIBILITIES

Upon our achievement of greater vitality and strength at home hang our fate and future in the world: our ability to sustain and supply the security of free men and nations; our ability to command their respect for our leadership; our ability to expand our trade without threat to our balance of payments; and our ability to adjust to the changing demands of cold war competition and challenge.

State of the Union Message, Jan. 14, 1963

104 / AMERICA'S BURDEN

It is customary, both here and around the world, to regard life in these United States as easy. Our advantages are many. But more than any other people in the world, we bear burdens and accept risks unprecedented in their size and duration, not for ourselves alone but for all who wish to be free. No other generation of free men in a single nation has ever faced so many and such difficult challenges.

Address, University of Washington, Seattle, Nov. 16, 1961

105 / UNIVERSAL CAUSE

I think in a very real sense the cause of all mankind is the cause of America.

Campaign address, VFW Convention, Detroit, Aug. 26, 1960

106 / EFFECTIVE FOREIGN POLICY

We want for other people what we want for ourselves, and I think that is the most effective foreign policy that we can carry out.

Campaign remarks, Niagara Falls, N.Y., Sept. 28, 1960

107 / STRENGTHENING THE FREE WORLD

Peace requires an America standing shoulder to shoulder with other free nations, united by close ties of commerce, friendship, and mutual respect. Americans cannot stand alone as a tiny minority in a hostile world, without friends and allies, without international effort to stem aggression from any source. But if we want the support and cooperation of others, we must earn that friendship and respect. We must consider their problems as well as ours, and joined by other free nations of the West whom we helped so greatly at the end of the Second World War, we must help strengthen the political, economic, and social independence of those countries in the bottom half of the globe who are now emerging on the road to independence, to prevent those countries from succumbing to the chaos and despair which comes with poverty, with no hope of release.

Campaign address, Democratic Women's luncheon, New York City, Sept. 14, 1960

108 / NATIONAL PURPOSE

Our national purpose is not merely to survive but to prevail. Our national purpose is not only to preserve a free society here in the United States but we also realize that there cannot be a free society here unless there is a free world.

Campaign address via telephone to AMVET Convention, Miami Beach, Aug. 26, 1960

109 / DEMANDS OF LEADERSHIP

Only an America which is strong and developing, only an America which is using its own resources to the maximum, only an America which is rebuilding its cities and distributing its food in a way that benefits our people and the free world, only an America which has a strength second to none, can lead the free world.

Campaign remarks, Nashville, Tenn., Sept. 21, 1960

110 / BEST AID TO THE DEVELOPING NATIONS

Nothing we could do to help the developing countries would help them half as much as a booming American economy, which consumes their raw materials. And nothing our opponents could do to encourage their own ambitions would encourage them half so much as a lagging U.S. economy.

State of the Union Message, Jan. 14, 1963

111 / TOTAL EFFORT

Only an America which is applying its full resources of imagination and thought and strength to the resolution of the world's great problems— only such an America will be able to maintain its position as the champion of peace and the protector of freedom everywhere.

Campaign address, Raleigh, N.C., Sept. 17, 1960

112 / RESOURCES

America has the human and material resources to meet the demands of national security and the obligations of world leadership while at the same time advancing well-being at home.

Message to Congress on the American economy, Feb. 2, 1961

113 / A SINGLE GOAL

[The] various elements in our foreign policy lead . . . to a single goal— the goal of a peaceful world of free and independent states.

This is our guide for the present and our vision for the future—a free community of nations, independent but interdependent, uniting north and south, east and west, in one great family of man, outgrowing and transcending the hates and fears that rend our age.

We will not reach that goal today or tomorrow. We may not reach it in our lifetime. But the quest is the great adventure of our century. We sometimes chafe at the burdens of our obligations, the complexity of our decisions, the agony of our choices, but there is no comfort or security for us in evasion, no relief in irresponsibility.

State of the Union Message, Jan. 11, 1962

114 / AMERICAN INTEREST IN THE SELF-DETERMINATION OF NEW NATIONS

Since the close of World War II, a worldwide declaration of independence has transformed nearly 1 billion people and 9 million square miles into 42 free and independent states. Less than 2 percent of the world's population now lives in "dependent" territories. . . . Within the limits of our responsibilities in such matters, my country intends to be a participant and not merely an observer, in the peaceful, expeditious movement of nations from the status of colonies to the partnership of equals. That continuing tide of self-determination, which runs so strong, has our sympathy and our support.

Address, U.N. General Assembly, Sept. 25, 1961

115 / PRIDE IN LEADERSHIP

. . . only the United States, and our power and strength and commitment, permits dozens of countries scattered all over the world to maintain their freedom. . . . Other countries look to their own interests. Only the United States . . . bears this kind of burden.

Remarks at dinner honoring Sen. Carl Hayden, Phoenix, Ariz., Nov. 17, 1961

116 / AMERICA'S COMMITMENT TO EUROPE

The United States cannot withdraw from Europe, unless and until Europe should wish us gone. We cannot distinguish its defenses from our own. We cannot diminish our contributions to Western security or abdicate the responsibilities of power.

Address, Conference on Trade Policy, Washington, D.C., May 17, 1962

117 / AMERICA'S VITAL ROLE IN MAINTAINING WORLD FREEDOM

If we were to resign from the United Nations, break off with all countries of whom we disapprove, end foreign aid, call for the resumption of atmospheric nuclear testing and turn our back on the rest of mankind, we would not only be abandoning American influence in the world—we would be inviting a Communist expansion which every Communist power would welcome.

Address, Mormon Tabernacle, Salt Lake City, Sept. 26, 1963

118 / REALITIES OF FOREIGN POLICY

We must recognize that foreign policy in the modern world does not lend itself to easy, simple black and white solution. If we were to have diplomatic relations only with those countries whose principles we approve of, we would have relations with very few countries in a very short time. If we were to withdraw our assistance from all governments who are run differently from our own, we would relinquish half the world immediately to our adversaries. If we were to treat foreign policy as merely a medium for delivering self-righteous sermons to supposedly inferior people, we would give up all thought of world influence or world leadership.

For the purpose of foreign policy is not to provide an outlet for our own sentiments of hope or indignation; it is to shape real events in a real world.

Ibid.

119 / UNITED EFFORT

My fellow citizens of the world: ask not what America will do for you, but what together we can do for the freedom of man.

Inaugural address, Jan. 20, 1961

120 / STANDARDS OF SACRIFICE

Whether you are citizens of America or citizens of the world, ask of us here the same high standards of strength and sacrifice which we ask of you.

Ibid.

121 / THE REALITIES

While we believe not only in the force of arms, but in the force of right and reason, we have learned that reason does not always appeal to unreasonable men, that it is not always true that "a soft answer turneth away wrath" and that right does not always make might. In short, we must face problems which do not lend themselves to easy, quick or permanent solutions. And we must face the fact that the United States is neither omnipotent nor omniscient, that we are only 6 per cent of the world's population, and that we cannot right every wrong or reverse each adversity, and that therefore there cannot be an American solution for every world problem.

Address, University of Washington, Seattle, Nov. 16, 1961

122 / PRAYER FOR WISDOM AND WORTHINESS

We in this country, in this generation, are—by destiny rather than choice —the watchmen on the walls of world freedom. We ask, therefore, that we may be worthy of our power and responsibility—that we may exercise our strength with wisdom and restraint—and that we may achieve in our time and for all time the ancient vision of peace on earth, goodwill toward men. That must always be our goal—and the righteousness of our cause must always underlie our strength. For as was written long ago; "Except the Lord keep the city, the watchman waketh but in vain."

Text of undelivered Dallas address, Nov. 22, 1963

123 / FREEDOM'S EXAMPLE

It is our task to maintain our country as a strong example of what a free society can be.

Address at political rally, Trenton, N.J., Nov. 2, 1961

124 / FREEDOM AT HOME

The quality and spirit of our own society must justify and support our efforts abroad.

Commencement address, American University, Washington, D.C., June 10, 1963

125 / PREREQUISITE FOR WORLD LEADERSHIP

We cannot lead for long the cause of peace and freedom, if we ever cease to set the pace at home.

State of the Union Message, Jan. 14, 1963

126 / LEADERSHIP FOR FREEDOM

I believe that we have a responsibility as the chief defenders of freedom to build the kind of society here which will cause people all around the globe to say, "There is the direction that I wish to go; there is the way of the future. Their high noon is yet to come."

Campaign remarks, ILGWU rally, New York City, Oct. 27, 1960

127 / WHAT WE DO

We shall be judged more by what we do at home than what we preach abroad.

State of the Union Message, Jan. 14, 1963

128 / PRACTICE OF DEMOCRACY

We preach the doctrine of democracy. It is the most difficult of all doctrines. But we have to live up to it. We have to practice what we preach.

Campaign remarks, Los Angeles, Nov. 1, 1960

129 / WORLD SHOWCASE

We sit on a conspicuous stage. The kind of society we build, the kind of country we maintain, the principles for which we fight identify us with countries around the world. The United States was a great revolutionary country. As long as we maintain that spirit, we are going to hold the imagination of the world.

Campaign remarks, Marion, Ill., Oct. 3, 1960

130 / SETTING THE PATTERN

I think it most important that we develop for our own people not only a more fruitful and productive life but we also demonstrate to the world that a system of freedom offers an example which they can hopefully follow.

Address, American Society of Newspaper Editors, Washington, D.C., April 19, 1963

131 / CHALLENGE TO DEMOCRACY

If the Communist system is able, through scientific or economic [achievements] or subversion, to demonstrate that it is on the advance, that we are standing still, that it holds the initiative and we merely respond, then all those people around the world who stand today poised on the razor-edge of decision will make a determination that perhaps the future belongs not to us but to our adversaries. Therefore, our response must be clear. We must be willing to devote our national energies to demonstrating in every form of human endeavor we are second to none, that we are first and will continue to be first regardless of what challenges may be hurled against us.

Campaign address via telephone to AMVET Convention, Miami Beach, Aug. 26, 1960

132 / INITIATIVE

If America stands still Mr. Khrushchev will try to run over us.

Campaign address, Alexandria, Va., Aug. 24, 1960

133 / AMERICAN WAY

We intend to build a still greater America where every man has a chance to work, a decent house to live in, and decent schools for his children because we believe in a decent life for all our citizens—and because we who first lit man's hope for the good life are determined that freedom shall continue to show the way to progress.

Campaign address, Raleigh, N.C., Sept. 17, 1960

134 / DEMOCRACY'S RESPONSIBILITY

If we succeed in this country, if we make this a great country to live in, if we reflect our vitality and energy and strength around the world, then the cause of freedom is strengthened. But if we fail, all fail.

Campaign address, Detroit, Sept. 5, 1960

135 / PRESTIGE

Our prestige in the world, our strength in the world, our influence in the world—all of these are directly related to the strength, energy, and drive of the United States itself.

Campaign address, Faneuil Hall, Boston, Nov. 7, 1960

136 / DEMOCRACY'S IMPACT

Peace requires an America that stands as the model of harmonious relations all around the world. . . . If a country is moving ahead, if the government and the people are engaged together in great enterprises, if the government and the people are associating themselves together in securing equal opportunity for all their citizens, then quite obviously this spills over, this has its influence in those countries which stand today on the razor-edge of decision and attempt to make a judgment which way history is moving.

Campaign address, Democratic Women's luncheon, New York City, Sept. 14, 1960

137 / DOMESTIC ISSUES AND WORLD FREEDOM

Today the safety of the world—the very future of freedom—depends as never before upon the sensible and clear-headed management of the domestic affairs of the United States.

Commencement address, Yale University, New Haven, June 11, 1962

138 / FOREIGN POLICY

The United States cannot be strong in its foreign policy unless it is also strong domestically.

Campaign address, Zembo Mosque Temple, Harrisburg, Pa., Sept. 15, 1960

139 / A STRONG ECONOMY: BULWARK OF FREEDOM

Unless the economy is functioning properly, our people will not be employed at good wages, our businessmen will not produce efficiently and profitably, our farmers will not receive fair prices, and our nation will lack funds for defense, schools, roads and other public services, and the means to help strengthen the cause of world freedom. Today, as never before, America needs a strong economy—not only to sustain our defenses—but also to demonstrate to other nations—particularly those wavering between our system and the Communists'—that the way of freedom is the way to strength and security—that their future lies with us and not with the Soviet Union.

> Campaign address, Associated Business Publications Conference, New York City, Oct. 12, 1960

140 / BUSINESS IN DEFENSE OF FREEDOM

We are committed to the defense of freedom around the world. When business does well in this country, we have full employment, and this country is moving ahead, then it strengthens our image as a prosperous and vital country in this great fight in which we are engaged. When you do well, the United States does well and our policies abroad do well. And when you do badly, all suffer.

> Address, National Association of Manufacturers, New York City, Dec. 6, 1961

141 / WHAT ARE WE FOR?

Today the Communists stir up . . . anti-American resentment that festers in too many countries, particularly among the people who are hungry, sick, and poor, and almost every area of crisis in the last years has been in countries where the people are poor, Laos and Cuba and the Congo and Algeria and Iraq and Guatemala and all the rest. These nations know that we are against communism, but they want to know are we also for the people. They judge us abroad by what we do here at home.

> Campaign address, Washington, D.C., Sept. 20, 1960

142 / PARADOXES

How can a nation as rich as ours tolerate substandard wages? How can we justify the absence of a decent program of health care for our older citizens? Why must so many of our children attend crowded and inadequate schools, and live in squalid homes? Why must we continue to have unfair and arbitrary restrictions on labor's right to use its economic power in support of its legitimate collective bargaining objectives?

Campaign remarks, New York State AFL-CIO Convention, via telephone from Washington, D.C., Aug. 30, 1960

143 / DENIAL OF RIGHTS

The denial of constitutional rights to some of our fellow Americans on account of race—at the ballot box and elsewhere—disturbs the national conscience, and subjects us to the charge of world opinion that our democracy is not equal to the high promise of our heritage.

State of the Union Message, Jan. 30, 1961

144 / SOCIAL JUSTICE

No nation can seek social justice abroad that does not practice it at home.

Luncheon given by Adolfo Lopez Mateos, President of Mexico, Mexico City, June 29, 1962

145 / UNDILUTED FREEDOM

We must present to the world a concept of freedom which has not been diluted by the evils of prejudice and discrimination.

Campaign statement on Citizenship Day, Washington, D.C., Sept. 17, 1960

146 / WORLDWIDE REPERCUSSIONS

Every time we deny to one of our citizens the right of equality of opportunity before the law, the right to send their children to schools on the basis of equality, so much weaker are we in Africa, Asia, and Latin America, where we are a white minority in a colored world.

Campaign address, Portland, Me., Sept. 2, 1960

147 / INEQUITABLE IMMIGRATION RESTRICTIONS

We cannot afford . . . to continue to keep on our books an immigration law which rates people of one national origin as better than people of another national origin. Such a law is not in keeping with the ideals of American democracy, not with the spirit of the American Constitution.

Campaign statement on Citizenship Day, Washington, D.C., Sept. 17, 1960

148 / IMMIGRATION POLICIES

Ours is a nation of immigrants. The men and women who have come here from abroad have built America into the greatest country in the world. If

America is to move ahead, we will have to draw on the skills of men and women of other nations, just as we have in the past. And if our country is to be the leader of democracy in the world, our immigration policies should conform more fully to the principles of equal justice on which our country was founded.

> Letter to Rep. Alfred E. Santangelo, Oct. 8, 1960

149 / SPIRITUAL VALUES

I have advocated the pathway of strength—a stronger America—the strongest sentinel at the gate of freedom—a nation prepared to put force behind law so that we will not be destroyed by the law of force. But I mean spiritually and morally stronger as well.

For it is a harsh fact that we have tended in recent times to neglect these deeper values in favor of our material strength. We have traveled in 100 years from the age of the pioneer to the age of payola. We boast to foreign visitors of our great dams and cities and wealth—but not our free religious heritage. We have become missionaries abroad of a wide range of doctrines—free enterprise, anticommunism, and pro-Americanism—but rarely the doctrine of religious liberty.

> Campaign address, Mormon Tabernacle, Salt Lake City, Sept. 23, 1960

150 / VOICE OF AMERICA BROADCASTS SHOULD TELL THE GOOD AND THE BAD

On the one hand . . . it is your task to bring our story around the world in a way which serves to represent democracy and the United States in its most favorable light. But on the other hand, as part of the cause of freedom, and the arm of freedom, you are obliged to tell our story in a truthful way, to tell it, as Oliver Cromwell said about his portrait, "Paint us with all our blemishes and warts, all those things about us that may not be so immediately attractive."

. . . the things that go bad in America, you must tell that also. And we hope that the bad and the good is sifted together by people of judgment and discretion and taste and discrimination, that they will realize what we are trying to do here.

> Remarks to Voice of America employees on the Voice's 20th anniversary, Washington, D.C., Feb. 26, 1962

151 / KEEPING FAITH AT HOME

Our overriding obligation . . . is to fulfill the world's hope by fulfilling our own faith. That task must begin at home. For if we cannot fulfill our own ideals here, we cannot expect others to accept them.

> State of the Union Message, Jan. 11, 1962

2

The Atlantic Community

Atlantic Partnership: Strength in Unity

I / DECLARATION OF INTERDEPENDENCE

With the passing of ancient empires, today less than 2 per cent of the world's population live in territories officially termed dependent. As this effort for independence, inspired by the American Declaration of Independence, now approaches a successful close, a great new effort for interdependence is transforming the world about us. And the spirit of that new effort is the same spirit which gave birth to the American Constitution.

That spirit is today most clearly seen across the Atlantic Ocean. The nations of Western Europe, long divided by feuds far more bitter than any which existed among the thirteen colonies, are today joining together, seeking, as our forefathers sought, to find freedom in diversity and unity in strength.

The United States looks on this vast new enterprise with hope and admiration. We do not regard a strong and united Europe as a rival, but a partner. To aid its progress has been the basic object of our foreign policy for seventeen years.

We believe that a united Europe will be capable of playing a greater role in the common defense, of responding more generously to the needs of poorer nations, of joining with the United States and others in lowering trade barriers, resolving problems of commerce and commodities and currency, and developing coordinated policies in all economic, political and diplomatic areas. We see in such a Europe a partner with whom we can deal on a basis of full equality in all the great and burdensome tasks of building and defending a community of free nations.

It would be premature at this time to do more than indicate the high regard with which we view the formation of this partnership. The first order of business is for our European friends to go forward in forming the more perfect union which will some day make this partnership possible.

A great new edifice is not built overnight. It was eleven years from the Declaration of Independence to the writing of the Constitution. The construction of workable Federal institutions required still another generation.

The greatest works of our nation's founders lay not in documents and in declarations, but in creative, determined action. The building of the new house of Europe has followed the same practical purposeful course. Building the Atlantic partnership now will not be easily or cheaply finished.

But I will say here and now, on this Day of Independence, that the United States will be ready for a declaration of interdependence, that we will be prepared to discuss with a United Europe the ways and means of forming a concrete Atlantic partnership, a mutually beneficial partnership between the new union now emerging in Europe and the old American union founded here 175 years ago.

Address, Independence Hall, Philadelphia, July 4, 1962

2 / WESTERN UNITY

The future of the West lies in Atlantic partnership—a system of cooperation, interdependence and harmony whose people can jointly meet their burdens and opportunities throughout the world. Some say this is only a dream, but I do not agree.

Address, Paulskirche, Frankfurt, West Germany, June 25, 1963

3 / STRONG ALLIANCE ESSENTIAL

To those old allies whose cultural and spiritual origins we share, we pledge the loyalty of faithful friends. United, there is little we cannot do in a host of cooperative ventures. Divided, there is little we can do—for we dare not meet a powerful challenge at odds and split asunder.

Inaugural address, Jan. 20, 1961

4 / INTERCONTINENTAL THINKING

In urging the adoption of the United States Constitution, Alexander Hamilton told his fellow New Yorkers "to think continentally." Today Americans must learn to think intercontinentally.

Acting on our own, by ourselves, we cannot establish justice throughout the world; we cannot insure its domestic tranquillity, or provide for its common defense, or promote its general welfare, or secure the blessings of liberty to ourselves and our posterity. But joined with other free nations, we can do all this and more. We can assist the developing nations to throw off the yoke of poverty. We can balance our worldwide trade and payments at the highest possible level of growth. We can mount a deterrent powerful enough to deter any aggression. And ultimately we can help to achieve a world of law and free choice, banishing the world of war and coercion.

For the Atlantic partnership of which I speak would not look inward only, preoccupied with its own welfare and advancement. It must look outward to cooperate with all nations in meeting their common concerns. It would serve as a nucleus for the eventual union of all free men—those who are now free and those who are vowing that some day they will be free.

Address, Independence Hall, Philadelphia, July 4, 1962

5 / DEFENSE AGAINST COMMUNISM

The reality of power is that the resources essential to defense against this danger are concentrated overwhelmingly in the nations of the Atlantic Alliance. In unity this Alliance has ample strength to hold back the expansion of communism until such time as it loses its force and momentum. Acting alone neither the United States nor Europe could be certain of success and survival. The reality of purpose, therefore, is that which serves to unite us is right, and what tends to divide us is wrong.

News conference, Washington, D.C., Jan. 24, 1963

6 / HISTORIC TRUST

If we are to be worthy of our historic trust, we must continue on both sides of the Atlantic to work together in trust.

Ibid.

7 / SHARING OF BENEFITS OF THE ATLANTIC ALLIANCE

We do not want this to be a rich man's club while the rest of the world gets poorer. We want the benefits of this kind of union to be shared.

News conference, Washington, D.C., July 5, 1962

8 / A WELCOME PARTNER

Far from resenting the new Europe, we regard her as a welcome partner, not a rival. For the road to world peace and freedom is still very long, and there are burdens which only full partners can share—in supporting the common defense, in expanding world trade, in aligning our balance of payments, in aiding the emergent nations, in concerting political and economic policies, and in welcoming to our common effort other industrialized nations, notably Japan, whose remarkable economic and political development of the 1950's permits it now to play on the world scene a major constructive role.

State of the Union Message, Jan. 14, 1963

9 / WISH FOR A UNIFIED EUROPE

We look forward to a Europe united and strong—speaking with a common voice—acting with a common will—a world power capable of meeting world problems as a full and equal partner.

Address, Paulskirche, Frankfurt, West Germany, June 25, 1963

10 / WESTERN UNITY REQUIRES A "COHESIVE EUROPE"

It is only a fully cohesive Europe that can protect us all against fragmentation of our alliance. Only such a Europe will permit full reciprocity of treatment across the ocean, in facing the Atlantic agenda. With only such a Europe can we have a full give-and-take between equals, and equal sharing of responsibilities, and an equal level of sacrifice. . . . The choice of paths to the unity of Europe is a choice which Europe must make. But as you continue this great effort, undeterred by either difficulty or delay, you should know that this new European greatness will be not an object of fear, but a source of strength for the United States of America.

Ibid.

11 / WESTERN COOPERATION

We in the West must move together in building military strength. We must consult one another more closely than ever before. We must together design our proposals for peace, and labor together as they are pressed at the conference table. And together we must share the burdens and the risks of this effort.

The Atlantic Community, as we know it, has been built in response to challenge: the challenge of European chaos in 1947, of the Berlin blockade in 1948, and the challenge of Communist aggression in Korea in 1950.

Now, standing strong and prosperous, after an unprecedented decade of progress, the Atlantic Community will not forget either its history or the principles which gave it meaning.

Address to the nation on the Berlin crisis, Washington, D.C., July 25, 1961

12 / COMMITMENT TO DEFEND WESTERN EUROPE

The United States will risk its cities to defend yours because we need your freedom to protect ours. Hundreds of thousands of our soldiers serve with yours on this continent, as a tangible evidence of this pledge. Those who would doubt our pledge or deny this indivisibility—those who would separate Europe from America or split one ally from another—would only give aid and comfort to the men who make themselves our adversaries and welcome any Western disarray.

Address, Paulskirche, Frankfurt, West Germany, June 25, 1963

13 / COMMON CONCERNS OF THE ATLANTIC COMMUNITY

The Atlantic Community is no longer concerned with purely military aims. As its common undertakings grow at an ever-increasing pace, we are, and increasingly will be, partners in aid, trade, defense, diplomacy and monetary affairs.

The emergence of a new Europe is being matched by the emergence of new ties across the Atlantic. It is a matter of undramatic daily cooperation in hundreds of workaday tasks: of currencies kept in effective relation, of development loans meshed together, of standardized weapons and concerted diplomatic positions. The Atlantic Community grows, not like a volcanic mountain, but like a coral reef, from the accumulating activity of all.

Thus, we in the free world are moving steadily toward unity and cooperation, in the teeth of that old Bolshevik prophecy, and at the very time when extraordinary rumbles of discord can be heard across the Iron Curtain. It is not free societies which bear within them the seeds of inevitable disunity.

State of the Union Message, Jan. 11, 1962

Free World Economy: America and the European Economic Community

14 / AMERICAN ENTERPRISE AND THE EUROPEAN COMMON MARKET

Our business men, workers and farmers are in need of new markets and the fastest-growing market in the world is the European Common Market. Its consumers will soon be nearly 250,000,000 people. Its sales possibilities have scarcely begun to be tapped. Its demand for American goods is without precedent—if only we can obtain the tools necessary to open the doors.

Our own markets here at home expand as our economy and population expand. But think of the tremendous demand in the Common Market countries, where most consumers have never had the goods which we take so much for granted! Think of the opportunities in a market where, compared to the ratio of ownership in this country, only one-fourth as many consumers have radios, one-seventh television sets, one-fifth automobiles, washing machines, refrigerators.

If our American producers can share in this market it will mean more investment and more plants, and more jobs and a faster rate of growth. To share in that market we must strike a bargain. We must have something to offer the Europeans. We must be willing to give them increased access to our market. Let us not avoid the fact: we cannot sell unless we buy. And there will be those who will be opposed to this competition.

But let those who believe in competition, those who welcome the challenge of world trade as our predecessors have done, let them recognize the value that will come from this exchange of goods. It will enrich the choice of consumers; it will make possible a higher standard of living. It will help hold the lid on the cost of living. It will stimulate our producers to modernize their products.

Address on world trade, dock ceremonies, New Orleans, May 4, 1962

15 / THE PROSPECT: WESTERN ECONOMIC UNITY

We are moving toward a full partnership with all the free nations of the world—a partnership which will have in this area 90 per cent of the industrial productive power of the free world, which will have the greatest market that the world has ever known, a productive power far greater than that of the Communist bloc, a trillion-dollar economy, where goods can flow freely back and forth. That is the prospect that lies before us, that faces this country in the year 1962.

For those who preach the doctrine of the inevitability of a collapse by us and a Communist success must realize that in the last few years the great effort which has been made to unify economically the countries of the free world offers far greater promise than the broken promises of the Communist system.

Against the Communist system of iron discipline the Atlantic partnership will present a world of free choice. Against their predictions of our collapse it will present a challenge of free nations working in harmony and it will provide economically an overwhelming and growing productivity preventing their ultimately overtaking us.

Ibid.

16 / TRADE POLICIES AND WESTERN UNITY

Our efforts to promote the strength and unity of the West are . . .
directly related to the strength and unity of Atlantic trade policies. An
expanded export program is necessary to give this nation both the balance
of payments equilibrium and the economic growth we need to sustain our
share of Western military security and economic advance. Equally important, a freer flow of trade across the Atlantic will enable the two
giant markets on either side of the ocean to impart strength and vigor to
each other, and to combine their resources and momentum to undertake
the many enterprises which the security of free peoples demands. For the
first time, as the world's greatest trading nation, we can welcome a single
partner whose trade is even larger than our own—a partner no longer divided and dependent, but strong enough to share with us the responsibilities and initiatives of the free world.

The Communist bloc, largely self-contained and isolated, represents an economic power already by some standards larger than that of
Western Europe and hoping someday to overtake the United States. But
the combined output and purchasing power of the United States and
Western Europe—nearly a trillion dollars a year—is more than twice as
great as that of the entire Sino-Soviet world. Though we have only half
the population, and far less than half the territory, we can pool our resources and resourcefulness in an open trade partnership strong enough to
outstrip any challenge, and strong enough to undertake all the many enterprises around the world which the maintenance and progress of freedom require. If we can take this step, Marxist predictions of "capitalistic"
empires warring over markets and stifling competition would be shattered
for all time—Communist hopes for a trade war between these two great
economic giants would be frustrated—and Communist efforts to split the
West would be doomed to failure.

Message to Congress on trade, Jan. 25, 1962

17 / "TEARING DOWN WALLS"

It is time now to write a new chapter in the evolution of the Atlantic
community. The success of our foreign policy depends in large measure
upon the success of our foreign trade, and our maintenance of Western
political unity depends in equally large measure upon the degree of Western economic unity. An integrated Western Europe joined in trading
partnership with the United States, will further shift the world balance of
power to the side of freedom.

Our efforts to prove the superiority of free choice will thus be advanced immeasurably. We will prove to the world that we believe in peacefully "tearing down walls" instead of arbitrarily building them. We will be opening new vistas of choice and opportunity to the producers and consumers of the free world. In answer to those who say to the world's poorer countries that economic progress and freedom are no longer compatible, we—who have long boasted about the virtues of the market place and of free competitive enterprise, about our ability to compete and sell in any market, and about our willingness to keep abreast of the times—will have our greatest opportunity since the Marshall Plan to demonstrate the vitality of free choice.

Ibid.

18 / WESTERN TRADE PROGRAM

If the Nations of the West can weld together on . . . [trade] problems a common program of action as extraordinary in economic history as NATO was unprecedented in military history, the long-range Communist aim of dividing and encircling us all is doomed to failure.

Address, National Association of Manufacturers, New York City, Dec. 6, 1961

19 / AMERICA MUST LEAD

The United States did not rise to greatness by waiting for others to lead. This nation is the world's foremost manufacturer, farmer, banker, consumer and exporter. The Common Market is moving ahead at an economic growth rate twice ours. The Communist economic offensive is under way. The opportunity is ours—the initiative is up to us.

State of the Union Message, Jan. 11, 1962

20 / A NEW TRADING COMMUNITY

The Common Market will not fulfill its own high promise unless its outside tariff walls are low. The dangers of restriction or timidity in our own policy have counterparts for our friends in Europe. For together we face a common challenge: to enlarge the prosperity of free men everywhere, to build in partnership a new trading community in which all free nations may gain from the productive energy of free competitive effort.

Ibid.

21 / AMERICAN TARIFF POLICY: ITEM-BY-ITEM NEGOTIATION INADEQUATE

A trade policy adequate to negotiate item by item tariff reductions with a large number of small independent states will no longer be adequate to assure ready access for ourselves—and for our traditional trading partners in Canada, Japan, Latin America and elsewhere—to a market [the European Common Market] nearly as large as our own, whose negotiators can speak with one voice but whose internal differences make it impossible for them to negotiate item by item.

Message to Congress on trade, Jan. 25, 1962

22 / TRADING TARIFF REDUCTIONS

The traditional technique of trading one brick at a time off our respective tariff walls will not suffice to assure American farm and factory exports the kind of access to the European market which they must have if trade between the two Atlantic markets is to expand. We must talk instead in terms of trading whole layers at a time in exchange for other layers, as the Europeans have been doing in reducing their internal tariffs, permitting the forces of competition to set new trade patterns. . . . But . . . we mean to see to it that all reductions and concessions are reciprocal.

Ibid.

23 / TRADE ADJUSTMENT ASSISTANCE

Just as the Federal Government has assisted in personal readjustments made necessary by military service, just as the Federal Government met its obligation to assist industry in adjusting to war production and again to return to peacetime production, so there is an obligation to render assistance to those who suffer as a result of national trade policy.

Ibid.

24 / REDUCING THE EXPORT OF CAPITAL FUNDS

If we can lower the external tariff wall of the Common Market through negotiation our manufacturers will be under less pressure to locate their plants behind that wall in order to sell in the European market, thus reducing the export of capital funds to Europe.

Ibid.

25 / TRADE EXPANSION AIM

To increase our markets through trade expansion so that capital does not leave us, but instead manufactured goods.

Address, United Auto Workers Convention, Atlantic City, N.J., May 8, 1962

26 / ECONOMIC STABILITY THROUGH EXPANDED TRADE

Our efforts to prevent inflation will be reinforced by expanded trade. Once given a fair and equal opportunity to compete in overseas markets, and once subject to healthy competition from overseas manufacturers for our own markets, American management and labor will have additional reason to maintain competitive costs and prices, modernize their plants and increase their productivity. The discipline of the world market place is an excellent measure of efficiency and a force to stability. To try to shield American industry from the discipline of foreign competition would isolate our domestic price level from world prices, encourage domestic inflation, reduce our exports still further and invite less desirable governmental solutions.

Message to Congress on trade, Jan. 25, 1962

27 / BENEFITS OF LIBERAL TRADE POLICY

A more liberal trade policy will in general benefit our most efficient and expanding industries—industries which have demonstrated their advantage over other world producers by exporting on the average twice as much of their products as we import—industries which have done this while paying the highest wages in our country. Increasing investment and employment in these growth industries will make for a more healthy, efficient and expanding economy and a still higher American standard of living. Indeed, freer movement of trade between America and the Common Market would bolster the economy of the entire free world, stimulating each nation to do what it does best and helping to achieve the O.E.C.D. [Organization for Economic Cooperation and Development] target of a 50 per cent combined Atlantic Community increase in gross national product by 1970.

Ibid.

28 / NEED FOR EXPANSION OF EXPORTS

Our efforts to expand our economy will be importantly affected by our ability to expand our exports—and particularly upon the ability of our farmers and business men to sell to the Common Market. There is arising across the Atlantic a single economic community which may soon have a population half again as big as our own, working and competing together with no more barriers to commerce and investment than exist among our fifty states—in an economy which has been growing roughly twice as fast as ours—representing a purchasing power which will some day equal our own and a living standard growing faster than our own. As its consumer incomes grow, its consumer demands are also growing, particularly for the type of goods that we produce best, which are only now beginning to be widely sold or known in the markets of Europe or in the homes of its middle-income families.

Some 30 per cent of our exports—more than $4,000,000,000 in industrial goods and materials and nearly $2,000,000,000 in agricultural products—already goes to the members and prospective members of the European Economic Community. European manufacturers, however, have increased their share of this rapidly expanding market at a far greater rate than American manufacturers. Unless our industry can maintain and increase its share of this attractive market, there will be further temptation to locate additional American financed plants in Europe in order to get behind the external tariff wall of the E.E.C. This would enable the American manufacturer to contend for the vast consumer potential on more competitive terms with his European counterparts; but it will also mean a failure on our part to take advantage of this growing market to increase jobs and investment in this country.

Ibid.

29 / "TRADE OR FADE"

In May of 1962 we stand at a great divide: we must either trade or fade. We must either go backward or go forward. For more than a quarter of a century the reciprocal trade legislation, fathered by Cordell Hull of Tennessee and sponsored by Franklin Roosevelt, has served this country well and on eleven different occasions it has been renewed by Congressmen from both parties.

But that act is no longer adequate to carry us through the channels and the locks of world trade today. For the whole pattern of trade is changing and we must change with it.

The Common Market uniting the countries of Western Europe together in one great trading group indicates both a promise or a threat to our economy.

Our international balance of payments is in deficit, requiring an increase in our exports. Japan has regained force as a trading nation—nearly fifty nations of Asia and Africa are seeking new markets—our friends in Latin America need to trade to develop their capital—and the Communist bloc has developed a large new arsenal of trading weapons which can be used against us. And they are ready to take and sell any area in which we leave a gap—wherever American leadership should falter. And we do not intend to give way.

I believe that American trade leadership must be maintained. . . . I believe it must be furthered and I have therefore submitted to the Congress the Trade Expansion Act of 1962.

Address on world trade at dock ceremonies, New Orleans, May 4, 1962

30 / FREEDOM ENDANGERED

If American industry cannot increase its sales to the Common Market, and increase this nation's surplus of exports over imports, our international payments position and our commitments to the defense of freedom will be endangered.

Address, National Association of Manufacturers, New York City, Dec. 6, 1961

31 / TRADE EXPANSION BILL AND FREEDOM

Trade expansion will emphasize the modern instead of the obsolete, the strong instead of the weak, the new frontiers of trade instead of the ancient strongholds of protection.

And we cannot continue to bear the burdens that we must take of helping freedom defend itself all the way from the American soldier guarding the Brandenburg Gate, to the Americans now in Vietnam, or the Peace Corpsmen in Colombia, unless we have the resources to finance those great expenditures which in the last year totaled over three billion dollars.

Unless we are able to increase our surplus of balance of payments then the United States will be faced with a hard choice of either lessening those commitments or beginning to withdraw this great national effort.

One answer to this problem is a negative answer: raise our tariffs, restrict our capital, pull back from the walls and our adversaries would only be too glad to fill any gap that we should leave. This Administration was not elected to preside over the resignation of American responsibilities in these great years.

There is another answer and that is to increase our exports, to meet our commitments and maintain our defense of freedom. I have every confidence that once this bill is passed the ability of American initiative and know-how will increase our export and our export surplus by competing successfully with any country in the world.

Address on world trade, dock ceremonies, New Orleans, May 4, 1962

32 / CREATION OF JOBS THROUGH TRADE EXPANSION

Let us not miss the main point: the new jobs opened through trade will be far greater than any jobs which will be adversely affected. And these new jobs will come in those enterprises that are today leading the economy of the country.

Ibid.

33 / COMMON MARKET PROGRESS

The experience of the European Common Market, where tariffs were gradually cut down, has shown that increased trade brings employment. They have full employment in the Common Market and its economic growth rate is twice that of the United States.

Ibid.

34 / THE CROSSROADS

In the life of every nation, as in the life of every man, there comes a time when a nation stands at the crossroads, when it can either shrink from the future and retire into its shell or can move ahead asserting its will and its faith against uncertain circumstance. I believe that we stand at such a juncture in our foreign economic policy and . . . I believe . . . the United States should move ahead.

Ibid.

35 / COMMON ECONOMIC GOALS OF TRADE AND GROWTH

We believe . . . that closer economic ties among all free nations are essential to prosperity and peace. And neither we nor the members of the Common Market are so affluent that we can long afford to shelter high-cost farms or factories from the winds of foreign competition, or to restrict the channels of trade with other nations of the free world. If the Common Market should now move toward protectionism and restrictionism, it would undermine its own basic principles. This Government means to use the authority conferred on it last year by the Congress to encourage trade expansion on both sides of the Atlantic and around the world.

State of the Union Message, Jan. 14, 1963

36 / TRANSATLANTIC ECONOMIC COOPERATION

I would hope in 1963, when the trail is still uphill, when we have great challenges from the Communist world, that we would not break apart and that the Atlantic would not be regarded as a wall between us.

News conference, Bonn, West Germany, June 24, 1963

3

The Underprivileged Areas of the World

The Moral Responsibility to Help and to Share

1 / AID WITH INTEGRITY

To those peoples in the huts and villages across the globe struggling to break the bonds of mass misery, we pledge our best efforts to help them help themselves, for whatever period is required—not because the Communists may be doing it, not because we seek their votes, but because it is right.

Inaugural address, Jan. 20, 1961

2 / TO CONQUER POVERTY

Our purpose is not to buy friends or hire allies. Our purpose is to defeat poverty.

Campaign address, Democratic Women's luncheon, New York City, Sept. 14, 1960

3 / TRADITIONAL GENEROSITY

America has a proud tradition of helping people when dire emergency strikes.

Campaign statement to Polish-American leaders, Hyannis, Mass., Aug. 6, 1960

4 / USE OF SURPLUS

The product of our abundance must be more effectively used to relieve hunger and help economic growth in all corners of the globe.

State of the Union Message, Jan. 30, 1961

5 / GLOBAL EFFORTS AGAINST POVERTY AND INJUSTICE

More will be needed than good will missions or talking back to Soviet politicians or increasing the tempo of the arms race. More will be needed than good intentions, for we know where that paving leads.

Acceptance Speech, Liberal Party Convention, New York City, Sept. 14, 1960

6 / MOTIVATING DRIVES

The people of the world are not so much interested in being allies of the United States as they are in joining a great effort to maintain their freedom, to defeat ignorance, disease, and those enemies of the human race which make life so difficult for people around the globe. That is the great struggle of the sixties. Unless we are prepared to associate with them in their efforts to provide a better life for their own people, they will not associate with us in the defense of freedom.

Campaign remarks, Philadelphia, Oct. 31, 1960

7 / PARADOX

We live in a land of abundance, a land of such great abundance of food and fiber, in fact, that our "cup runneth over." At the same time we live in a world where over 60 percent of the population lives under the shadow of hunger and malnutrition. This is the great paradox of the 1950's.

Campaign statement on food for peace, Washington, D.C., Oct. 31, 1960

8 / HALF-STARVED WORLD

Half of humanity is still undernourished or hungry. In 70 developing nations—with over 2,000,000,000 people—malnutrition is widespread and persistent.

Address, World Food Congress, Washington, D.C., June 4, 1963

9 / "FOR ALL MANKIND"

It is right that we should be grateful for the plenty amidst which we live; the productivity of our farms, the output of our factories, the skill of our artisans and the ingenuity of our inventors. But in the midst of our Thanksgiving, let us not be unmindful of the plight of those in many parts of the world to whom hunger is no stranger and the plight of those millions more who live without the blessings of liberty and freedom. With some we are able to share our material abundance through our Food-for-Peace Program and through our support of the United Nations Freedom From Hunger Campaign. To all we can offer the sustenance of hope that we shall not fail in our unceasing efforts to make this a peaceful and prosperous world for all mankind.

> Thanksgiving proclamation, Nov. 21, 1961

10 / QUALITIES OF LEADERSHIP

We want an America whose qualities of initiative and leadership have earned the respect of the entire free world—not merely because of our size or strength, but because we stand for freedom and progress and the pursuit of peace. This means that we must help the developing and newly emerging nations of the world to achieve the economic progress on which their political freedom depends. We must be sure that they are strong and stable enough to resist the steady and ruthless infiltration of Communist subversion.

> Campaign address, Raleigh, N.C., Sept. 17, 1960

11 / TO ELIMINATE STARVATION

The challenge of world hunger is one that we must meet, knowing that the burden is greater today than it has ever been before. But it is heartening to know that we are now joined in a worldwide alliance, the Freedom From Hunger Campaign, to eliminate hunger from the earth.

> Remarks at ceremony for Freedom From Hunger Foundation, Washington, D.C., Nov. 22, 1962

The Crucial Third of Humanity

12 / THE THREE THIRDS

One third of the world, it has been said, may be free—but one third is the victim of cruel repression—and the other one third is racked by the pangs of poverty, hunger and envy.

> Acceptance speech, Democratic National Convention, Los Angeles, July 15, 1960

13 / THE DEVELOPING NATIONS: ROLE IN SHAPING THE WORLD

In some 80 developing nations, countless large and small decisions will be made in the days and months and years ahead—decisions which, taken together, will establish the economic and social system, determine the political leadership, shape the political practices, and mold the structure of the institutions which will promote either consent or coercion for one-third of humanity. And these decisions will drastically affect the shape of the world in which our children grow to maturity.

Message to Congress on foreign aid, April 2, 1963

14 / WHITE MINORITY

Do you know the greatest minority in the world today? The greatest minority in the world today is the whites. The whole world, Africa, Asia, the Middle East—people who are colored, yellow, brown, black, they look to us, they look to the Communists, and they want to decide which road they will take.

Campaign remarks, Los Angeles, Nov. 1, 1960

15 / THE TWO ROADS

The Communists are determined to convince the emerging and developing nations of Asia and Africa and Latin America that only communism will eliminate their poverty and hunger and disease—that the Communist road is the only road to a better life. We know that this is not true—for our own greatness is living proof that the road to abundance is freedom's road.

Campaign address, Raleigh, N.C., Sept. 17, 1960

16 / COMMUNISM THRIVES IN POVERTY

It is hard for any nation to focus on an external or subversive threat to its independence when its energies are drained in daily combat with the forces of poverty and despair.

State of the Union Message, Jan. 14, 1963

17 / THE GOADS

Bitter want and hunger in the newly developing nations have goaded their people into restless action and revolution as they have sought to better their lives. Some have turned to the tyranny of communism as a means to rapid economic development.

Campaign statement on food for peace, Washington, D.C., Oct. 31, 1960

The Underdeveloped Nations, New and Old

18 / SOCIAL EXPLOSION

More energy is released by the awakening of new nations than by the fission of the atom itself.

Acceptance speech, Democratic National Convention, Los Angeles, July 15, 1960

19 / TO THE NEWLY INDEPENDENT STATES

To those new States whom we welcome to the ranks of the free, we pledge our word that one form of colonial control shall not have passed away merely to be replaced by a far greater tyranny. We shall not always expect to find them supporting our view. But we shall always hope to find them strongly supporting their own freedom—and to remember that, in the past, those who foolishly sought power by riding the back of the tiger ended up inside.

Inaugural address, Jan. 20, 1961

20 / STRENGTHENING UNDERDEVELOPED NATIONS

We should know by now that where weakness and dependence are not transformed into strength and self-reliance, we can expect only chaos, and then tyranny, to follow.

Message to Congress on foreign aid, March 13, 1962

21 / INDIVISIBLE INSECURITY

So long as freedom from hunger is only half achieved—so long as two-thirds of the nations of the world have food deficits—no citizen, no nation can afford to feel satisfied or secure.

Address, World Food Congress, Washington, D.C., June 4, 1963

22 / TO STRENGTHEN FREEDOM

Wherever nations are willing to help themselves, we stand ready to help them build new bulwarks of freedom. We are not purchasing votes for the cold war; we have gone to the aid of imperiled nations, neutrals and allies alike. What we do ask—and all that we ask—is that our help be used to the best advantage, and that their own efforts not be diverted by needless quarrels with other independent nations.

State of the Union Message, Jan. 14, 1963

23 / COMMUNIST AID AND TRADE OFFENSIVE

The Communist aid and trade offensive has . . . become more apparent in recent years. Soviet bloc trade with forty-one non-Communist countries in the less-developed areas of the globe has more than tripled in recent years; and bloc trade missions are busy in nearly every continent attempting to penetrate, encircle and divide the free world.

Message to Congress on trade, Jan. 25, 1962

24 / FREE LABOR BASIC TO FREEDOM

We do not want to leave the people of some countries a choice between placing their destiny in the hands of a few who hold in their hands most of the property, and on the other side the Communist movement. . . . We want them to have the instruments of freedom to protect themselves and provide for progress in their countries, and a strong free labor movement can do it.

Address, AFL-CIO Convention, Miami, Dec. 7, 1961

25 / LABOR UNIONS IN NEW COUNTRIES

No greater service to the cause of the free world could possibly come forward than the development of effective, liberal free trade unions in the newly emerging countries. These are the areas where the Communists concentrate. If they are able to have a great mass of the people living in misery and a few in luxury it suits them to a T. And the way that progress can be made over a wide spectrum for the great majority of the people is by having an effective labor movement.

Address, United Auto Workers Convention, Atlantic City, N.J., May 8, 1962

26 / PROGRAMS OF REFORM IN UNDERDEVELOPED NATIONS

The United States recognizes that it takes time—to develop careful programs for national development and the administrative capacity necessary to carry out such a program—to go beyond the enactment of land reform measures and actually transfer the land and make the most productive use of it—to pass new tax laws and then achieve their acceptance and enforcement.

Message to Congress on foreign aid, March 13, 1962

27 / INDEPENDENCE OF NEW STATES

We support the independence of those newer or weaker states whose history, geography, economy or lack of power impels them to remain outside "entangling alliances" as we did for more than a century. For the independence of nations is a bar to the Communists' "grand design." It is the basis of our own.

State of the Union Message, Jan. 11, 1962

American Foreign Aid

28 / VITAL PROGRAM

Our economic assistance program . . . is vital in the continuing struggle against tyranny and oppression, and the poverty on which they feed.

Message to Congress on U.S. balance of payments, Feb. 6, 1961

29 / OUR INTEREST IN THE UNDERDEVELOPED NATIONS

The economic collapse of those free but less-developed nations which now stand poised between sustained growth and economic chaos would be disastrous to our national security, harmful to our comparative prosperity, and offensive to our conscience.

Message to Congress on foreign aid, March 22, 1961

30 / THE GOAL

Our new aid policy aims at strengthening the political and economic independence of developing countries—which means strengthening their capacity both to master the inherent stress of rapid change and to repel Communist efforts to exploit such stress from within or without.

Message to Congress on foreign aid, March 13, 1962

31 / NATIONAL AUTONOMY

We must . . . recognize that we cannot remake the world simply by our own command. . . . Every nation has its own traditions, its own values, its own aspirations. Our assistance from time to time can help other nations preserve their independence and advance their growth, but we cannot remake them in our own image. We cannot enact their laws, nor can we operate their governments or dictate our policies.

Address, Mormon Tabernacle, Salt Lake City, Sept. 26, 1963

32 / NECESSITY

Is a foreign aid program really necessary? Why should we not lay down this burden which our nation has now carried for some 15 years? The answer is that there is no escaping our obligations: our moral obligations as a wise leader and good neighbor in the interdependent community of free nations—our economic obligations as the wealthiest people in a world of largely poor people, as a nation no longer dependent upon the loans from abroad that once helped us develop our own economy—and our political obligations as the single largest counter to the adversaries of freedom.

To fail to meet those obligations now would be disastrous; and, in the long run, more expensive. For widespread poverty and chaos lead to a collapse of existing political and social structures which would inevitably invite the advance of totalitarianism into every weak and unstable area. Thus our own security would be endangered and our prosperity imperiled. A program of assistance to the underdeveloped nations must continue because the nation's interest and the cause of political freedom require it.

Message to Congress on foreign aid, March 22, 1961

33 / TO AID FREEDOM

I realize that there are among us those who are weary of sustaining this continual effort to help other nations. But I would ask them to look at a map and recognize that many of those whom we help live on the "frontlines" of the long twilight struggle for freedom—that others are new nations posed between order and chaos—and the rest are older nations now undergoing a turbulent transition of new expectations. Our efforts to help them help themselves, to demonstrate and to strengthen the vitality of free institutions, are small in cost compared to our military outlays for the defense of freedom. Yet all of our armies and atoms combined will be of little avail if these nations fall, unable to meet the needs of their own people, and unable to stave off within their borders the rise of forces that threaten our security.

Message to Congress on foreign aid, March 13, 1962

34 / AMERICA'S OBLIGATION

I think our people get awfully impatient and maybe fatigued and tired, and saying, "We have been carrying this burden for 17 years; can we lay it down?" We can't lay it down, and I don't see how we are going to lay it down in this century.

Television and radio interview, Dec. 17, 1961

35 / JUSTIFIABLE EXPENDITURE

The United States today is spending over 10 percent of its gross national product on programs primarily aimed at improving our national security. Somewhat less than $\frac{1}{20}$ of this amount, and less than 0.7 percent of our GNP, goes into the mutual assistance program: Roughly half for economic development, and half for military and other short-term assistance. The richest nation in the world would surely be justified in spending less than 1 percent of its national income on assistance to its less fortunate sister nations solely as a matter of international responsibility; but inasmuch as these programs are not merely the right thing to do, but clearly in our national self-interest, all criticisms should be placed in that perspective. That our aid programs can be improved is not a matter of debate. But that our aid programs serve both our national traditions and our national interests is beyond all reasonable doubt.

Message to Congress on foreign aid, April 2, 1963

36 / AS VITAL AS ARMS

The aid program is just as important as any military spending we do abroad. You cannot separate guns from roads and schools when it comes to resisting Communist subversion in underdeveloped countries.

Statement on House Appropriations Committee recommendation for a cut in foreign aid, Sept. 19, 1962

37 / HISTORICAL MOMENT

We live at a very special moment in history. The whole southern half of the world—Latin America, Africa, the Middle East, and Asia—are caught up in the adventures of asserting their independence and modernizing their old ways of life. These new nations need aid in loans and technical assistance just as we in the northern half of the world drew successively on one another's capital and know-how as we moved into industrialization and regular growth.

But in our time these new nations need help for a special reason. Without exception they are under Communist pressure. In many cases, that pressure is direct and military. In others, it takes the form of intense subversive activity designed to break down and supersede the new—and often frail—modern institutions they have thus far built.

Message to Congress on foreign aid, March 22, 1961

38 / BASIC AIM

The fundamental task of our foreign aid program in the 1960's is not negatively to fight communism: Its fundamental task is to help make a historical demonstration that in the 20th century, as in the 19th—in the southern half of the globe as in the north—economic growth and political democracy can develop hand in hand.

Ibid.

39 / AMERICA'S INTEREST

Our new program should not be based merely on reaction to Communist threats or short-term crises. We have a positive interest in helping less-developed nations provide decent living standards for their people and achieve sufficient strength, self-respect, and independence to become self-reliant members of the community of nations. And thus our aid should be conditioned on the recipients' ability and willingness to take the steps necessary to reach that goal.

Ibid.

40 / AN UPHILL STRUGGLE

Free world development will still be an uphill struggle. Governmental aid can only supplement the role of private investment, trade expansion, and commodity stabilization, and, above all, internal self-improvement. The processes of growth are gradual—bearing fruit in a decade, not in a day. Our successes will neither be quick nor dramatic. But if these programs were ever to be ended, our failures in a dozen countries would be sudden and would be certain.

State of the Union Message, Jan. 14, 1963

41 / NEED FOR LONG-TERM PLANNING

Piecemeal projects, hastily designed to match the rhythm of the fiscal year are no substitute for orderly long-term planning.

Message to Congress on foreign aid, March 22, 1961

42 / SKILLED SERVICE

The program requires a highly professional skilled service, attracting substantial numbers of high-caliber men and women capable of sensitive dealing with other governments, and with a deep understanding of the process of economic development.

Ibid.

43 / "HISTORIC OPPORTUNITY"

There exists, in the 1960's, a historic opportunity for a major economic assistance effort by the free industrialized nations to move more than half the people of the less-developed nations into self-sustained economic growth, while the rest move substantially closer to the day when they, too, will no longer have to depend on outside assistance.

Ibid.

44 / "DECADE OF DEVELOPMENT"

The 1960's can be—and must be—the crucial "decade of development" —the period when many less-developed nations make the transition into self-sustained growth—the period in which an enlarged community of free, stable, and self-reliant nations can reduce world tensions and insecurity. The goal is in our grasp if, and only if, the other industrialized nations now join us in developing with the recipients a set of commonly agreed criteria, a set of long-range goals, and a common undertaking to meet those goals, in which each nation's contribution is related to the contributions of others, and to the precise needs of each less-developed nation. Our job, in its largest sense, is to create a new partnership between the northern and southern halves of the world, to which all free nations can contribute, in which each free nation must assume a responsibility proportional to its means.

Ibid.

45 / TOWARD A TURN-AROUND

We must say to the less-developed nations, if they are willing to undertake necessary internal reform and self-help—and to the other industrialized nations, if they are willing to undertake a much greater effort on a much broader scale—that we then intend during this coming decade of development to achieve a decisive turn-around in the fate of the less-developed world, looking toward the ultimate day when all nations can be self-reliant and when foreign aid will no longer be needed.

Ibid.

46 / BIPARTISAN EFFORT

Foreign aid—America's unprecedented response to world challenges—has not been the work of one party or one administration. It has moved forward under the leadership of two great Presidents—Harry Truman and

Dwight Eisenhower—and drawn its support from forward-looking members of both political parties in the Congress and throughout the nation.
Ibid.

47 / SHORTSIGHTED VIEW

It makes little sense for us to assail, in speeches and resolutions, the horrors of communism, to spend $50 billion a year to prevent its military advance, and then to begrudge spending, largely on American products, less than one-tenth of that amount to help other nations strengthen their independence and cure the social chaos in which communism always has thrived.

State of the Union Message, Jan. 14, 1963

48 / UNWARRANTABLE REDUCTIONS BY CONGRESS

Is this nation stating that it cannot afford an additional $600 million to help the developing nations of the world become strong and free—an amount less than this country's annual outlay for lipstick, face cream and chewing gum?

Address, Protestant Council of the City of New York, Nov. 8, 1963

49 / GIVING HOPE

History will record that today our technical assistance and development loans are giving hope where hope was lacking, sparking action where life was static, and stimulating progress around the earth—simultaneously supporting the military security of the free world, helping to erect barriers against the growth of Communism where those barriers count the most, helping to build the kind of world community of independent, self-supporting nations in which we want to live, and helping to serve the deep American urge to extend a generous hand to those working toward a better life for themselves and their children.

Message to Congress on foreign aid, April 2, 1963

50 / VICTORIES OF PEACE

"Peace hath her victories no less renowned than war," wrote Milton. And no peace-time victory in history has been as far-reaching in its impact, nor served the cause of freedom so well, as the victories scored in the last 17 years by this nation's mutual defense and assistance programs. These victories have been, in the main, quiet instead of dramatic. Their aim has been, not to gain territories for the United States or support in the

United Nations, but to preserve freedom and hope, and to prevent tyranny and subversion, in dozens of key nations all over the world.

Ibid.

51 / CONTINUING EFFORT FOR IMPROVEMENT

Despite all its past achievements, the continued progress of the mutual assistance program requires a persistent discontent with present progress. We have been reorganizing this program to make it a more effective and efficient instrument, and the process will continue.

State of the Union Message, Jan. 14, 1963

52 / MONEY'S WORTH

Dollar for dollar, in or out of Government, there is no better form of investment in our national security than our much-abused foreign aid program. We cannot afford to lose it. We can afford to maintain it. We can surely afford, for example, to do as much for our 19 needy neighbors of Latin America as the Communist bloc is sending to the island of Cuba alone.

Text of undelivered Dallas address, Nov. 22, 1963

53 / "WE DARE NOT WEARY OF THE TASK"

Our security and strength, in the last analysis, directly depend on the security and strength of others—and that is why our military and economic assistance plays such a key role in enabling those who live on the periphery of the Communist world to maintain their independence of choice. Our assistance to these nations can be painful, risky and costly—as is true in Southeast Asia today. But we dare not weary of the task.

Ibid.

The Peace Corps

54 / PROPOSAL FOR A PEACE CORPS

Throughout the world the people of the newly developing nations are struggling for economic and social progress which reflects their deepest desires. Our own freedom, and the future of freedom around the world, depend, in a very real sense, on their ability to build growing and independent nations where men can live in dignity, liberated from the bonds of hunger, ignorance, and poverty.

One of the greatest obstacles to the achievement of this goal is the lack of trained men and women with the skill to teach the young and assist in the operation of development projects—men and women with the capacity to cope with the demands of swiftly evolving economies, and with the dedication to put that capacity to work in the villages, the mountains, the towns, and the factories of dozens of struggling nations. The vast task of economic development urgently requires skilled people to do the work of the society—to help teach in the schools, construct development projects, demonstrate modern methods of sanitation in the villages, and perform a hundred other tasks calling for training and advanced knowledge.

To meet this urgent need for skilled manpower we are proposing the establishment of a Peace Corps—an organization which will recruit and train American volunteers, sending them abroad to work with the people of other nations.

Message to Congress on the establishment of a permanent Peace Corps, March 1, 1961

55 / COUNTERING COMMUNIST MISSIONARIES

The fact of the matter is that out of Moscow and Peiping and Czechoslovakia and Eastern Germany are hundreds of men and women, scientists, physicists, teachers, engineers, doctors, nurses, studying in . . . institutes, prepared to spend their lives abroad in the service of world communism. . . . This can only be countered by skill and dedication of Americans who are willing to spend their lives serving the cause of freedom.

Campaign address, Cow Palace, San Francisco, Nov. 2, 1960

56 / MORE VALUABLE THAN ABUNDANCE

An even more valuable national asset is our reservoir of dedicated men and women—not only on our college campuses but in every age group—who have indicated their desire to contribute their skills, their efforts, and a part of their lives to the fight for world order.

State of the Union Message, Jan. 30, 1961

57 / POTENTIAL MISSIONARIES FOR FREEDOM

I am convinced that the pool of people in this country of ours anxious to respond to the public service is greater than it has ever been in our history. I am convinced that our men and women, dedicated to freedom, are able to be missionaries, not only for freedom and peace, but join in a worldwide struggle against poverty and disease and ignorance.

Campaign address, Cow Palace, San Francisco, Nov. 2, 1960

58 / READINESS TO SERVE

Nowhere is the profile of the best of American youth better drawn than in our Peace Corps volunteers. In the 2 years of the Peace Corps' growth from idea to rewarding reality, almost 45,000 American men and women —the majority of them young in years, all of them young in spirit—have volunteered their services. In January 1963 alone, the Peace Corps received 4,345 applications, almost 5 times the number received during the same period last year. This response reveals much that is reassuring about the generation which is heir to this country's traditions.

Message to Congress on the nation's youth, Feb. 14, 1963

59 / ACCOMPLISHMENTS OF PEACE CORPS WORKERS

Americans clearly recognize their obligation to their country and to mankind. They are willing to devote 2 years of their lives to serve the cause of a better, more peaceful world, no matter how distant, inconvenient or even hazardous that task may prove to be. Both capable and adaptable, they have demonstrated throughout the world a sense of purpose which has brought increased respect and admiration to their country as well as to themselves. . . . Whether they work as teachers, farmers, health workers, surveyors, construction workers, or in a wide variety of other fields, they are making meaningful contributions to international understanding. The most objective and effective appraisal of their contributions can best be found in the fact that every single country where Peace Corps volunteers are at work has requested more of them.

Ibid.

60 / RECOMMENDATION FOR EXPANSION

At the beginning of 1962, there were 750 volunteers at work or in training for service in 12 countries. By the same date in 1963 there were 4,350 volunteers—almost 4,000 of them 30 years old or younger—in training or in service in 44 countries. By the end of the summer, their number is expected to increase to 9,000. And requests for more volunteers continue to be received more rapidly than they can be met. I recommend, therefore, that the existing Peace Corps authority be renewed and expanded to permit a corps of 13,000 volunteers by September of 1964.

Ibid.

61 / ABILITY AND DEDICATION

The Peace Corps has permitted more Americans from more walks of life to exhibit more of these qualities on a more generous scale than ever before in the history of this country.

Ibid.

62 / VEHICLE OF AMERICAN IDEALISM

Neither money nor technical assistance . . . can be our only weapon against poverty. In the end, the crucial effort is one of purpose—requiring not only the fuel of finance but the torch of idealism. And nothing carries the spirit of American idealism more effectively to the far corners of the earth than the Peace Corps.

State of the Union Message, Jan. 14, 1963

4

The Americas

Inter-American Relations

1 / DEMOCRATIC DEVELOPMENT

For the first time in the history of inter-American relations our energies are concentrated on the central task of democratic development.

Address, reception for Latin American diplomats, Washington, D.C., March 13, 1962

2 / REDEDICATION TO HEMISPHERIC WELFARE

We in the United States have made many mistakes in our relations with the other American republics. We have not always understood the magnitude of your problems, or accepted our share of responsibility for the welfare of the hemisphere. But we have long dedicated the energy and will of the United States to an untiring pursuit of that welfare and I . . . reaffirm that dedication.

Address at state dinner, San Carlos Palace, Bogotá, Colombia, Dec. 17, 1961

3 / ECONOMIC SECURITY

Economic security, the bringing of a better life to all of our people, must now in the 1960's be the principal object and goal of the inter-American system.

Address at an agrarian reform project, La Morita, Venezuela, Dec. 16, 1961

4 / NOT MERELY SLOGANS

Now, today, in 1961, it is our obligation to move ahead and to bring to fruition the conception that along with national independence and individual liberties goes the well-being of the people themselves. We do not merely talk of slogans of democracy and freedom. It is our function here in this hemisphere in 1961 to make it possible for all the people not only to be free but to have a home, to educate their children, to have a job for themselves and their security, and that is what we are determined to do.

Ibid.

5 / SOCIAL REFORMS REQUIRED: A DIFFICULT TASK

Our own history shows how fierce the resistance can be to changes which later generations regard as part of the framework of life. And the course of rational social change is even more hazardous for those progressive governments [of the Western Hemisphere] who often face entrenched privilege of the Right and subversive conspiracies on the Left.

For too long my country, the wealthiest nation on a poor continent, failed to carry out its full responsibilities to its sister republics. We have now accepted that responsibility. In the same way those who possess wealth and power in poor nations must accept their own responsibilities. They must lead the fight for those basic reforms which alone can preserve the fabric of their own societies. Those who make peaceful revolution impossible will make violent revolution inevitable.

These social reforms are at the heart of The Alliance for Progress. They are the pre-condition to economic modernization. And they are the instrument by which we assure to the poor and hungry, to the worker and the campesino his full participation in the benefits of our development and in the same dignity which is the purpose of free societies. At the same time we sympathize with the difficulties of remaking deeply rooted and traditional social structures. We ask that substantial and steady progress toward reform accompany the effort to develop the economies of the American nations.

Address, reception for Latin American diplomats, Washington, D.C., March 13, 1962

6 / EQUALITY OF PEOPLE

Today we seek . . . to establish the principle that all the people of this hemisphere are entitled to a decent way of life and to transform that principle into the reality of economic advance and social justice on which political equality is based. This is the most demanding goal of all. For we seek not merely the welfare and equality of nations, but the welfare and equality of the people of these nations.

     Ibid.

7 / THE PROBLEMS OF THE UNDERPRIVILEGED

The people of the world respect a nation which can see beyond its own image. To us, the major issue is the fight against communism, but to them, those who live to the south of us, the fighting is against poverty and disease and illiteracy and ignorance.

     Campaign address, Portland, Ore., Sept. 7, 1960

8 / DETERMINATION TO IMPROVE

Throughout Latin America millions of people are struggling to free themselves from the bonds of poverty and hunger and ignorance. To the north and east they see the abundance which modern science can bring. They know the tools of progress are within their reach. And they are determined to have a better life for themselves and their children.

     Message to Congress on the Inter-American Fund for Social Progress, March 14, 1961

9 / MESSAGE FOR THE PEOPLE OF LATIN AMERICA

My real message is for millions of people in a thousand cities and villages throughout the mountains and plains of this majestic land. To you—to the workers, to the campesinos on the farms, to the women who toil wearily each day for the survival of their children—to you I bring a message of hope. Every day, every hour, in far-off Washington and in the capital of your own country, dedicated men are struggling to bring nearer the day when you will have more to eat and a decent roof over your head and schools for your children—when you will have a better and more abundant life to accompany that great human dignity and love of freedom from which all of us have much to learn. And . . . I pledge to you that, with your help, that day will come.

     Address at state dinner, San Carlos Palace, Bogotá, Colombia, Dec. 17, 1961

10 / LATIN AMERICANS: SENSE OF RESPONSIBILITY—FAITH IN THE UNITED STATES

Latin Americans, by an overwhelming majority, are ready to work, to sacrifice, to fight if necessary, to maintain their own freedom, and to build societies which serve the welfare of all their people. They lack only the full measure of resources necessary to build a hemisphere where all can be secure and free. They know that they bear the fundamental responsibility for their own welfare and progress, but . . . they also know that we in the United States today have a deep concern for their problems, a common dedication to their aspirations, and a faithful commitment to help them in their efforts.

News conference, Washington, D.C., March 21, 1963

11 / CHALLENGE

Today we face the greatest challenge to the vitality of our American revolution. Millions of our people—scattered across a vast and rich continent —endure lives of hopeless misery. We must prove to them that free institutions can best answer their implacable demand for social justice, for food, for material welfare and above all, for new hope—hope for themselves and for their children. And in so proving the blessings of freedom in Latin America, we will be teaching the same lesson to a watching and impatient world.

Address at state dinner, San Carlos Palace, Bogotá, Colombia, Dec. 17, 1961

12 / LEADERSHIP IN LATIN AMERICAN STATES

The leaders of Latin America, the industrialists and the land owners are, I am sure . . . ready to admit past mistakes and accept new responsibilities. For unless they are willing to contribute your resources to national development, unless they are prepared not merely to accept, but initiate, basic land and tax reforms, unless they take the lead in improving the welfare of the people of your country—then that leadership will be taken from them and the heritage of centuries of Western civilization will be consumed in a few months of violence.

Ibid.

13 / FREEDOM'S LIGHT

We are a young and strong people. Our Doctrines—the flames lit by Bolivar and Washington and San Martin—now burn brightly in Africa and Asia and wherever men struggle to be free. And here in our own hemisphere we have successfully resisted every effort to impose the despotism of the old world on the nations of the new.

Ibid.

14 / FREEDOM FROM FOREIGN RULE

. . . if there is one principle which has run through the long history of this hemisphere it is a common determination to prevent the rule of foreign systems or nations in the Americas.

Address, Inter-American Press Association, Miami Beach, Nov. 18, 1963

15 / GOALS OF FREEDOM

The achievement of . . . two freedoms—freedom from dictatorship and freedom from the bonds of economic and social injustice—must be the contribution of our generation in this decade.

Address at an agrarian reform project, La Morita, Venezuela, Dec. 16, 1961

16 / HISTORIC LESSONS FOR THE AMERICAS

I do not hold the view which some now preach that the only way we can make economic progress is through dictatorship. I believe the reverse. I believe that the experiences of Eastern Europe, the wall in Berlin, the famine in China, the hardships in our hemisphere show that liberty and economic progress go hand in hand provided the people and the Government together are permitted to progress for the people.

Ibid.

17 / PRIMARY OBJECTIVE

One of the first goals of the new spirit of this hemisphere must be the elimination of tyranny from the north to the south until it is a hemisphere that Simon Bolivar once predicted of free men, of free countries, living under a system of liberty.

Ibid.

18 / A PLEDGE

We are pledged to work with our sister republics to free the Americas of all such foreign domination and all tyranny, working toward the goal of a free hemisphere of free governments, extending from Cape Horn to the Arctic Circle.

State of the Union Message, Jan. 30, 1961

19 / "POWER OF DEMOCRACY"

The history of the Americas is a tribute to the creative force of free men, to the unparalleled power of democracy to reshape society to meet its new needs without violence, without repression, without a discipline which destroys liberty. It is this knowledge and experience which is the great contribution of our young nations to world history.

Address at state dinner, San Carlos Palace, Bogotá, Colombia, Dec. 17, 1961

20 / DEMOCRACIES DEMAND PEACEFUL CHANGE

Democratic governments demand that those in opposition accept the defects of today and work towards remedying them within the machinery of peaceful change. Otherwise, in return for momentary satisfaction, we tear apart the fabric and hope of lasting democracy.

Address, Inter-American Press Association, Miami Beach, Nov. 18, 1963

21 / BIRTHPLACE OF REVOLUTIONARY FORCES

We live in a hemisphere whose own revolution has given birth to the most powerful forces of the modern age—the search for the freedom and self-fulfillment of man.

Message to the Inter-American Economic and Social Conference, Punta del Este, Uruguay, Aug. 5, 1961

Alliance for Progress

22 / A SPECIAL PLEDGE

To our sister republics south of our border, we offer a special pledge—to convert our good words into good deeds, in a new alliance for progress, to assist free men and free governments in casting off the chains of poverty. But this peaceful revolution of hope cannot become the prey of hostile powers. Let all our neighbors know that we shall join with them to oppose aggression or subversion anywhere in the Americas. And let every other power know that this hemisphere intends to remain the master of its own house.

Inaugural address, Jan. 20, 1961

23 / OBJECTIVE

To our sister republics to the south, we have pledged a new alliance for progress—*alianza para progreso*. Our goal is a free and prosperous Latin America, realizing for all its states and their citizens a degree of economic and social progress that matches their historic contributions of culture, intellect, and liberty.

State of the Union Message, Jan. 30, 1961

24 / THE CALL IS SOUNDED

. . . I have called on all people of the hemisphere to join in a new Alliance for Progress—*Alianza para Progreso*—a vast cooperative effort, unparalleled in magnitude and nobility of purpose, to satisfy basic needs of the American people for homes, work and land, health and schools—*techo, trabajo y tierra, salud y escuela.*

> Address, reception for Latin American diplomats, Washington, D.C., March 13, 1961

25 / ACT OF BOGOTÁ

The Act of Bogotá marks an historic turning point in the evolution of the Western Hemisphere. For the first time the American nations have agreed to join in a massive cooperative effort to strengthen democratic institutions through a program of economic development and social progress.

> Message to Congress on the Inter-American Fund for Social Progress, March 14, 1961

26 / STEP FOR DEVELOPMENT

The Act [of Bogotá] itself is only a single step in our program for the development of the hemisphere—a program I have termed the Alliance for Progress—*Alianza para Progreso*. In addition to the social fund, hemispheric development will require substantial outside resources for economic development, a major self-help effort by the Latin American nations themselves, inter-American cooperation to deal with the problems of economic integration and commodity markets and other measures designed to speed economic growth and improve understanding among the American nations.

> *Ibid.*

27 / SELF-IMPROVEMENT PREREQUISITE

It is clear that the Bogotá program cannot have any significant impact if its funds are used merely for the temporary relief of conditions of distress. Its effectiveness depends on the willingness of each recipient nation to improve its own institutions, make necessary modifications in its own social patterns, and mobilize its own domestic resources for a program of development.

> *Ibid.*

28 / SOCIAL PROGRESS

The fund which I am requesting today will be devoted to social progress. Social progress is not a substitute for economic development. It is an effort to create a social framework within which all the people of a nation can share in the benefits of prosperity, and participate in the process of growth. Economic growth without social progress lets the great majority of the people remain in poverty, while a privileged few reap the benefits of rising abundance. In addition the process of growth largely depends on the existence of beneficial social conditions. Our own experience is witness to this. For much of our own great productivity and industrial development is based on our system of universal public education.

Thus the purpose of our special effort for social progress is to overcome the barriers of geographical and social isolation, illiteracy and lack of educational opportunities, archaic tax and land tenure structures, and other institutional obstacles to broad participation in economic growth.

Ibid.

29 / THE LAND PROBLEM

The uneven distribution of land is one of the gravest social problems in many Latin American countries. In some nations 2 percent of the farms account for three-fourths of the total farm area. And in one Central American country, 40 percent of the privately owned acreage is held in one-fifth of 1 percent of the number of farms. It is clear that when land ownership is so heavily concentrated, efforts to increase agricultural productivity will only benefit a very small percentage of the population. Thus if funds for improving land usage are to be used effectively they should go only to those nations in which the benefits will accrue to the great mass of rural workers.

Ibid.

30 / THE SEEDS OF UNREST

Improved land use and rural living conditions were rightly given top place in the Act of Bogotá. Most of the Latin American peoples live and work on the land. Yet agricultural output and productivity have lagged far behind both industrial development and urgent needs for consumption and export. As a result poverty, illiteracy, hopelessness, and a sense of injustice—the conditions which breed political and social unrest—are almost universal in the Latin American countryside.

Ibid.

31 / TO PREVENT COMMUNISM

The people of Latin America are the inheritors of a deep belief in political democracy and the freedom of man—a sincere faith that the best road to progress is freedom's road. But if the Act of Bogotá becomes just another empty declaration—if we are unwilling to commit our resources and energy to the task of social progress and economic development— then we face a grave and imminent danger that desperate peoples will turn to communism or other forms of tyranny as their only hope for change. Well-organized, skillful, and strongly financed forces are constantly urging them to take this course.

Ibid.

32 / CHARTER OF PUNTA DEL ESTE: GOAL, PEACEFUL REVOLUTION

The Charter of Punta del Este, which last August established the Alliance for Progress, is the framework of goals and conditions for what has been called "a peaceful revolution on a hemispheric scale."

That revolution had begun before the Charter was drawn. It will continue after its goals are reached. If its goals are not achieved, the revolution will continue, but its methods and results will be tragically different. History has removed for governments the margin of safety between the peaceful revolution and the violent revolution. The luxury of a leisurely interval is no longer available.

Message to Congress on foreign aid, March 12, 1962

33 / DOCTRINE OF FREEDOM

We must not forget that our Alliance for Progress is more than a doctrine of development, a blueprint for economic advance. Rather it is an expression of the noblest goals of our civilization. It says that want and despair need not be the lot of man. It says that no society is free until all its people have an equal opportunity to share the fruits of their own land and their own labor. And it says that material progress is meaningless without individual freedom and political liberty. It is a doctrine of the freedom of man in the most spacious sense of that freedom.

Address, reception for Latin American diplomats, Washington, D.C., March 13, 1962

34 / NATIONAL ECONOMIC FREEDOM AND INTERNATIONAL INTEGRITY

In pursuit of economic welfare the *Alianza* does not dictate to any nation how to organize its economic life. Every nation is free to shape its own economic institutions, in accordance with its own national needs and will. However, just as no country can tell another how it must order its economy, no nation should act within its own borders so as to violate the rights of others under accepted principles of international law.

Address, Inter-American Press Association, Miami Beach, Nov. 18, 1963

35 / RESPECT FOR NATIONAL SOVEREIGNTY

We are determined to reinforce the inter-American principle of absolute respect for the sovereignty and independence of every nation. That principle was at the heart of the Good Neighbor Policy—and we remain good neighbors today. That principle is the foundation of our Alliance—and we shall always be allies for progress.

Address at luncheon given by Adolfo Lopez Mateos, President of Mexico, Mexico City, June 29, 1962

36 / UNITY AGAINST COMMUNIST MENACE

If the Alliance is to succeed, we must continue to support measures to halt Communist infiltration and subversion and to assist governments menaced from abroad. The American states must be ready to come to the aid of any government requesting aid to prevent a take-over linked to the policies of foreign Communism rather than to an internal desire for change. My own country is prepared to do this.

Address, Inter-American Press Association, Miami Beach, Nov. 18, 1963

37 / UNITED STATES CONTRIBUTION

The Alliance for Progress . . . means a greatly increased effort by the United States both in terms of material resources and deeper comprehension of the basic needs of Latin America. My country has already begun its contribution.

Message to the Inter-American Economic and Social Conference, Punta del Este, Uruguay, Aug. 5, 1961

38 / INTER-AMERICAN UNITY

From this day forward, the inter-American system represents not merely the unity of governments that are involved but the unity of people, not only a common goal for a political alignment but a common vow by all of our governments and all of our people to improve man's economic, social and political well-being. Not just an alliance for the protection of our country, but an alliance for progress for our people. We will be in the

Nineteen Sixties more than good neighbors. We will be partners in building a better life for our people.

Address at an agrarian reform project, La Morita, Venezuela, Dec. 16, 1961

39 / A COOPERATIVE EFFORT

The men and women of this hemisphere know that the Alliance would not succeed if it were only another name for U.S. handouts—that it can succeed only as the Latin American nations themselves devote their best effort to fulfilling its goals.

State of the Union Message, Jan. 14, 1963

40 / EFFORTS OF LATIN AMERICAN NATIONS VITAL

Let me stress that only the most determined efforts of the American nations themselves can bring success to this effort. They, and they alone, can mobilize their resources, enlist the energies of their people, and modify their social patterns so that all, and not just a privileged few, share in the fruits of growth.

Address, reception for Latin American diplomats, Washington, D.C., March 13, 1961

41 / SELF-FULFILLMENT

It means full recognition of the right of all the people to share fully in our progress. For there is no place in democratic life for institutions which benefit the few while denying the needs of the many even though the elimination of such institutions may require far-reaching and difficult changes such as land reform and tax reform and a vastly increased emphasis on education and health and housing. Without these changes our common effort cannot succeed.

Message to the Inter-American Economic and Social Conference, Punta del Este, Uruguay, Aug. 5, 1961

42 / TOWERING EFFORT

Only an effort of towering dimension—an effort similar to that which was needed to rebuild the economies of Western Europe—can insure fulfillment of our Alliance for Progress. This heroic effort is not for governments alone. Its success demands the participation of all our people—of workers and farmers, business men and intellectuals and, above all, of the young people of the Americas. For to them and to their children belongs the new world we are resolved to create.

Ibid.

43 / "HISTORIC MOMENT"

The tasks before us are vast, the problems difficult, the challenges unparalleled. But we carry with us the vision of a new and better world, and the unlimited power of free men guided by free governments. And I believe that our ultimate success will make us proud to have lived and worked at this historic moment in the life of our hemisphere.

Ibid.

44 / SOME CONCRETE ACHIEVEMENTS

I do not underestimate the difficulties that we face in this mutual effort among our close neighbors, but the free states of this hemisphere, working in close collaboration, have begun to make this Alliance a reality. Today it is feeding one out of every four school-age children in Latin America an extra food ration from our farm surplus. It has distributed 1.5 million schoolbooks and is building 17,000 classrooms. It has helped resettle tens of thousands of farm families on land they can call their own. It is stimulating our good neighbors to more self-help and reform—fiscal, social, institutional, and land reforms. It is bringing housing and hope and health to millions who were previously forgotten.

State of the Union Message, Jan. 14, 1963

45 / ENDURING FAITH

In 1961 the American nations signed the Charter of Punta del Este. Today, more than two years later, despite dangers and difficulties, I support and believe in the Alliance for Progress more strongly than ever before.

Address, Inter-American Press Association, Miami Beach, Nov. 18, 1963

5

Disarmament

For Mankind's Security and Survival

I / A REQUEST

To those nations who make themselves our adversary, we offer not a pledge but a request: that both sides begin anew the quest for peace, before the dark powers of destruction unleashed by science engulf all humanity in planned or accidental self-destruction.

Inaugural address, Jan. 20, 1961

2 / MUTUALLY UNSATISFACTORY COURSE

. . . neither can two great and powerful groups of nations take comfort from our present course—both sides overburdened by the cost of modern weapons, both rightly alarmed by the steady spread of the deadly atom, yet both racing to alter that uncertain balance of terror that stays the hand of mankind's final war.

Ibid.

3 / UNITED STATES AND SOVIET UNION CAUGHT UP IN VICIOUS CYCLE

. . . in the cold war, which brings burdens and dangers to so many countries, including this nation's closest allies—our two countries bear the heaviest burdens. For we are both devoting massive sums of money to weapons that could better be devoted to combating ignorance, poverty and disease. We are both caught up in a vicious and dangerous cycle in which suspicion on one side breeds suspicion on the other, and new weapons beget counterweapons. In short, both the United States and its allies, and the Soviet Union and its allies, have a mutually deep interest in a just and genuine peace and in halting the arms race.

    Commencement address, American University, Washington, D.C., June 10, 1963

4 / CONTINUING ENDEAVORS

Disarmament, so difficult and so urgent, has been much discussed . . . but progress has not been made. Recrimination in such matters is seldom useful, and we for our part are determined to try again. In so doing, we note that, in the public position of both sides in recent years, the determination to be strong has been coupled with announced willingness to negotiate. For our part, we know there can be dialectical truth in such a position, and we shall do all we can to prove it in action. . . . If genuine progress is made, then as tension is reduced, so will be our arms.

    Message to Congress on the defense budget, March 28, 1961

5 / SUPREME EFFORT

Peace in space will help us naught once peace on earth is gone. World order will be secured only when the whole world has laid down weapons which seem to offer us present security but threaten future survival of the human race. That armistice day seems very far away. The vast resources of this planet are being devoted more and more to the means of destroying, instead of enriching, human life.

    But the world was not meant to be a prison in which man awaits his executioner. Nor has mankind survived the tests and the trials of thousands of years to surrender everything including its existence now.

    This nation has the will and the faith to make a supreme effort to break the logjam on disarmament and nuclear tests—and we will persist until we prevail, until the rule of law has replaced the ever-dangerous use of force.

    State of the Union Message, Jan. 11, 1962

6 / SHRINKING SECURITY

Men no longer maintain that disarmament must await the settlement of all disputes, for disarmament must be a part of any permanent settlement. And man may no longer pretend that the quest for disarmament is a sign of weakness, for in a spiraling arms race a nation's security may be shrinking even as its arms increase.

    Address, U.N. General Assembly, Sept. 25, 1961

7 / A CRUCIAL DEVELOPMENT

. . . the fact that the immediate and practical significance of the task . . . has come to be so fully realized by the peoples of the world is one of the crucial developments of our time. For men know that amassing of destructive power does not beget security; they know that polemics do not bring peace.

> Letter to Secretary of State Dean Rusk on disarmament, Washington, D.C., March 14, 1962

8 / THE WILL FOR DISARMAMENT

Men's minds, men's hearts, and men's spiritual aspirations alike demand no less than a reversal of the course of recent history—a replacement of ever-growing stockpiles of destruction by ever-growing opportunities for human achievement. . . . This task, the foremost item on the agenda of humanity, is not a quick or easy one. It must be approached both boldly and responsibly. It is a task whose magnitude and urgency justifies our bringing to bear upon it the highest resources of creative statesmanship the international community has to offer, for it is the future of the community of mankind that is involved.

We must pledge ourselves at the outset to an unceasing effort to continue until the job is done. We must not be discouraged by initial disagreements nor weakened in our resolve by the tensions that surround us and add difficulties to our task. For verifiable disarmament arrangements are not a fair weather phenomenon.

A sea wall is not needed when the seas are calm. Sound disarmament agreements, deeply rooted in mankind's mutual interest in survival, must serve as a bulwark against the tidal waves of war and its destructiveness. Let no one, then, say that we cannot arrive at such agreements in troubled times, for it is then their need is greatest.

> *Ibid.*

9 / URGENCY FOR A BEGINNING

If a beginning can be made by breaking the arms race and moving toward general disarmament, mankind will have turned a corner of history. Although the difficulties and frustrations are great, the task of achieving disarmament is not an impossible one. Each day its importance and urgency increase.

> Statement on resumption in Geneva of East-West disarmament talks, Hyannis Port, Mass., July 14, 1962

10 / MANKIND'S CHOICE

Mankind must put an end to war or war will put an end to mankind.

Address, U.N. General Assembly, Sept. 25, 1961

11 / STRIVING FOR DISARMAMENT

Peace requires an America that is planning and preparing and striving for disarmament. . . . the hour has grown late. The weapons are more deadly. Atomic know-how has spread, and the next administration must devote the same effort to the struggle for peace, the same resources and energies, that we now put into the preparation for war.

Campaign address at Democratic Women's luncheon, New York City, Sept. 14, 1960

12 / URGENCY FOR LIMITATION

The deadly arms race, and the huge resources it absorbs, have too long overshadowed all else we must do. We must prevent that arms race from spreading to new nations, to new nuclear powers, and to the reaches of outer space.

State of the Union Message, Jan. 30, 1961

13 / UNCEASING PURSUIT OF PEACE

Our commitment to national safety is not a commitment to expand our Military Establishment indefinitely. We do not dismiss disarmament as an idle dream. For we believe that, in the end, it is the only way of assuring the security of all without impairing the interests of any. Nor do we mistake honorable negotiation for appeasement. While we shall never weary in the defense of freedom, neither shall we abandon the pursuit of peace.

State of the Union Message, Jan. 14, 1963

14 / FOR MANKIND'S BENEFIT

All men will benefit if we can invoke the wonders of science instead of its terrors.

News conference, Washington, D.C., Feb. 21, 1962

15 / HUMANITY'S POSSIBILITIES

If the future holds great potentialities for destruction, the possibilities for a better life, for human dignity, and for a real enduring peace are even greater, if we but have the will, the patience, and the skill to bring them about.

Campaign message to the nation's new voters, Washington, D.C., Oct. 5, 1960

The Threat of Nuclear War

16 / THE POWER OF HUMAN EXTERMINATION

The world has been close to war before—but now man, who has survived all previous threats to his existence, has taken into his mortal hands the power to exterminate the entire species some seven times over.

Acceptance speech, Democratic National Convention, Los Angeles, July 15, 1960

17 / SOURCE OF UNIVERSAL TENSION

Men no longer debate whether armaments are a symptom or a cause of tension. The mere existence of modern weapons—ten million times more powerful than any that the world has ever seen, and only minutes away from any target on earth—is a source of horror and discord and distrust.

Address, U.N. General Assembly, Sept. 25, 1961

18 / AMERICA'S PEACE EFFORTS OBSTRUCTED

For fifteen years we have sought to make the atom an instrument of peaceful growth rather than of war. But for fifteen years our concessions have been matched by obstruction, our patience by intransigence, and the pleas of mankind for peace have been met with disregard.

Ibid.

19 / UNREMITTING EFFORTS FOR EARLY ACTION

In . . . negotiations the United States will continue to seek agreement which will meet the dangers of the nuclear threat. These dangers will only increase if early action is not taken to halt the growth of stockpiles of modern armaments, the spread of nuclear weapons into the arsenals of a widening number of countries and to outer space, and the possibilities of outbreak of war by accident, miscalculation or failure of communication.

Statement on resumption in Geneva of East-West disarmament talks, Hyannis Port, Mass., July 14, 1962

20 / MISJUDGMENTS

Three times in my lifetime our country and Europe have been involved in major wars. In each case serious misjudgments were made on both sides of the intentions of others which brought about great devastation. Now in the thermonuclear age any misjudgments on either side about the intentions of the other could rain more devastation in several hours than has been wrought in all the wars of human history.

Address to the nation on the Berlin crisis, Washington, D.C., July 25, 1961

21 / NUCLEAR DANGER

Today, every inhabitant of this planet must contemplate the day when this planet may no longer be habitable. Every man, woman and child lives under a nuclear sword of Damocles, hanging by the slenderest of threads, capable of being cut at any moment by accident, or miscalculation or by madness. The weapons of war must be abolished before they abolish us.

Address, U.N. General Assembly, Sept. 25, 1961

22 / COMMON INTEREST

In a nuclear age, all nations have a common interest in preserving their mutual security against the growing perils of the arms race.

Statement on resumption in Geneva of East-West disarmament talks, Hyannis Port, Mass., July 14, 1962

23 / NUCLEAR DISASTER

Unconditional war can no longer lead to unconditional victory. It can no longer concern the great powers alone. For a nuclear disaster, spread by wind and water and fear, could well engulf the great and the small, the rich and the poor, the committed and the uncommitted alike.

Address, U.N. General Assembly, Sept. 25, 1961

24 / FREE-WORLD EFFORT TO AVERT DISASTER

We move for the first time in our history through an age in which two opposing powers have the capacity to destroy each other, and while we do not intend to see the free world give up, we shall make every effort to prevent the world from being blown up.

Address, University of North Carolina, Chapel Hill, Oct. 12, 1961

25 / AMERICA'S OBJECTIVE: VICTORY FOR FREEDOM WITHOUT NUCLEAR WAR

. . . every American . . . wants the United States to be secure and at peace and they want the cause of freedom around the world to prevail. Quite obviously that is our national objective. And what we are anxious to do, of course, is protect our national security, protect the freedom of countries, permit what Thomas Jefferson called "the disease of liberty" to be caught in areas which are now held by Communists and some areas where people are imprisoned.

We want to do that, of course, without having a nuclear war. Now, if someone thinks we should have a nuclear war in order to win, I can inform them that there will not be winners in the next nuclear war if there is one, and that this country and other countries will suffer very heavy blows. So that we have to proceed with responsibility and with care in an age where the human race can obliterate itself.

And that—the objective of this Administration, and I think the objective of the country—is to protect our security, keep the peace, protect our vital interests, make it possible for what we believe to be a system of government which is in accordance with the basic aspirations of people everywhere to ultimately prevail.

News Conference, Washington, D.C., Feb. 14, 1962

26 / NUCLEAR WAR TODAY

A war today or tomorrow, if it led to nuclear war, would not be like any war in history. A full-scale nuclear exchange, lasting less than 60 minutes, could wipe out more than 300,000,000 Americans, Europeans and Russians, as well as untold numbers elsewhere. And the survivors, as Chairman Krushchev warned the Communist Chinese, "would envy the dead." For they would inherit a world so devastated by the explosions and poison and fire that today we cannot even conceive of all its horrors.

Address to the nation on the Nuclear Test Ban Treaty, Washington, D.C., July 26, 1963

27 / THERMONUCLEAR DESTRUCTIVE FORCE

If only one thermonuclear bomb were to be dropped on any American, Russian or other city—whether it was launched by accident or design, by a madman or by an enemy, by a large nation or small, from any corner of the world—that one bomb could release more destructive force on the inhabitants of that one helpless city than all the bombs dropped in the Second World War.

Ibid.

28 / IS THE UNITED STATES ORIENTED TOWARD WAR?

I think that we have made it very clear that there is not going to be any winner of the next war. No one who is a rational man can possibly desire to see hostilities break out, particularly between the major powers which are equipped with nuclear weapons. So your view of the United States in this regard is really inaccurate.

We certainly desire peace. I am not aware of any action which the United States has taken since the end of the second war which has not been in the direction of securing peace.

Exchange with Brazilian university students, Washington, D.C., July 31, 1962

29 / PATIENCE FROM UNDERSTANDING

No man who witnessed the tragedies of the last war, no man who can imagine the unimaginable possibilities of the next war can advocate war out of irritability or frustration or impatience.

Veterans Day address, Arlington National Cemetery, Nov. 11, 1961

The Nuclear Test Ban Treaty: A Step toward Peace

30 / A BEGINNING

The logical place to begin is a treaty assuring the end of nuclear tests of all kinds, in every environment, under workable controls. The United States and the United Kingdom have proposed such a treaty that is both reasonable, effective and ready for signature. We are still prepared to sign that treaty today.

Address, U.N. General Assembly, Sept. 25, 1961

31 / TOP PRIORITY

. . . you should seek as a matter of highest priority agreement on a safeguarded nuclear test ban. At this juncture in history no single measure in the field of disarmament would be more productive of concrete benefit in the alleviation of tensions and the enhancement of prospects for greater progress.

Letter to Secretary of State Dean Rusk on disarmament, Washington, D.C., March 14, 1962

32 / VERIFICATION

Our position is a simple one and it is that whatever disarmament obligations are undertaken must be subject to satisfactory verification.
Message to Premier Khrushchev, Palm Beach, Fla., Feb. 25, 1962

33 / TO PREVENT NUCLEAR DIFFUSION

. . . those who sign the treaty would use all the influence that they had in their possession to persuade others not to grasp the nuclear nettle.
News conference, Bonn, West Germany, June 24, 1963

34 / SO NEAR, YET SO FAR

The only major area of . . . negotiations where the end is in sight—yet where a fresh start is badly needed—is a treaty to outlaw nuclear tests. The conclusion of such a treaty—so near and yet so far—would check the spiraling arms race in one of its most dangerous areas. It would place the nuclear powers in a position to deal more effectively with one of the greatest hazards which man faces in 1963—the further spread of nuclear weapons. It would increase our security—it would decrease the prospects of war.
Commencement address, American University, Washington, D.C., June 10, 1963

35 / ACT OF FAITH

To make clear our good faith and solemn convictions . . . the United States does not propose to conduct nuclear tests in the atmosphere so long as other states do not do so. We will not be the first to resume. Such a declaration is no substitute for a formal binding treaty—but I hope it will help us achieve one. Nor would such a treaty be a substitute for disarmament—but I hope it will help us achieve it.
Ibid.

36 / "IN A SPIRIT OF HOPE"

I speak to you tonight in a spirit of hope. Eighteen years ago the advent of nuclear weapons changed the course of the world as well as the war. Since that time, all mankind has been struggling to escape from the darkening prospects of mass destruction. . . . Yesterday, a shaft of light cut into the darkness. Negotiations were concluded in Moscow on a treaty to ban all nuclear tests in the atmosphere, in outer space and under water. For the first time, an agreement has been reached on bringing the forces of nuclear destruction under international control.

Address to the nation on the Nuclear Test Ban Treaty, Washington, D.C., July 26, 1963

37 / "VICTORY FOR MANKIND"

The achievement of this goal is not a victory for one side; it is a victory for mankind.

Ibid.

38 / LIMITED PURPOSES ELIMINATE INSPECTION

. . . in 1946 . . . Bernard Baruch submitted our comprehensive plan to the members of the United Nations. That plan, and many subsequent disarmament plans, large and small, have all been blocked by those opposed to international inspection. A ban on nuclear tests, however, requires on-the-spot inspection only for underground tests. This nation now possesses a variety of techniques to detect the nuclear tests of other nations which are conducted in the air or under water, for such tests produce unmistakable signs which our modern instruments can pick up. The treaty initialed yesterday, therefore, is a limited treaty which permits continued underground testing and prohibits only those tests that we ourselves can police. It requires no control posts, no onsite inspection, no international body.

Ibid.

39 / PROVISION FOR WITHDRAWAL

Any nation which signs the treaty will have an opportunity to withdraw if it finds that extraordinary events related to the subject matter of the treaty have jeopardized its supreme interests; and no nation's right to self-defense will be impaired.

Ibid.

40 / A FIRST STEP

This treaty is not the millennium. It will not resolve all conflicts, or cause the Communists to forgo their ambitions, or eliminate the dangers of war. It will not reduce our need for arms or allies or programs of assistance to others. But it is an important first step—a step toward peace—a step toward reason—a step away from war.

Ibid.

41 / AVENUE TO BROADER AGREEMENT

This treaty can be a step toward reduced world tensions and broader areas of agreement. The Moscow talks reached no agreement on any other subject, nor is this treaty conditioned on any other matter.

Ibid.

42 / POSSIBLE SYMBOL OF NEW ERA

Nuclear test ban negotiations have long been a symbol of East-West disagreement. If this treaty can also be a symbol—if it can symbolize the end of one era and the beginning of another—if both sides can by this treaty gain confidence and experience in peaceful collaboration—then this short and simple treaty may well become an historic mark in man's age-old pursuit of peace.

Ibid.

43 / TOWARD ENDING FALLOUT PERIL

The treaty can be a step freeing the world from fears and dangers of radioactive fallout.

Ibid.

44 / FALLOUT AND RESPECT FOR HUMAN LIFE

The loss of even one human life or the malformation of even one baby—who may be born long after we are gone—should be of concern to us all. Our children and grandchildren are not merely statistics toward which we can be indifferent.

Ibid.

45 / PREVENTING SPREAD OF NUCLEAR WEAPONS

This treaty can be a step toward preventing the spread of nuclear weapons to nations not now possessing them. During the next several years, in addition to the four current nuclear powers [United States, Soviet Union, United Kingdom and France], a small but significant number of nations will have the intellectual, physical and financial resources to produce both nuclear weapons and the means of delivering them. In time, it is estimated, many other nations will have either this capacity or other ways of obtaining nuclear warheads, even as missiles can be commercially purchased today.

I ask you to stop and think for a moment what it would mean to have nuclear weapons in many hands—in the hands of countries large and small, stable and unstable, responsible and irresponsible, scattered throughout the world. There would be no rest for anyone then, no stability, no real security, and no chance of effective disarmament. There would only be increased chances of accidental war, and an increased necessity for the great powers to involve themselves in what would otherwise be local conflicts.

Ibid.

46 / OBLIGATION OF THE NUCLEAR POWERS

We have a great obligation—all four nuclear powers have a great obligation—to use whatever time remains to prevent the spread of nuclear weapons, to persuade other countries not to test, transfer, acquire, possess or produce such weapons.

This treaty can be the opening wedge in that campaign. It provides that none of the parties will assist other nations to test in the forbidden environments. It opens the door for further agreements on the control of nuclear weapons. And it is open for all nations to sign. For it is in the interest of all nations—and already we have heard from a number of countries who wish to join with us promptly.

Ibid.

47 / AID TO SECURITY

This treaty can limit the nuclear arms race in ways, which, on balance, will strengthen our nation's security far more than the continuation of unrestricted testing. . . . We have, and under this treaty we will continue to have, all the nuclear strength that we need.

Ibid.

48 / POSSIBILITY OF SECRET VIOLATIONS

Nations cannot afford in these matters to rely simply on the good faith of their adversaries. We have not therefore overlooked the risk of secret violations. There is at present a possibility that deep in outer space, hundreds of thousands and millions of miles away from the earth, illegal tests might go undetected. But we already have the capability to construct a system of observation that make such tests almost impossible to conceal. . . . Any violation, moreover, involves along with the risk of detection, the end of the treaty, and the worldwide consequences for the violator.

Ibid.

49 / VIGILANCE MAINTAINED

Our own vigilance and strength must be maintained as we remain ready to withdraw and to resume all forms of testing, if we must. But it would be a mistake to assume that this treaty will be quickly broken. The gains of illegal testing are obviously slight compared to their cost, and the hazard of discovery.

Ibid.

50 / SELF-INTEREST THE MOTIVATION

The nations which have initialed and will sign this treaty prefer it, in my judgment, to unrestricted testing as a matter of their own self-interest. For these nations, too, and all nations, have a stake in limiting the arms race, in halting the spread of nuclear weapons and breathing air that is not radioactive.

Ibid.

51 / SAFER COURSE

This limited test ban in our most careful judgment is safer by far for the United States than an unlimited nuclear arms race.

Ibid.

52 / DEBATE CALLED FOR

A document which may mark an historic and constructive opportunity for the world deserves an historic and constructive debate. It is my hope that all of you will take part in that debate, for this treaty is for all of us. It is particularly for our children and our grandchildren, and they have no lobby in Washington.

Ibid.

53 / PEOPLE'S RESPONSIBILITY

This debate will involve military, scientific and political experts, but it must not be left to them alone. The right and the responsibility are yours.

Ibid.

54 / NOT PEACE—BUT PERHAPS THE PATH OF PEACE

Nothing could more greatly damage our cause than if we and our allies were to believe that peace has already been achieved and that our strength and unity were no longer required. But now for the first time in many years the path of peace may be open. No one can be certain what the future will bring. No one can say whether the time has come for an easing of the struggle, but history and our own conscience will judge us harshly if we do not now make every effort to test our hopes by action, and this is the place to begin.

Ibid.

55 / "LET US TAKE THAT FIRST STEP"

According to the ancient Chinese proverb, a journey of 1,000 miles must begin with a single step. My fellow Americans, let us take that first step. Let us, if we can, step back from the shadows of war and seek out the way of peace. And if that journey is 1,000 miles, or even more, let history record that we, in this land, at this time, took the first step.

Ibid.

56 / MESSAGE OF HOPE

In its first two decades, the age of nuclear energy has been full of fear, yet never empty of hope. Today the fear is a little less and the hope a little greater. For the first time, we have been able to reach an agreement which can limit the dangers of this age.

The agreement itself is limited, but its message of hope has been heard and understood, not only by the peoples of the three originating nations, but by the peoples and Governments of the hundred other countries that have signed. This treaty is the first fruit of labors in which multitudes have shared—citizens, legislators, statesmen, diplomats, and soldiers, too.

Soberly and unremittingly this nation—but never this nation alone —has sought the doorway to effective disarmament into a world where peace is secure. Today we have a beginning and it is right for us to acknowledge all whose work across the years has helped make this beginning possible.

What the future will bring, no one of us can know. This first fruit of hope may or may not be followed by larger harvests. Even this limited treaty, great as it is with promise, can survive only if it has from others the determined support in letter and spirit which I hereby pledge in behalf of the United States.

If this treaty fails, it will not be our doing, and even if it fails we shall not regret that we have made this clear and honorable national commitment to the cause of man's survival. For under this treaty, we can and must still keep our vigil in defense of freedom.

But this treaty need not fail. This small step toward safety can be followed by others longer and less limited, if also harder in the taking. With our courage and understanding enlarged by this achievement, let us press on in quest of man's essential desire for peace.

As President of the United States and with the advice and consent of the Senate, I now sign the instruments of ratification of this treaty.

Statement on ratifying the Treaty to Limit Nuclear Testing, Washington, D.C., Oct. 7, 1963

6

Preparedness in the Pursuit of Peace

Defense for Peace

1 / ARMS FOR DETERRENCE

So long as fanaticism and fear brood over the affairs of men, we must arm to deter others from aggression.

State of the Union Message, Jan. 11, 1962

2 / DETERRING WOULD-BE ADVERSARIES

We dare not tempt them with weakness. For only when our arms are sufficient beyond doubt can we be certain beyond doubt that they will never be employed.

Inaugural address, Jan. 20, 1961

3 / A PERILOUS FUTURE

Peace and freedom do not come cheap, and we are destined, all of us here today, to live out most if not all of our lives in uncertainty and challenge and peril. Our policy must therefore blend, whatever degree of firmness and flexibility, which are necessary to protect our vital interests, by peaceful means if possible, by resolute action if necessary.

Address, University of North Carolina, Chapel Hill, Oct. 12, 1961

4 / ARMS SECURITY

This nation can afford to be strong—it cannot afford to be weak.

Message to Congress on the defense budget, March 28, 1961

5 / STRENGTH

Neither smiles nor frowns, neither good intentions nor harsh words, are a substitute for strength.

Campaign address, Alexandria, Va., Aug. 24, 1960

6 / PREREQUISITE

It is an unfortunate fact that we can secure peace only by preparing for war.

Campaign address, Seattle, Sept. 6, 1960

7 / FROM STRENGTH

We can convince Mr. Khrushchev to bargain seriously at the conference table if he respects our strength.

Ibid.

8 / FIVE SOURCES OF STRENGTH FOR PEACE

At times our goal has been obscured by crisis or endangered by conflict, but it draws sustenance from five basic sources of strength:

The moral and physical strength of the United States;

The united strength of the Atlantic community;

The regional strength of our hemispheric relations;

The creative strength of our efforts in the new and developing nations;

And the peace-keeping strength of the United Nations.

State of the Union Message, Jan. 11, 1962

9 / MILITARY STRENGTH ESSENTIAL

We are moving into a period of uncertain risk and great commitment in which both the military and diplomatic possibilities require a free world force so powerful as to make any aggression clearly futile.

State of the Union Message, Jan. 30, 1961

10 / "MAKING IT CLEAR"

Our strategic arms and defenses must be adequate to deter any deliberate nuclear attack on the United States or our allies—by making it clear to any potential aggressor that sufficient retaliatory forces will be able to survive a first strike and penetrate his defenses in order to inflict unacceptable losses upon him.

Message to Congress on the defense budget, March 28, 1961

11 / UNMISTAKABLE DEFENSE POSTURE

Our defense posture must be both flexible and determined. Any potential aggressor contemplating an attack on any part of the free world with any kind of weapons, conventional or nuclear, must know that our response will be suitable, selective, swift, and effective.

Ibid.

12 / REQUIREMENT FOR PEACE

Peace requires, unfortunately, an American defense posture strong enough to convince any potential aggressor that a war would be a mistake —his mistake.

Campaign address, Democratic Women's luncheon, New York City, Sept. 14, 1960

13 / UNTIL THE SOVIET UNION CHOOSES PEACE

If all trends and developments can persuade the Soviet Union to walk the path of peace, then let her know that all free nations will join with her. But until that choice is made, and until the world can develop a reliable system of international security, the free peoples have no choice but to keep their arms near.

State of the Union Message, Jan. 14, 1963

14 / AMERICAN TRADITION OF NONAGGRESSION

Our arms will never be used to strike the first blow in any attack. This is not a confession of weakness but a statement of strength. It is our national tradition. We must offset whatever advantage this may appear to hand an aggressor by so increasing the capability of our forces to respond swiftly and effectively to any aggressive move as to convince any would-be aggressor that such a movement would be too futile and costly to undertake. In the area of general war, this doctrine means that such capability must rest with that portion of our forces which would survive the initial attack. We are not creating forces for a first strike against any other nation. We shall never threaten, provoke or initiate aggression—but if aggression should come, our response will be swift and effective.

Message to Congress on the defense budget, March 28, 1961

15 / THE PRIMARY PURPOSE

The primary purpose of our arms is peace, not war—to make certain that they will never have to be used—to deter all wars, general or limited, nuclear or conventional, large or small—to convince all potential aggressors that any attack would be futile—to provide backing for diplomatic settlement of disputes—to insure the adequacy of our bargaining power for an end to the arms race. The basic problems facing the world today are not susceptible to a military solution. Neither our strategy nor our psychology as a nation—and certainly not our economy—must become dependent upon the permanent maintenance of a large Military Establishment. Our military posture must be sufficiently flexible and under control to be consistent with our efforts to explore all possibilities and to take every step to lessen tensions, to obtain peaceful solutions and to secure arms limitations. Diplomacy and defense are no longer distinct alternatives, one to be used where the other fails—both must complement each other.

Ibid.

16 / PREPARATION

The new preparations that we shall make to defend the peace . . . are based on our needs to meet a worldwide threat. . . . Our primary purpose is neither propaganda nor provocation, but preparation.

Address to the nation on the Berlin crisis, Washington, D.C., July 25, 1961

17 / MILITARY FLEXIBILITY

We have rejected any all-or-nothing posture which would leave no choice but inglorious retreat or unlimited retaliation.

State of the Union Message, Jan. 11, 1962

18 / FLEXIBILITY IN MAINTAINING SECURITY

Our national security, in a period of rapid change, will depend on constant reappraisal of our present doctrine, on alertness to new developments, on imagination and resourcefulness and new ideas.

> Commencement address, U.S. Air Force Academy, Colorado Springs, June 5, 1963

19 / PREVENTION OF ACCIDENTAL WAR

Our defense posture must be designed to reduce the danger of irrational or unpremeditated general war—the danger of an unnecessary escalation of a small war into a large one, or of miscalculation or misinterpretation of an incident or enemy intention. Our diplomatic efforts to reach agreements on the prevention of surprise attack, an end to the spread of nuclear weapons—indeed all our efforts to end the arms race—are aimed at this objective.

> Message to Congress on the defense budget, March 28, 1961

20 / AMERICAN VIEW

We are neither warmongers nor appeasers, neither hard nor soft. We are Americans, determined to defend the frontiers of freedom by an honorable peace, if peace is possible, but by arms if arms are used against us.

> Address, University of Washington, Seattle, Nov. 16, 1961

21 / MEETING TERRORISM

Terror is not a new weapon. Throughout history it has been used by those who could not prevail either by persuasion or example. But inevitably they fail, either because men are not afraid to die for a life worth living, or because the terrorists themselves came to realize that free men cannot be frightened by threats and that aggression would meet its own response. And it is in the light of that history that every nation today should know, be he friend or foe, that the United States has both the will and the weapons to join free men in standing up to their responsibilities.

> Address, U.N. General Assembly, Sept. 25, 1961

22 / UNTIL WAR IS BANISHED

Seventeen years ago, man unleashed the power of the atom. He thereby took into his mortal hands the power of self-extinction. Throughout the years that have followed, under three successive Presidents, the United States has sought to banish this weapon from the arsenals of individual nations. For of all the awesome responsibilities entrusted to this office, none is more somber to contemplate than the special statutory authority to employ nuclear arms in the defense of our people and freedom.

But until mankind has banished both war and its instruments of destruction, the United States must maintain an effective quantity and quality of nuclear weapons, so deployed and protected as to be capable of surviving any surprise attack and devastating the attacker. Only through such strength can we be certain of deterring a nuclear attack, or an overwhelming ground attack, upon our forces and our allies.

Only through such strength can we in the free world—should that deterrent fail—face the tragedy of another war with any hope of survival. And that deterrent strength, if it is to be effective and credible when compared with that of any other nation, must embody the most modern, the most reliable and the most versatile nuclear weapons our research and development can produce.

Address to the nation on nuclear testing and disarmament, Washington, D.C., March 2, 1962

23 / IF NECESSARY, THE LAST FULL MEASURE

Let no nation confuse our perseverance and patience with fear of war or unwillingness to meet our responsibilities. We cannot save ourselves by abandoning those who are associated with us or rejecting our responsibilities.

In the end, the only way to maintain the peace is to be prepared in the final extreme to fight for our country and to mean it. As a nation we have little capacity for deception. We can convince friend and foe alike that we are in earnest about the defense of freedom only if we are in earnest. And I can assure the world that we are.

Veterans Day address, Arlington National Cemetery, Nov. 11, 1961

24 / STRENGTH FOR PEACE

We increase our arms at a heavy cost, primarily to make certain we will never use them. We must face up to the chance of war if we are to have a chance for peace.

Address, University of Washington, Seattle, Nov. 16, 1961

25 / COST OF PREPAREDNESS

There is no discount price on defense.

Annual budget message to Congress, Jan. 17, 1963

26 / OUR GOALS: STRENGTH AND PEACE

On the Presidential coat of arms, the American eagle holds in his right talon the olive branch, while in his left is held a bundle of arrows. We intend to give equal attention to both.

State of the Union Message, Jan. 30, 1961

27 / ROLE OF THE MILITARY

The basic problems facing the world today are not susceptible of a final military solution. While we will long require the services and admire the dedication and commitment of the fighting men of this country, neither our strategy nor our psychology as a nation . . . must become permanently dependent upon an ever-increasing Military Establishment.

Commencement address, U.S. Military Academy, West Point, N.Y., June 6, 1962

28 / CIVILIAN CONTROL

Our arms must be subject to ultimate civilian control and command at all times, in war as well as peace. The basic decisions on our participation in any conflict and our response to any threat . . . will be made by the regularly constituted civilian authorities.

Message to Congress on the defense budget, March 28, 1961

29 / STRENGTHENING DEFENSE AGAINST NON-NUCLEAR WEAPONS

The Free World's security can be endangered not only by a nuclear attack, but also by being slowly nibbled away at the periphery, regardless of our strategic power, by forces of subversion, infiltration, intimidation, indirect or non-overt aggression, internal revolution, diplomatic blackmail, guerrilla warfare, or a series of limited wars.

Ibid.

30 / ROLE OF OUR OVERSEA FORCES

The strength and deployment of our forces in combination with those of our allies should be sufficiently powerful and mobile to prevent the steady erosion of the Free World through limited wars; and it is this role that should constitute the primary mission of our oversea forces. Non-nuclear wars, and sub-limited or guerrilla warfare, have since 1945 constituted the most active and constant threat to Free World security.

Ibid.

31 / "ANOTHER TYPE OF WARFARE"

Korea has not been the only battleground since the end of the Second World War. Men have fought and died in Malaya, in Greece, in the Philippines, in Algeria and Cuba and Cyprus and almost continuously on the Indochinese Peninsula. No nuclear weapons have been fired—no massive nuclear retaliation has been considered appropriate.

This is another type of warfare—new in its intensity, ancient in its origin—war by guerrillas, subversives, insurgents, assassins—war by ambush instead of by combat, by infiltration instead of aggression—seeking victory by eroding and exhausting the enemy instead of engaging him. It is a form of warfare uniquely adapted to what has been strangely called "wars of liberation," to undermine the efforts of new and poor countries to maintain the freedom that they have finally achieved. It preys on economic unrest and ethnic conflict.

It requires in those situations where we must counter it—and these are the kinds of challenges that will be before us in the next decade—if freedom is to be saved, a whole new kind of strategy, a wholly different kind of military training.

> Commencement address, U.S. Military Academy, West Point, N.Y., June 6, 1962

America's Goal: A Just and Lasting Peace

32 / PRIMACY

The most important topic on earth: world peace.

> Commencement address, American University, Washington, D.C., June 10, 1963

33 / RELENTLESS PURSUIT

While we shall never weary in the defense of freedom, neither shall we ever abandon the pursuit of peace.

> State of the Union Message, Jan. 14, 1963

34 / ESSENCE OF PEACE

Is not peace, in the last analysis, basically a matter of human rights—the right to live out our lives without fear of devastation—the right to breathe air as nature provided it—the right of future generations to a healthy existence?

> Commencement address, American University, Washington, D.C., June 10, 1963

35 / PRACTICAL PEACE ATTAINABLE

Too many of us think it is impossible. Too many think it is unreal. But that is a dangerous, defeatist belief. It leads to the conclusion that war is inevitable—that mankind is doomed—that we are gripped by forces we cannot control. We need not accept that view. Our problems are man-made. Therefore they can be solved by man. And man can be as big as he wants. No problem of human destiny is beyond human beings. Man's reason and spirit have often solved the seemingly unsolvable—and we believe they can do it again.

Ibid.

36 / RELENTLESS PURSUIT

When history writes its verdict, let it be said that we pursued the peace with all the courage, all the strength, and all the resourcefulness at our command.

Campaign address, Zionists of America Convention, New York City, Aug 26, 1960

37 / BUILDING A WORLD OF PEACE

We are not helpless before that task or hopeless of its success. Confident and unafraid, we labor on—not towards a strategy of annihilation but towards a strategy of peace.

Commencement address, American University, Washington, D.C., June 10, 1963

38 / ANTICIPATED CONVERSION

In a world of danger and trial, peace is our deepest aspiration, and when peace comes, we will gladly convert not our swords into plowshares, but our bombs into peaceful reactors, and our planes into space vessels.

Campaign address, Seattle, Sept. 6, 1960

39 / AMERICA'S ASPIRATION

Peace is man's greatest aspiration—a just peace, a secure peace, without appeasement. We will not accept the peace of foreign domination—we do not seek the peace of the grave. We want more than this so-called peace that is merely an interval between wars.

Campaign remarks at Farm Conference, Des Moines, Iowa, Aug. 21, 1960

40 / PEACEMAKERS

The generation which I speak for has seen enough of warmongers. Let our great role in history be that of peacemakers.
>Campaign address, Cow Palace, San Francisco, Nov. 2, 1960

41 / PEACEFUL SOLUTIONS

We do not want military considerations to dominate the thinking of either East or West.
>Address to the nation on the Berlin crisis, Washington, D.C., July 25, 1961

42 / AMBASSADORS OF PEACE

We cannot discontinue training our young men as soldiers of war, but we also want them to be ambassadors of peace.
>Campaign address, Cow Palace, San Francisco, Nov. 2, 1960

43 / FREEDOM'S GOAL: "VICTORY OF MEN"

We seek not the worldwide victory of one nation or system but a world-wide victory of men. The modern globe is too small, its weapons too destructive—they multiply too fast—and its disorders too contagious to permit any other kind of victory.
>State of the Union Message, Jan. 14, 1963

Paths to Peace

44 / EAST-WEST EFFORTS

Let both sides explore what problems unite us instead of laboring those problems which divide us.
>Inaugural address, Jan. 20, 1961

45 / INVITATION FOR COOPERATIVE ENDEAVORS

Let both sides seek to invoke the wonders of science instead of its terrors. Together let us explore the stars, conquer the deserts, eradicate disease, tap the ocean depths, and encourage the arts and commerce.
>*Ibid.*

46 / COOPERATION FOR HUMAN BETTERMENT

Where nature makes natural allies of us all, we can demonstrate that beneficial relations are possible even with those with whom we most deeply disagree, and this must someday be the basis of world peace and world law.

State of the Union Message, Jan. 30, 1961

47 / "WE ARE ALL MORTAL"

If we cannot end our differences, at least we can help make the world safe for diversity. For, in the final analysis, our most basic common link is that we all inhabit this small planet. We all breathe the same air. We all cherish our children's future. And we are all mortal.

Commencement address, American University, Washington, D.C., June 10, 1963

48 / THE GULF

Let us re-examine our attitude towards the Soviet Union. It is discouraging to think that their leaders may actually believe what their propagandists write. It is discouraging to read a recent authoritative Soviet text on military strategy and find, on page after page, wholly baseless and incredible claims—such as the allegation that "American imperialist circles are preparing to unleash different types of wars . . . that there is a very real threat of a preventive war being unleashed by American imperialists against the Soviet Union . . . [and that] the political aims of the American imperialists are to enslave economically and politically the European and other capitalist countries . . . [and] to achieve world domination . . . by means of aggressive wars."

Truly as it was written long ago: "The wicked flee when no man pursueth." Yet it is sad to read these Soviet statements, to realize the extent of the gulf between us. But it is also a warning—a warning to the American people not to fall into the same trap as the Soviets, not to see only a distorted and desperate view of the other side, not to see conflict as inevitable, accommodation as impossible, and communication as nothing more than an exchange of threats.

Ibid.

49 / HUMANITY'S KINSHIP

Across the gulfs and barriers that now divide us we must remember that there are no permanent enemies. Hostility today is a fact, but it is not a ruling law.

Address to Irish Parliament, Dublin, June 28, 1963

50 / COMMUNICATION

I think that communication, an exchange of views, an honest report of what our countries are like and what they want and what the people wish, is in the interests of both our countries and in the interests of peace.

Interview by Aleksei I. Adzhubei, Washington, D.C., Nov. 28, 1961

51 / PEACEFUL COMPETITION WITH COMMUNIST POWERS WELCOMED

Our task is to convince them that aggression and subversion will not be profitable routes to pursue. Open and peaceful competition—for prestige, for markets, for scientific achievement, even for men's minds—is something else again. For if freedom and communism were to compete for man's allegiance in a world at peace, I would look to the future with ever increasing confidence.

State of the Union Message, Jan. 30, 1961

52 / PEACEFUL NEGOTIATION

The world has long passed that time when armed conflict can be the solution to international problems.

Message to Premier Nikita Khrushchev, Hyannis Port, Mass., July 5, 1963

53 / NO PUSH-BUTTON PEACE

We can push a button to start the next war but there is no push button magic to winning a lasting and enduring peace.

Campaign address, Cow Palace, San Francisco, Nov. 2, 1960

54 / A LONG, TOUGH TASK

Peace and security and the survival of the United States can only be won by work, perseverance, will, carried out over a long period of time without cease, without fail.

Campaign remarks, Providence, Nov. 7, 1960

55 / DANGER OF HUMAN FOLLY

Nor will national security in the years ahead be achieved simply by piling up bigger bombs or burying our missiles under bigger loads of concrete.

For in an imperfect world, where human folly has been the rule and not the exception, the surest way to bring on "the war that can never happen" is to sit back and assure ourselves it will not happen.

> Commencement address, U.S. Air Force Academy, Colorado Springs, June 5, 1963

56 / "PATIENCE, PERSEVERANCE AND COURAGE"

We shall achieve peace only with patience and perseverance and courage. The patience and perseverance necessary to work with allies, of diverse interests, of common goals, the courage necessary over a long period of time to overcome an adversary skilled in the arts of harassment and obstruction. There is no way to maintain the frontiers of freedom without cost and commitment and risk. There is no swift and easy path to peace in our generation.

> Veterans Day address, Arlington National Cemetery, Nov. 11, 1961

57 / NEVER FROM FEAR

Let us never negotiate out of fear. But let us never fear to negotiate.

> Inaugural address, Jan. 20, 1961

58 / INEXHAUSTIBLE PATIENCE

Our patience at the bargaining table is nearly inexhaustible, though our credulity is limited . . . our hopes for peace are unfailing.

> Address, American Society of Newspaper Editors, Washington, D.C., April 20, 1961

59 / NEGOTIATION

While we are ready to defend our interests, we shall also be ready to search for peace—in quiet exploratory talks, in formal or informal meetings.

> Address to the nation on the Berlin crisis, Washington, D.C., July 25, 1961

60 / HONORABLE ALTERNATIVES

We intend to have a wider choice than humiliation or all-out nuclear action.

> *Ibid.*

61 / USES OF NEGOTIATION

If vital interests under duress can be preserved by peaceful means, negotiations will find that out. If our adversary will accept nothing less than a concession of our rights, negotiations will find that out. And if negotiations are to take place, this nation cannot abdicate to its adversaries the task of choosing the forum and the framework and the time.

Address, University of Washington, Seattle, Nov. 16, 1961

62 / MATURE OUTLOOK ON NEGOTIATION

No one should be under the illusion that negotiations for the sake of negotiations always advance the cause of peace. If, for lack of preparation or respect, they break up in bitterness, the prospects of peace have been endangered. If they are made a mere forum for propaganda or a cover for aggression, the processes of peace have been abused.

But it is a test of our national maturity to accept the fact that negotiations are not a contest spelling victory or defeat. They may succeed, they may fail. But they are likely to be successful only if both sides reach an agreement which both regard as preferable to the status quo, an agreement in which each side can consider that its own situation has been improved, and this is most difficult to obtain.

Ibid.

63 / MORAL DUTY TO NEGOTIATE

As long as we know precisely what comprises our vital interest and our long-range goals, we have nothing to fear from negotiations at the appropriate time, and nothing to gain by refusing them. At a time when a single clash could escalate overnight into a holocaust of mushroom clouds, a great power does not prove its firmness by leaving the task of exploring the other's intentions to sentries or those without full responsibility. Nor can ultimate weapons rightfully be employed, or the ultimate sacrifice rightfully demanded of our citizens, until every reasonable solution has been explored.

Ibid.

64 / READINESS FOR DISCUSSION

As signers of the UN Charter, we shall always be prepared to discuss international problems with any and all nations that are willing to talk—and listen—with reason. If they have proposals—not demands—we shall hear them. If they seek genuine understanding—not concessions of our rights—we shall meet with them.

Address to the nation on the Berlin crisis, Washington, D.C., July 25, 1961

65 / EFFECTIVENESS IN NEGOTIATION

We must make certain that our negotiators are better informed and better prepared—to formulate workable proposals of our own and to make sound judgments about the proposals of others.

> State of the Union Message, Jan. 30, 1961

66 / FIRMNESS

This generation learned from bitter experience that either brandishing or yielding to threats can only lead to war. But firmness and reason can lead to the kind of peaceful solution in which my country profoundly believes.

> Address, U.N. General Assembly, Sept. 25, 1961

67 / "PEACE RACE"

We are well aware that all issues of principle are not settled—and that principles alone are not enough. It is therefore our intention to challenge the Soviet Union, not to an arms race but a peace race; to advance together step by step, stage by stage, until general and complete disarmament has been achieved. We invite them now to go beyond agreement in principle to reach agreement on actual plans.

> *Ibid.*

68 / MUTUAL TOLERANCE AND JUSTICE

World peace, like community peace, does not require that each man love his neighbor—it requires only that they live together with mutual tolerance, submitting their disputes to a just and peaceful settlement.

> Commencement address, American University, Washington, D.C., June 10, 1963

69 / "PROBLEM OF POLITICS AND PEOPLE"

Peace is not solely a matter of military or technical problems—it is primarily a problem of politics and people. And unless man can match his strides in weaponry and technology with equal strides in social and political development, our great strength, like that of the dinosaur, will become incapable of proper control—and like the dinosaur vanish from the earth.

> Address, U.N. General Assembly, Sept. 25, 1961

70 / WORLDWIDE LAW

To destroy arms . . . is not enough. We must create even as we destroy, creating worldwide law and law enforcement as we outlaw worldwide war and weapons.

Ibid.

71 / PEACE THROUGH LAW

Disarmament without checks is but a shadow, and a community without law is but a shell.

Ibid.

72 / ULTIMATE OBJECTIVE

Our primary long-range interest in Geneva is general and complete disarmament—designed to take place by stages, permitting parallel political developments to build the new institutions of peace which would take the place of arms.

Commencement address, American University, Washington, D.C., June 10, 1963

73 / CHIEF CAUSE OF TENSION

It is our hope—and the purpose of allied policies—to convince the Soviet Union that she, too, should let each nation choose its own future, so long as that choice does not interfere with the choices of others. The Communist drive to impose their political and economic system on others is the primary cause of world tension today. For there can be no doubt that, if all nations could refrain from interfering in the self-determination of others, the peace would be much more assured. This will require a new effort to achieve world law—a new context for world discussions. It will require increased understanding between the Soviets and ourselves. And increased understanding will require increased contact and communication.

Ibid.

74 / "LET US BEGIN"

If a beachhead of cooperation may push back the jungle of suspicion, let both sides join in creating a new endeavor, not a new balance of power, but a new world of law, where the strong are just and the weak secure and the peace preserved.

All this will not be finished in the first 100 days. Nor will it be finished in the first 1,000 days, nor in the life of this administration, nor even perhaps in our lifetime on this planet. But let us begin.

Inaugural address, Jan. 20, 1961

7

The Trouble Spots

Berlin

1 / A DIVIDED CITY

To divide a country, to divide a city, to put up a wall in a city, we believe, only increases tensions rather than diminish them. And we believe that, if the German people were permitted to be reunified, adequate steps could be taken to protect the security of all involved.

Interview by Aleksei I. Adzhubei, Washington, D.C., Nov. 25, 1961

2 / THE SIMPLE ISSUES

This is not the time or the place for immoderate tones, but the world community is entitled to know the very simple issues as we see them.

If there is a crisis, it is because an existing island of free people is under pressure, because solemn agreements are being treated with indifference. Established international rights are being threatened with unilateral usurpation. Peaceful circulation has been interrupted by barbed wire and concrete blocks. . . .

It is absurd to allege that we are threatening a war merely to prevent the Soviet Union and East Germany from signing a so-called "treaty" of peace. The Western allies are not concerned with any paper arrangement the Soviets may wish to make with a regime of their own creation, on territory occupied and governed by their own agents. No such action, however, can affect either our rights or our responsibilities.

If there is a dangerous crisis in Berlin—and there is—it is because of threats against the vital interests and the deep commitments of the Western powers, and the freedom of West Berlin. We cannot yield these interests. We cannot fail these commitments. We cannot surrender the freedom of these people for whom we are responsible.

A "peace treaty" which carried with it provisions which destroy the peace would be a fraud. A "free city" which was not genuinely free would suffocate freedom and would be an infamy. For a city or a people to be truly free, they must have the secure right, without economic, political or police pressure, to make their own choice and to live their own lives. And as I have said before, if anyone doubts the extent to which our presence is desired by the people of West Berlin, we are ready to have that question submitted to a free vote in all Berlin and, if possible, among all the German people.

The elementary fact about this crisis is that it is unnecessary. The elementary tools for a peaceful settlement are to be found in the [U.N.] charter. Under its law, agreements are to be kept, unless changed by all those who make them. Established rights are to be respected. The political disposition of peoples should rest upon their own wishes, freely expressed in plebiscites and free elections. If there are legal problems, they can be solved by legal means. If there is a threat of force it must be rejected. If there is a desire for change, it must be a subject for negotiation, it must be rooted in mutual respect and concern for the rights of others.

The Western powers have calmly resolved to defend, by whatever means are forced upon them, their obligations and their access to the free citizens of West Berlin and the self-determination of those citizens.

Address, U.N. General Assembly, Sept. 25, 1961

3 / SOVIET CHOICE

The source of world trouble and tension is Moscow, not Berlin. And if war begins, it will have begun in Moscow and not Berlin. For the choice of peace or war is largely theirs, not ours. It is the Soviets who have stirred up this crisis. It is they who are trying to force a change. It is they who have opposed free elections. It is they who have rejected an all-German peace treaty and the rulings of international law.

Address to the nation on the Berlin crisis, Washington, D.C., July 25, 1961

4 / DANGEROUS MISTAKE

We do not want to fight—but we have fought before. And others in earlier times have made the same dangerous mistake of assuming that the West was too selfish and too soft and too divided to resist invasions of freedom in other lands.

Ibid.

5 / "ICH BIN EIN BERLINER"

Two thousand years ago the proud boast was "*civis Romanus sum* [I am a Roman citizen]." Today, in the world of freedom, the proudest boast is "*Ich bin ein Berliner* [I am a Berliner]." . . . All free men, wherever they may live, are citizens of Berlin, and, therefore, as a free man, I take pride in the words "*Ich bin ein Berliner*."

Address, City Hall, West Berlin, June 26, 1963

6 / PLEDGE

Those who threaten to unleash the forces of war on a dispute over West Berlin should recall the words of the ancient philosopher: "A man who causes fear cannot be free from fear." We cannot and will not permit the Communists to drive us out of Berlin—either gradually or by force. For the fulfillment of our pledge to that city is essential to the morale and security of West Germany, to the unity of Western Europe and to the faith of the entire free world.

Address to the nation on the Berlin crisis, Washington, D.C., July 25, 1961

7 / PEACE—BUT NO SURRENDER

We seek peace—but we shall not surrender. That is the central meaning of this crisis, and the meaning of your government's policy.

Ibid.

8 / WESTERN UNITY

The solemn vow we each of us gave to West Berlin in time of peace will not be broken in time of danger. If we do not meet our commitments to Berlin, where will we later stand? If we are not true to our word there, all that we have achieved in collective security, which relies on these words, will mean nothing. And if there is one path above all others to war, it is the path of weakness and disunity.

Ibid.

9 / "WE SHALL STAY"

On this anniversary of the Prince of Peace, my fellow Americans and I extend our greetings to you, the people of Berlin. We observe this season of peace and spiritual rededication at a time of crisis.

Peace, peace on earth, goodwill to men, real peace, real goodwill is more of a goal than a reality. Until truly there is goodwill among men, not walls to divide them, our pursuit of peace shall continue.

During these days which ought to bring families together, many of you are thinking of loved ones forcibly separated from you. Our deepest sympathy goes out to all those who suffer from this imposed separation, especially at this time of year.

For all of us, for freedom itself, this is a time of trial. I need not remind you in Berlin of America's determination to support and sustain you in freedom. The bonds which tie us have been tested before: we are at your side now—as before. We shall stay.

The Christmas lights of free Berlin cast a glow which penetrates deep into the darkness surrounding. No wall can keep out this light. We know that this beacon will continue to shine brightly, for many years to come.

With confidence and conviction, therefore, let us rededicate ourselves to the principles of peace and goodwill toward men which guided the life of Him whose birth we celebrate on Christmas. This rededication will be a source of inspiration to men everywhere.

Christmas message to the people of West Berlin, Washington, D.C., Dec. 25, 1961

10 / REAFFIRMATION OF COMMITMENT TO WEST GERMANY

The United States is here on this continent to stay. So long as our presence is desired and required, our forces and commitments will remain. For your safety is our safety, your liberty is our liberty, and any attack on your soil is an attack on our own. Out of necessity as well as sentiment, in our approach to peace as well as war, our fortunes are one.

Reply to welcoming address by Chancellor Konrad Adenauer, Bonn, West Germany, June 23, 1963

11 / REASSURANCE ON AMERICAN COMMITMENT

The shield of moral and military commitment with which we guard the freedom of the West Berliners will not be lowered or put aside so long as its presence is needed.

Address, Free University of Berlin, Germany, June 26, 1963

12 / PEACEFUL AGREEMENT POSSIBLE

We are committed to no rigid formulas. We seek no perfect solution. We recognize that troops and tanks can, for a time, keep a nation divided against its will, however unwise that policy may seem to us. But we believe a peaceful agreement is possible which protects the freedom of

West Berlin and Allied presence and access, while recognizing the historic and legitimate interests of others in assuring European security.

Address, U.N. General Assembly, Sept. 25, 1961

13 / RESPONSE TO THE CRISIS

Our response to the Berlin crisis will not be merely military or negative. It will be more than merely standing firm. For we do not intend to leave it to others to choose and monopolize the forum and framework of discussion. We do not intend to abandon our duty to mankind to seek a peaceful solution.

Address to the nation on the Berlin crisis, Washington, D.C., July 25, 1961

14 / FREEDOM NOT NEGOTIABLE

We have . . . indicated our readiness to remove any actual irritants in West Berlin. But the freedom of that city is not negotiable. We cannot negotiate with those who say, "What's mine is mine and what's yours is negotiable."

Ibid.

15 / NEGOTIATING WITH MR. GROMYKO

You have offered to trade us an apple for an orchard. We don't do that in this country.

Comment to Soviet Foreign Minister Andrei A. Gromyko during conference on Berlin-Germany problems, Washington, D.C., Oct. 6, 1961

16 / KEY TO PEACE

I think we could have peace in this century in Central Europe if we can reach an accord over West Berlin. To pursue another course in the name of ending World War II—a course which threatens to increase the chance of World War III—represents a wholly unwise policy, for you and for us.

Interview by Aleksei I. Adzhubei, Washington, D.C., Nov. 25, 1961

17 / PEOPLES' HOPES

Today, the endangered frontier of freedom runs through divided Berlin. We want it to remain a frontier of peace. This is the hope of every citizen of the Atlantic community; every citizen of Eastern Europe; and, I am confident, every citizen of the Soviet Union. For I cannot believe that the Russian people—who bravely suffered enormous losses in the Second World War—would now wish to see the peace upset once more in Germany. The Soviet Government alone can convert Berlin's frontier of peace into a pretext of war.

Address to the nation on the Berlin crisis, Washington, D.C., July 25, 1961

18 / REUNIFICATION: FAITH WITHOUT FALSE OPTIMISM

Reunification, I believe, will someday be a reality. The lessons of history support that belief. But we all know that a police state regime has been imposed on the eastern sector of this city and country. The peaceful reunification of Berlin and Germany will, therefore, not be either quick or easy. We must first bring others to see their own true interest better than they do today. What will count in the long run are the realities of Western strength.

Address, Free University of Berlin, Germany, June 26, 1963

Cuba

19 / UNKEPT COMMITMENT

In the case of Cuba . . . the Castro revolution was originally supported by the great majority of the people. When Castro was leading the revolution, the statement was made that there would be free elections, and freedom for the people and progress for the people. But Castro has not kept that commitment. Until the present Government of Cuba will allow free and honest elections, in our opinion, it cannot claim to represent the majority of the people. That is our dispute with Cuba.

Interview by Aleksei I. Adzhubei, Washington, D.C., Nov. 25, 1961

20 / DICTATORSHIP

The Cuban people were promised by the revolution political liberty, social justice, intellectual freedom, land for the campesinos [peasants] and an end to economic exploitation. They have received a police state, the elimination of the dignity of land ownership, the destruction of free speech and of free press, and the complete subjugation of individual human welfare to the service of the state and of foreign states.

Address, rally of Cuban exiles, Miami, Dec. 29, 1962

21 / SOVIET SATELLITE

It's quite obvious now to the hemisphere and, in fact, to the world that Castro is merely a Soviet satellite.

Address, American Society of Newspaper Editors, Washington, D.C., April 19, 1963

22 / HEMISPHERIC CONCERN

All Americans as well as all of our friends in this hemisphere have been concerned over the recent moves of the Soviet Union to bolster the military power of the Castro regime in Cuba.

Statement on Cuba, Washington, D.C., Sept. 4, 1962

23 / CUBA PART OF THE COMMUNIST CHALLENGE

The Cuban question must be considered as a part of the worldwide challenge posed by Communist threats to the peace. It must be dealt with as a part of that larger issue as well as in the context of the special relationships which have long characterized the inter-American system.

Ibid.

24 / PLEDGE TO BAR CUBAN AGGRESSION

It continues to be the policy of the United States that the Castro regime will not be allowed to export its aggressive purposes by force or the threat of force. It will be prevented by whatever means may be necessary from taking action against any part of the Western Hemisphere.

Ibid.

25 / AMERICAN WATCHFULNESS

The United States in conjunction with other hemisphere countries will make sure that, while increased Cuban armaments will be a heavy burden to the unhappy people of Cuba themselves, they will be nothing more.

Ibid.

26 / DOCTRINE ON CUBA

If at any time the Communist build-up in Cuba were to endanger or interfere with our security in any way, including our base at Guantanamo, our passage to the Panama Canal, our missile and space activities in Cape Canaveral or the lives of American citizens in this country, or if Cuba should ever attempt to export its aggressive purposes by force or the threat of force against any nation in this hemisphere or become an offensive military base of significant capacity for the Soviet Union, then this country will do whatever must be done to protect its own security and that of its allies. We shall be alert to and fully capable of dealing swiftly with any such development.

News conference, Washington, D.C., Sept. 13, 1962

27 / THE LINE

We shall neither initiate nor permit aggression in this hemisphere.

Ibid.

28 / LOOSE TALK

Unilateral military intervention [in Cuba] on the part of the United States cannot currently be either required or justified, and it is regrettable that loose talk about such action in this country might serve to give a thin color of legitimacy to the Communist pretense that such a threat exists.

Ibid.

29 / AMERICAN STABILITY

. . . while I recognize that rash talk is cheap, particularly on the part of those who do not have the responsibility, I would hope that the future record will show that the only people talking about a war or an invasion at this time are the Communist spokesmen in Moscow and Havana, and that the American people defending as we do so much of the free world, will in this nuclear age, as they have in the past, keep both their nerve and their head.

Ibid.

30 / DEDICATION TO CUBAN FREEDOM

We shall continue to work with Cuban refugee leaders who are dedicated as we are to that nation's future return to freedom.

Ibid.

31 / A PROVOCATIVE, UNACCEPTABLE CHANGE

This secret, swift, extraordinary build-up of Communist missiles in an area well-known to have a special and historical relationship to the United States and the nations of the Western Hemisphere, in violation of Soviet assurances and in defiance of American and hemispheric policy—this sudden, clandestine decision to station strategic weapons for the first time outside of Soviet soil—is a deliberately provocative and unjustified change in the status quo which cannot be accepted by this country if our courage and commitments are ever to be trusted again, by either friend or foe.

Address to the nation on the Soviet build-up in Cuba, Washington, D.C., Oct. 22, 1962

32 / A DEFINITE THREAT

Neither the United States of America nor the world community of nations can tolerate deliberate deception and offensive threats on the part of any nation, large or small. We no longer live in a world where only the actual firing of weapons represents a sufficient challenge to a nation's security to constitute maximum peril. Nuclear weapons are so destructive and ballistic missiles are so swift that any substantially increased possibility of their use or any sudden change in their deployment may well be regarded as a definite threat to peace.

Ibid.

33 / OUR OBJECTIVE

Our unswerving objective . . . must be to prevent the use of these missiles against this or any other country; and to secure their withdrawal or elimination from the Western Hemisphere.

Ibid.

34 / "IN THE DEFENSE OF OUR OWN SECURITY"

Acting . . . in the defense of our own security and of the entire Western Hemisphere and under the authority entrusted to me by the Constitution as endorsed by the resolution of the Congress, I have directed that the following initial steps be taken immediately:

First, to halt this offensive build-up, a strict quarantine on all offensive military equipment under shipment to Cuba is being initiated. All ships of any kind bound for Cuba from whatever nation or port will, where they are found to contain cargoes of offensive weapons, be turned back. This quarantine will be extended if needed to other types of cargo and carriers. We are not at this time, however, denying the necessities of life as the Soviets attempted to do in their Berlin blockade of 1948.

Second, I have directed the continued and increased close surveillance of Cuba and its military build-up. The foreign ministers of the O.A.S. in their communiqué of October 6 rejected secrecy on such matters in this hemisphere. Should these offensive military preparations continue, thus increasing the threat to the hemisphere, further action will be justified.

I have directed the armed forces to prepare for any eventualities, and I trust that in the interests of both the Cuban people and the Soviet technicians at the sites, the hazards to all concerned of continuing this threat will be recognized.

Third, it shall be the policy of this nation to regard any nuclear missile launched from Cuba against any nation in the Western Hemisphere as an attack by the Soviet Union on the United States requiring a full retaliatory response upon the Soviet Union.

Fourth, as a necessary military precaution, I have reinforced our base at Guantanamo, evacuated today the dependents of our personnel there and ordered additional military units to be on a stand-by alert basis.

Fifth, we are calling tonight for an immediate meeting of the organization of consultation under the Organization of American States to consider this threat to hemispheric security and to invoke Articles 6 and 8 of the Rio Treaty in support of all necessary action. The United Nations Charter allows for regional security arrangements and the nations of this hemisphere decided long ago against the military presence of outside powers. Our other allies around the world have also been alerted.

Sixth, under the Charter of the United Nations we are asking tonight that an emergency meeting of the Security Council be convoked without delay to take action against this latest Soviet threat to world peace. Our resolution will call for the prompt dismantling and withdrawal of all offensive weapons in Cuba under the supervision of U.N. observers before the quarantine can be lifted.

Seventh, and finally, I call upon Chairman Khrushchev to halt and eliminate this clandestine, reckless and provocative threat to world peace and to stable relations between our two nations. I call upon him further to abandon this course of world domination and to join in an historic effort to end the perilous arms race and to transform the history of man.

Ibid.

35 / NEVER SUBMISSION

The cost of freedom is always high, but Americans have always paid it. And one path we shall never choose, and that is the path of surrender, or submission.

Ibid.

36 / A HAZARDOUS PATH

The path we have chosen for the present is full of hazards, as all paths are. But it is the one most consistent with our character and courage as a nation and our commitments around the world.

Ibid.

37 / A CONTRIBUTION TO PEACE

I welcome Chairman Khrushchev's statesmanlike decision to stop building bases in Cuba, dismantling offensive weapons and returning them to the Soviet Union under United Nations verification.

This is an important and constructive contribution to peace.

We shall be in touch with the Secretary General of the United Nations with respect to reciprocal measures to assure peace in the Caribbean area.

It is my earnest hope that the governments of the world can, with a solution of the Cuban crisis, turn their urgent attention to the compelling necessity for ending the arms race and reducing world tensions.

This applies to the military confrontation between the Warsaw Pact and NATO countries as well as to other situations in other parts of the world where tensions lead to the wasteful diversion of resources to weapons of war.

Statement on Soviet pledges to remove Cuban missile bases, Washington, D.C., Oct. 28, 1962

38 / "AS WE STEP BACK FROM DANGER"

Mr. Chairman, both our countries have unfinished tasks and I know that your people as well as the United States can ask for nothing better than to pursue them free from the fear of war. Modern science and technology have given us the possibility of making labor fruitful beyond anything that could have been dreamed of a few decades ago.

I agree with you that we must devote urgent attention to the problem of disarmament, as it relates to the whole world and also to critical areas. Perhaps now, as we step back from danger, we can together make real progress in this vital field. I think we should give priority to questions relating to the proliferation of nuclear weapons, on earth and in outer space, and to the great effort for a nuclear test ban. But we should also work hard to see if wider measures of disarmament can be agreed to and put into operation at an early date.

The United States Government will be prepared to discuss these questions urgently, and in a constructive spirit, at Geneva or elsewhere.

Message in reply to Premier Khrushchev's proposal to remove Cuban missile bases, Washington, D.C., Oct. 28, 1962

39 / RETAINING FAITH IN THE CUBAN PEOPLE

We cannot write the Cuban people off as lost. Neither should we drive them inextricably into Soviet hands. But let us make the American Revolution the chief import of Latin America, not the Cuban Revolution. And if we do so then some day on the island of Cuba itself, there will be a government constituted to secure the rights of life, liberty, and the pursuit of happiness.

Campaign remarks, Johnstown, Pa., Oct. 15, 1960

40 / COMMUNIST EFFORTS

In Latin America, Communist agents seeking to exploit that region's peaceful revolution of hope have established a base on Cuba, only 90 miles from our shores. Our objection with Cuba is not over the people's drive for a better life. Our objection is to their domination by foreign and domestic tyrannies. Cuban social and economic reforms should be encouraged. Questions of economic and trade policy can always be negotiated. But Communist domination in this hemisphere can never be negotiated.

State of the Union Message, Washington, D.C., Jan. 30, 1961

41 / RESISTANCE TO COMMUNIST RULE

At the very time that newly independent nations rise in the Caribbean the people of Cuba have been forcibly compelled to submit to a new imperialism, more ruthless, more powerful, and more deadly in its pursuit of power than any this hemisphere has ever known. Just when it was hoped that Cuba was about to enter upon a new era of democracy and social justice, the Soviet Union, through its Cuban puppets, absorbed the Cuban nation into its empire—and it now seeks to extend its rule to the shores of the continent itself.

But other foreign powers have discovered that the American Hemisphere is not a fertile ground for foreign tyranny, and that any effort to spread such rule will meet with fierce and unyielding resistance. For Americans will not yield up those freedoms they shed so much blood to achieve.

Opening address, Presidents' Conference, San José, Costa Rica, March 18, 1963

42 / CHALLENGE OF FOREIGN DOMINATION

. . . every effort to reimpose the despotisms of the Old World on the people of the New has ultimately been beaten back—because within this system 20 Republics have attained the full recognition of their dignity as sovereign nations—and because this system has maintained an unmatched record of peaceful relations among its members. . . .

In the first three centuries of our history, the seeds of Western civilization and culture were planted here. In the next century, we established an inter-American system which helped to complete and maintain our freedom from foreign rule. This freedom has often been challenged—as today it is challenged in Cuba. But with the help of dedicated and brave men—men such as those who drove out Maximilian or men such as those who prevented the Spanish reconquest in 1866, men such as Costa Rica's Mora, who helped to drive out William Walker—with such help we have destroyed all efforts at foreign conquest in the past, as we will ultimately triumph over the new conquerors of today.

    Ibid.

43 / STEPS TAKEN TO IMPLEMENT OUR STAND AGAINST COMMUNISM IN
    CUBA

We have—and the other countries of the free world have—cut free world trade [with Cuba] in the last two years from $800,000,000 to 80. We are working with the O.A.S. to set up an organization which will limit the movement of potential guerrillas in and out of Cuba. We have —the O.A.S.—have almost diplomatically isolated Castro in this hemisphere. I think the members of the O.A.S. have made it very clear that Marxist-Leninism and the Soviet presence is not a matter which is acceptable to the people of the hemisphere.

    News conference, Washington, D.C., April 24, 1963

44 / WORLDWIDE RESPONSIBILITIES DETERMINE AMERICAN POLICY

. . . since the last two years, the United States has taken a good many actions to contain the spread of Communism in the hemisphere. . . . there are two additional policies which could be carried out. . . . the two remaining policies are, one, a blockade which of course brings us once again to a confrontation with the Soviet Union, and the other is invasion of Cuba. In my judgment, it would be a mistake to carry out either one of those policies today.

I don't know what conditions are going to bring in the future. . . . I think that we should maintain our strength and our determination, but I don't think that it would serve the interests of the United States or of our allies to carry out either an invasion or blockade under these present conditions.

The United States is responsible for the independence of dozens of countries stretching from South Korea to Berlin. It is responsible for the defense, really, of Western Europe. It is responsible for the major struggle against the Communists in our own hemisphere. For 6 per cent of the world's population we carry tremendous burdens. I do not think we can indulge ourselves at this point, if that is the proper word, in concentrating all of our material strength in one section of the world, and be indifferent to its consequences elsewhere.

Address, American Society of Newspaper Editors, Washington, D.C., April 19, 1963

45 / A CHALLENGE TO CRITICS OF THE ADMINISTRATION'S CUBAN POLICY

. . . the question which is rather sidestepped . . . is, if the United States should go to war in order to remove Castro. That nettle is not grasped, and it would seem to me that we have pretty much done all those things that can be done to demonstrate hostility to the concept of a Soviet satellite in the Caribbean except take these other steps which bring in their wake violence, and may bring a good deal of worldwide difficulty. If they are advocating that, then I recognize that as an alternate policy, but if it's merely a policy which says we should do something without defining it except, perhaps, as I've said, unleashing the exiles, which cannot do the job, it seems to me we deserve on a question of this importance a good deal more precision in our prescriptions for its solution.

News conference, Washington, D.C., April 24, 1963

46 / LIMIT FOR SOVIET INTERFERENCE

We have made it very clear that we would not accept a Hungary in Cuba.
Ibid.

47 / PREVENTION OF AGGRESSION FROM CUBA

We've made it very clear that we would not permit the movement of troops from Cuba to another country for offensive purposes. We maintain surveillance.
Ibid.

48 / FAITH IN RETURN OF FREEDOM TO CUBA

I can't indicate the roads by which there will be a change, but I have seen enough—as we all have—enough of change in the last 15 years, to make me feel that time will see Cuba free again. And I think when that happens the record will show that the United States has played a significant role.

Address, American Society of Newspaper Editors, Washington, D.C., April 19, 1963

49 / "AS LONG AS CUBA IS A SOVIET SATELLITE"

The United States has indicated very clearly that we do not accept the existence and cannot coexist in the peaceful sense with a Soviet satellite in the Carribbean. . . . I don't see that any progress is going to be made along these lines as long as Cuba is a Soviet satellite.

News conference, Washington, D.C., July 17, 1963

50 / RESTATEMENT OF POLICY

It is important to restate what now divides Cuba from my country and from the other countries of this hemisphere. It is the fact that a small band of conspirators has stripped the Cuban people of their freedom and handed over the independence and sovereignty of the Cuban nation to forces beyond the hemisphere. They have made Cuba a victim of foreign imperialism, an instrument of the policy of others, a weapon in an effort dictated by external powers to subvert the other American republics.

This, and this alone, divides us.

As long as this is true, nothing is possible. Without it everything is possible.

Once this barrier is removed we will be ready and anxious to work with the Cuban people in pursuit of those progressive goals which a few short years ago stirred their hopes and the sympathy of many people throughout the hemisphere.

No Cuban need feel trapped between dependence on the broken promises of foreign Communism and the hostility of the rest of the hemisphere. For, once Cuban sovereignty has been restored, we will extend the hand of friendship and assistance to a Cuba whose political and economic institutions have been shaped by the will of the Cuban people.

Address, Inter-American Press Association, Miami Beach, Nov. 18, 1963

Vietnam

51 / AGGRESSION AGAINST SOUTH VIETNAM

The systematic aggression now bleeding that country is not a "war of liberation," for Vietnam is already free. It is a war of attempted subjugation, and it will be resisted.

State of the Union Message, Jan. 11, 1962

52 / AMERICA'S OBJECT

. . . our object [is] to . . . permit the South Vietnamese to maintain themselves as a free and independent country, and permit democratic forces within the country to operate.

News conference, Washington, D.C., Nov. 14, 1963

53 / IF SOUTH VIETNAM FALLS

China is so large, looms so high just beyond the frontiers, that if South Vietnam went, it would not only give them an improved geographic position for a guerrilla assault on Malaya, but would also give the impression that the wave of the future in Southeast Asia was China and the Communists.

> Television interview, Sept. 9, 1963

Laos

54 / AMERICAN OBJECTIVES

We seek in Laos what we seek in all Asia, and, indeed, in all the world— freedom for the people and independence for their government. This nation shall persevere in our pursuit of these objectives.

> State of the Union Message, Jan. 30, 1961

55 / NEUTRAL INDEPENDENCE VITAL

The security of all of Southeast Asia will be endangered if Laos loses its neutral independence. Its own safety runs with the safety of us all—in real neutrality observed by all. I want to make it clear to the American people and to all the world that all we want in Laos is peace, not war; a truly neutral government, not a cold war pawn; a settlement concluded at the conference table and not on the battlefield.

> News conference, Washington, D.C., March 23, 1961

56 / AMERICA SUPPORTS LAOTIAN FREEDOM

We support a truly neutral and independent Laos, its people free from outside interference, living at peace with themselves and with their neighbors, assured that their territory will not be used for attacks on others.

> Address, U.N. General Assembly, Sept. 25, 1961

The Congo

57 / UNITED STATES SUPPORT FOR UNITED NATIONS EFFORTS

In Africa, the Congo has been brutally torn by civil strife, political unrest, and public disorder. We shall continue to support the heroic efforts of the United Nations to restore peace and order—efforts which are now endangered by mounting tensions, unsolved problems, and decreasing support from many member states.

State of the Union Message, Jan. 30, 1961

58 / AMERICA'S OBJECTIVE

Eighteen months ago the tangled and turbulent Congo presented the United Nations with its gravest challenge. The prospect was one of chaos —or certain big-power confrontation, with all of its hazards and all of its risks to us and to others. Today the hopes have improved for peaceful conciliation within a united Congo. This is the objective of our policy in this important area.

State of the Union Message, Jan. 11, 1962

Matsu and Quemoy

59 / COMMITMENT TO DEFEND AGAINST AGGRESSION

The situation in the areas of the Taiwan Straits is a matter of serious concern to this government. . . . One possibility is that there might be aggressive action against the offshore islands of Matsu and Quemoy. In that event, the policy of this country will be that established seven years ago under the Formosa Resolution. The United States will take the action necessary to assure the defense of Formosa and the Pescadores.

News conference, Washington, D.C., June 27, 1962

The Middle East

60 / "IN THE EVENT OF AGGRESSION"

The United States supports social and economic and political progress in the Middle East. We support the security of both Israel and her neighbors. We seek to limit the Near East arms race, which obviously takes resources from an area already poor and puts them into an increasing race which does not really bring any great security. We strongly oppose the use of force or the threat of force in the Near East. And we also seek to limit the spread of Communism in the Middle East, which would, of course, destroy the independence of the people.

This Government has been, and remains, strongly opposed to the use of force, or the threat of force, in the Near East. In the event of aggression, or preparation for aggression, whether direct or indirect, we would support appropriate measures in the United Nations, and adopt other courses of action on our own to prevent or to put a stop to such aggression, which, of course, has been the policy which the United States has followed for some time.

News conference, Washington, D.C., May 8, 1963

8

The United Nations

Force for Peace

1 / "OUR LAST BEST HOPE"

To that world assembly of sovereign states, the United Nations, our last best hope in an age where the instruments of war have far outpaced the instruments of peace, we renew our pledge of support—to prevent it from becoming merely a forum for invective—to strengthen its shield of the new and the weak—and to enlarge the area in which its writ may run.

Inaugural address, Jan. 20, 1961

2 / THE QUESTION

The great question which confronted this body in 1945 is still before us: whether man's cherished hopes for progress and peace are to be destroyed by terror and disruption; whether the "foul winds of war" can be tamed in time to free the cooling winds of reason, and whether the pledges of our Charter are to be fulfilled or defied—pledges to secure peace, progress, human rights and world law.

Address, U.N. General Assembly, Sept. 25, 1961

3 / UNITED NATIONS, SOLE ALTERNATIVE TO WAR

It will either grow to meet the challenges of our age or it will be gone with the wind, without influence, without force, without respect. Were we to let it die, to enfeeble its vigor, to cripple its powers, we would condemn our future. For in the development of this organization rests the only true alternative to war—and war appeals no longer as a rational alternative.

Ibid.

4 / OUR INSTRUMENT FOR PEACE

Arms alone are not enough to keep the peace. It must be kept by men. Our instrument and our hope is the United Nations, and I see little merit in the impatience of those who would abandon this imperfect world instrument because they dislike our imperfect world. For the troubles of the world organization merely reflect the troubles of the world itself. And if the organization is weakened, these troubles can only increase.

We may not always agree with every detailed action taken by every officer of the United Nations, or with every voting majority. But as an institution, it has in the future, as it has had in the past since its inception, no stronger or more faithful member than the United States of America.

State of the Union Message, Jan. 11, 1962

5 / AMERICAN SUPPORT

We must increase our support of the United Nations as an instrument to end the cold war instead of an arena in which to fight it.

State of the Union Message, Jan. 30, 1961

6 / AMERICAN AIMS

We seek to strengthen the United Nations, to help solve its financial problems, to make it a more effective instrument for peace, to develop it into a genuine world security system—a system capable of resolving disputes on the basis of law, of insuring the security of the large and the small, and of creating conditions under which arms can finally be abolished.

Commencement address, American University, Washington, D.C., June 10, 1963

7 / AMERICA'S POSTURE

We can neither abandon nor control the international organization in which we now cast less than 1 per cent of the General Assembly votes.

Address, University of Washington, Seattle, Nov. 16, 1961

8 / TOWARD A WORLD OF LAW

Peace requires positive American leadership in a more effective United Nations, working toward the establishment of a worldwide system of law, enforced by worldwide sanctions of justice. In this age of jets and atoms, we can no longer put our faith in war as a method of settling international disputes. We can no longer tolerate a world which is like a frontier town, without a sheriff or a magistrate. But the United Nations can be no stronger and more effective than the nations which make it up. Unless we are willing to take the leadership in the United States, next week as well as next year, unless we are willing to channel more of our ideas and our programs and delegate power to that body in the fight for peace, then we may expect to see the last great hope of peace swallowed up in the oceans of indifference and hate.

> Campaign address, Democratic Women's luncheon, New York City, Sept. 14, 1960

9 / "LET NO MAN . . . DESPAIR"

I come here today to look across this world of threats to a world of peace. In that search we cannot expect any final triumph, for new problems will always arise. We cannot expect that all nations will adopt like systems, for conformity is the jailer of freedom and the enemy of growth. Nor can we expect to reach our goal by contrivance, by fiat or even by the wishes of all.

But however close we sometimes seem to that dark and final abyss, let no man of peace and freedom despair. For he does not stand alone. If we all can persevere, if we can in every land and office look beyond our own shores and ambitions, then surely the age will dawn in which the strong are just and the weak secure and the peace preserved.

> Address, U.N. General Assembly, Sept. 25, 1961

10 / PLEA TO SMALL NATIONS

I would address a special plea to the smaller nations of the world—to join with us in strengthening this organization, which is far more essential to their security than it is to ours—the only body in the world today where no nation need be powerful to be secure, where every nation has an equal voice, and where any nation can exert influence not according to the strength of its armies but according to the strength of its ideas. It deserves the support of all.

> State of the Union Message, Jan. 30, 1961

11 / STRONGER UNITED NATIONS

Let us call a truce to terror. Let us invoke the blessings of peace. And, as we build an international capacity to keep the peace, let us join in dismantling the national capacity to wage war. This will require new strength and new roles for the United Nations. For disarmament without checks is but a shadow, and a community without law is but a shell.

Address, U.N. General Assembly, Sept. 25, 1961

12 / PRACTICAL NECESSITY

For fifteen years this organization has sought the reduction and destruction of arms. Now that goal is no longer a dream; it is a practical matter of life or death. The risks inherent in disarmament pale in comparison to the risks inherent in an unlimited arms race.

Ibid.

13 / RESTRAINING INFLUENCE

Already the United Nations has become both the measure and the vehicle of man's most generous impulses. Already it has provided—in the Middle East, in Asia, in Africa this year in the Congo—a means of holding man's violence within bounds.

Ibid.

14 / QUEST FOR PEACE THROUGH LAW

In this quest, the United Nations requires our full and continued support. Its value in serving the cause of peace has been shown anew in its role in the West New Guinea settlement, in its use as a forum for the Cuban crisis, and in its task of unification in the Congo. Today the United Nations is primarily the protector of the small and the weak, and a safety valve for the strong. Tomorrow it can form the framework for a world of law—a world in which no nation dictates the destiny of another, and in which the vast resources now devoted to destructive means will serve constructive ends.

State of the Union Message, Jan. 14, 1963

15 / "UNITED NATIONS DECADE OF DEVELOPMENT"

The mysteries of outer space must not divert our eyes or our energies from the harsh realities that face our fellow men. Political sovereignty is but a mockery without the means of meeting poverty and illiteracy and disease. Self-determination is but a slogan if the future holds no hope.

That is why my nation, which has freely shared its capital and its technology to help others help themselves, now proposes officially designating this decade of the Nineteen Sixties as the United Nations Decade of

Development. Under the framework of that resolution, the United Nations' existing efforts in promoting economic growth can be expanded and coordinated. Regional surveys and training institutes can now pool the talents of many. New research, technical assistance and pilot projects can unlock the wealth of less developed lands and untapped waters. And development can become a cooperative and not a competitive enterprise —to enable all nations, however diverse in their systems and beliefs, to become in fact as well as in law free and equal nations.

    Address, U.N. General Assembly, Sept. 25, 1961

This Generation's Vow

16 / SOLEMN PLEDGE

We in this hall shall be remembered either as part of the generation that turned this planet into a flaming funeral pyre or the generation that met its vow "to save succeeding generations from the scourge of war." In the endeavor to meet that vow, I pledge you every effort that this nation possesses. I pledge you that we shall neither commit nor provoke aggression, that we shall neither flee nor invoke the threat of force, that we shall never negotiate out of fear and we shall never fear to negotiate.

    Ibid.

17 / "SAVE IT WE MUST"

Never have the nations of the world had so much to lose or so much to gain. Together we shall save our planet or together we shall perish in its flames. Save it we can and save it we must, and then shall we earn the eternal thanks of mankind and, as peacemakers, the eternal blessing of God.

    Ibid.

Part II

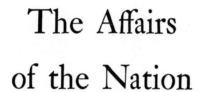

The Affairs
of the Nation

9

Political Democracy

Pillars of Free Government

1 / THE CONSTITUTION: EQUAL RIGHTS

Our Constitution is founded on the principle that all men are equal as citizens, and entitled to the same rights, whether they achieved citizenship by birth, or after coming here as immigrants, seeking to find in America new freedom and new opportunities.

Campaign statement on Citizenship Day, Washington, D.C., Sept. 17, 1960

2 / REVOLUTIONARY DOCUMENT

I hold the view that the Constitution is the most revolutionary document . . . ever written, and it should to the new countries serve as a source of stimulation and enterprise.

Campaign remarks, rally, Greensboro, N.C., Sept. 17, 1960

3 / INDIVISIBLE LIBERTY

As apt and applicable as the Declaration of Independence is today, we would do well to honor that other historic document drafted in this hall, the Constitution of the United States. For it stressed not independence, but interdependence; not the individual liberty of one, but the indivisible liberty of all.

Address, Independence Hall, Philadelphia, July 4, 1962

4 / HUMAN ACTIVATION

The American Constitution is an extraordinary document and it is certainly the most extraordinary written constitution in the history of the world, but it has required men to make it work, and it still does today. After all, the Constitution was written for an entirely different period in our nation's history. It was written under entirely different conditions. It was written during a period of isolation. It was written at a time when there were 13 different units which had to be joined together and which, of course, were extremely desirous of limiting the central power of the government. . . . It has to be made to work today in an entirely different world from the day in which it was written, both at home and abroad.

Talk to college students, White House lawn, Aug. 28, 1962

5 / THE PRESIDENCY

The Presidency is the well-spring of action in the American constitutional system. Only the President speaks for the United States.

Campaign address, Pocatello, Idaho, Sept. 6, 1960

6 / PRESIDENT'S FUNCTION

The function and responsibility of the President is to set before the American people the unfinished business, the things we must do if we are going to succeed as a nation.

Campaign remarks, Crestwood, Mo., Oct. 22, 1960

7 / PRESIDENT'S RESPONSIBILITIES

All of the problems which center upon the United States finally come to rest, in a free society, upon the desk of the President. He is not only the Commander in Chief, he is not only the head of his party, he is not only a legislative leader, he is not only charged with the power of appointment, he also is charged by the Constitution and by the force of events with the maintenance of our relations across the seas.

Campaign remarks, St. Charles, Ill., Oct. 25, 1960

8 / CONGRESS AND THE EXECUTIVE

The Constitution makes us not rivals for power but partners for progress.

State of the Union Message, Jan. 11, 1962

9 / MUTUAL RESPECT

Our Constitution wisely assigns both joint and separate roles to each branch of the Government; and a President and a Congress who hold each other in mutual respect will neither permit nor attempt any trespass.

State of the Union Message, Jan. 30, 1961

10 / THE HOUSE OF REPRESENTATIVES

The House of Representatives is given the two great powers which are the hallmark of a self-governing society: One, the power to appropriate money, and the second is the power to levy taxes.

Campaign remarks, Cheyenne, Wyo., Sept. 23, 1960

11 / LOCAL SELF-GOVERNMENT

Local self-government is among the most cherished of American democratic traditions. This basic concept has persisted in our country from the town meetings of Colonial days to the present pattern in which counties, cities, towns, boroughs, parishes and villages have vested in them the broadest authority to manage local affairs through instruments of their own creation and officials of their own choice.

Letter to Congress on proposed legislation granting greater self-rule to the Virgin Islands, April 6, 1962

12 / FREE SOCIETY

We [the Government] are not omniscient. We are not all-powerful. This is a free society, and management and labor and the farmer and the citizen have their rights. We did not give them their rights in government.

Address, AFL-CIO Convention, Miami, Dec. 7, 1961

Governmental Responsibility

13 / PRECIOUS OBLIGATION

Government is an art and a precious obligation; and when it has a job to do, I believe it should do it. And this requires not only great ends but that we propose concrete means of achieving them.

Acceptance Speech, Liberal Party Convention, New York City, Sept. 14, 1960

14 / GOVERNMENTAL ACTION

I believe in a government which acts, which exercises its full powers and its full responsibilities.

Ibid.

15 / ACHIEVEMENT OF OBJECTIVES

Our responsibility is not discharged by an announcement of virtuous ends. Our responsibility is to achieve these objectives with social invention, with political skill, and executive vigor.

Ibid.

16 / FAITHFUL ACCOUNTING

The prudent heir takes careful inventory of his legacies, and gives a faithful accounting to those whom he owes an obligation of trust.

> State of the Union Message, Jan. 30, 1961

17 / FEDERAL GOVERNMENT'S OBLIGATION

The Federal Government is not a remote bureaucracy. It must seek to meet those needs of the individual, the family and the community which can best be met by the nationwide cooperation of all and which cannot be met by state and local governments.

> Address, American Society of Newspaper Editors, Washington, D.C., April 19, 1963

18 / "TO GOVERN IS TO CHOOSE"

Because our system is designed to encourage both differences and dissent, because its checks and balances are designed to preserve the rights of the individual and the locality against pre-eminent central authority, you and I, Governors, both recognize how dependent we both are, one upon another, for the successful operation of our unique and happy form of Government. Our system and our freedom permit the legislative to be pitted against the executive, the state against the Federal Government, the city against the countryside, the party against party, interest against interest, all in competition or in contention one with another.

Our task—your task in the State House and my task in the White House—is to weave from all these tangled threads a fabric of law and progress. Others may confine themselves to debate, discussion and that ultimate luxury—free advice. Our responsibility is one of decision, for to govern is to choose.

> Apostrophe to State Governors, address, Independence Hall, Philadelphia, July 4, 1962

People's Government

19 / "THE FEDERAL GOVERNMENT IS . . . THE PEOPLE"

The Federal Government is not a stranger or an enemy. It is the people of 50 states joining in a national effort to seek progress in every state.

> Address, 30th anniversary of the Tennessee Valley Authority, Muscle Shoals, Ala., May 18, 1963

20 / THE PEOPLE'S CONTRIBUTION

The greatness of our Constitution comes not so much from the words that it contains. It is great because of the people who have lived and worked under it to add to its framework of words and ideas the work and sacrifice and passionate devotion of many generations of Americans.

Campaign statement on Citizenship Day, Washington, D.C., Sept. 17, 1960

21 / DEMOCRACY'S FORCE

We . . . have no greater asset than the willingness of a free and determined people, through its elected officials, to face all problems frankly and meet all dangers free from panic or fear.

State of the Union Message, Jan. 30, 1961

22 / THE PEOPLE DECIDE

All of us are involved in the discipline of self-government. All of us in this country, in a sense, are officeholders. All of us make an important decision as to what this country must be and how it must move and what its function shall be, and what its image shall be.

Campaign address, Wittenberg College Stadium, Springfield, Ohio, Oct. 17, 1960

23 / FREEDOM'S CHALLENGE

This is a free society, and the kind of country we have, the kind of strength we have, depends in the final analysis upon the people themselves.

Campaign remarks, Crestwood, Mo., Oct. 22, 1960

24 / DEMOCRACY'S PREMISE

Our greatness is based on the final premise that the people themselves, working among themselves, making their final decision, will make a judgment which fits the best interest of our country. If we did not accept that premise, then the whole concept upon which a democracy is based would be hollow.

Campaign remarks, Philadelphia, Oct. 29, 1960

25 / CITIZEN PARTICIPATION

While there may be some who say that the business of government is so important that it should be confined to those who govern, in this free society of ours the consent and, may I say, the support of the citizens of this country is essential, if . . . any . . . piece of progressive legislation is going to be passed.

> Address, National Council of Senior Citizens, New York City, May 20, 1962

26 / RIGHTS AND RESPONSIBILITIES

This nation was not founded solely on the principle of citizen rights. Equally important—though too often not discussed—is the citizen's responsibility. For our privileges can be no greater than our obligations. The protection of our rights can endure no longer than the performance of our responsibilities. Each can be neglected only at the peril of the other.

> Address, Vanderbilt University, Nashville, Tenn., May 18, 1963

27 / POWER OF THE BALLOT

In a free society, those with the power to govern are necessarily responsive to those with the right to vote.

> Message to Congress on civil rights, Feb. 28, 1963

28 / MOST DIFFICULT

A democracy is the most difficult kind of government to operate. It represents the last flowering, really, of the human experience.

> Campaign address, Pocatello, Idaho, Sept. 6, 1960

29 / SELF-DISCIPLINE

Self-government requires qualities of self-denial and restraint.

> Campaign address, Washington, D.C., Sept. 20, 1960

30 / DEMOCRACY'S DELAYS

Democracy involves delays and debates and dissension. It requires men to think as well as believe, to look ahead as well as back, to give up narrow views or interests that retard their nation's progress. But given an opportunity to work, it completely contradicts and isolates the false appeals of the extremists who would destroy democracy.

> Address at dinner given by President Antonio Segni of Italy, Rome, July 1, 1963

31 / CITIZEN'S RESPONSIBILITY

Political action is the highest responsibility of a citizen.

> Campaign remarks, Pat Clancy Dinner, Astor Hotel, New York City, Oct. 20, 1960

32 / APATHY IN ELECTIONS

Responsible Americans are increasingly concerned with the widespread failure of our citizens to exercise their right to vote.

Statement with executive order creating the President's Commission on Registration, March 30, 1963

Ethical Standards in Government

33 / BASIC RESPONSIBILITY

No responsibility of Government is more fundamental than the responsibility of maintaining the highest standards of ethical behavior by those who conduct the public business.

Message to Congress on ethical conduct in government, April 27, 1961

34 / INFLEXIBLE PRINCIPLE

There can be no dissent from the principle that all officials must act with unwavering integrity, absolute impartiality, and complete devotion to the public interest. This principle must be followed not only in reality but in appearance. For the basis of effective government is public confidence, and that confidence is endangered when ethical standards falter or appear to falter.

Ibid.

35 / OFFICIAL INTEGRITY

The essence of any government that belongs to the people must lie in the biblical injunction, "No man can serve two masters, for either he will hate one and love the other, or else he will hold to one and despise the other." All America seeks a government which no man holds to his own interest, and despises the public interest, and where all men serve only the public and love that master well.

Campaign address, Wittenberg College Stadium, Springfield, Ohio, Oct. 17, 1960

36 / ETHICAL BEHAVIOR

Improprieties occur in a good many different kinds of life, whether it's with labor, management, government. Not all people are able to withstand these pressures. But we intend that the personnel of the United

States Government will meet the highest ethical standards possible, and when they do not, action will be taken.

News conference, Washington, D.C., May 17, 1962

37 / STANDARD FOR OFFICEHOLDERS

To be above criminality is not enough. Good judgment is also required.

Campaign address, Wittenberg College Stadium, Springfield, Ohio, Oct. 17, 1960

38 / REGULATION OF CONDUCT IN PUBLIC OFFICE

No web of statute or regulation, however intricately conceived, can hope to deal with the myriad possible challenges to a man's integrity or his devotion to the public interest. Nevertheless formal regulation is required —regulation which can lay down clear guidelines of policy, punish venality and double-dealing, and set a general ethical tone for the conduct of public business.

Message to Congress on ethical conduct in government, April 27, 1961

39 / PRESIDENTIAL RESPONSIBILITY

No President can excuse or pardon the slightest deviation from irreproachable standards of behavior on the part of any member of the executive branch. For his firmness and determination is the ultimate source of public confidence in the Government of the United States. And there is no consideration that can justify the undermining of that confidence.

Ibid.

40 / EXECUTIVE EXAMPLE

Ultimately, high ethical standards can be maintained only if the leaders of Government provide a personal example of dedication to the public service—and exercise their leadership to develop in all Government employees an increasing sensitivity to the ethical and moral conditions imposed by public service. Their own conduct must be above reproach.

Ibid.

41 / SOCIETY'S MORAL STANDARDS

Public officials are not a group apart. They inevitably reflect the moral tone of the society in which they live. And if that moral tone is injured —by fixed athletic contests or television quiz shows—by widespread business conspiracies to fix prices—by the collusion of businessmen and unions with organized crime—by cheating on expense accounts, by the ignoring of traffic laws, or by petty tax evasion—then the conduct of our Government must be affected. Inevitably, the moral standards of a society influence the conduct of all who live within it—the governed and those who govern.

Ibid.

42 / THE ANSWER

The ultimate answer to ethical problems in Government is honest people in a good ethical environment.

Ibid.

43 / BIPARTISAN WEAKNESSES

History teaches us that no political party has a monopoly on honesty. Both parties attract their share of crooks and weaklings. But that does not mean that these problems are incapable of solution.

Campaign address, Wittenberg College Stadium, Springfield, Ohio, Oct. 17, 1960

Qualification for Government Office

44 / CAPACITY FOR OFFICE

The test of capacity to serve in key national security posts should not be a man's party affiliation. It should be how much talent and dedication he can contribute to the nation.

Campaign press conference, Washington, D.C., Aug. 30, 1960

45 / THE SUBSTANCE

No government is better than the men who compose it.

Campaign address, Wittenberg College Stadium, Springfield, Ohio, Oct. 17, 1960

46 / CALIBER OF PERSONNEL

No amount of reorganization or new procedures can be effective without, or substitute for, high quality personnel in charge of these agencies.

Message to Congress on government regulatory agencies, April 13, 1961

47 / QUALIFICATIONS

We need men of intellectual curiosity, far-sighted, concerned, interested, who want this country to be what it can and must be.

Campaign remarks, Kalamazoo, Mich., Oct. 14, 1960

48 / GOVERNMENT'S NEED OF TOPFLIGHT TALENT

Today's Government needs men and women with a broad range of experience, knowledge, and ability. It needs increasing numbers of people with topflight executive talent. It needs hundreds of occasional and intermittent consultants and part-time experts to help deal with problems of increasing complexity and technical difficulty. In short, we need to draw upon America's entire reservoir of talent and skill to help conduct our generation's most important business—the public business.

Message to Congress on ethical conduct in government, April 27, 1961

49 / THE EDUCATED CITIZEN'S OBLIGATION

The educated citizen has an obligation to serve the public. He may be a precinct worker or President. He may give his talents at the courthouse, the statehouse, the White House. He may be a civil servant or a Senator, a candidate or a campaign worker, a winner or a loser. But he must be a participant and not a spectator.

Address, Vanderbilt University, Nashville, Tenn., May 18, 1963

50 / INVOCATION FOR GOVERNMENTAL LEADERS

Do not pray for easy lives. Pray to be stronger men.

Address, Washington, D.C., Prayer Breakfast, Feb. 7, 1963

Separation of Church and State

51 / ABSOLUTE SEPARATION

I believe in an America where the separation of church and state is absolute—where no Catholic prelate would tell the President (should he be Catholic) how to act, and no Protestant minister would tell his parishioners for whom to vote—where no church or church school is granted any public funds or political preference—and where no man is denied public office merely because his religion differs from the President who might appoint him or the people who might elect him.

I believe in an America that is officially neither Catholic, Protestant nor Jewish—where no public official either requests or accepts instructions on public policy from the Pope, the National Council of Churches or any other ecclesiastical source—where no religious body seeks to impose its will directly or indirectly upon the general populace or the public acts of its officials—and where religious liberty is so indivisible that an act against one church is treated as an act against all. . . .

I believe in an America where religious intolerance will someday end—where all men and all churches are treated as equal—where every man has the same right to attend or not attend the church of his choice —where there is no Catholic vote, no anti-Catholic vote, no bloc voting of any kind—and where Catholics, Protestants and Jews, at both the lay and pastoral level, will refrain from those attitudes of disdain and division which have so often marred their works in the past, and promote instead the American ideal of brotherhood.

Campaign address, Greater Houston Ministerial Association, Sept. 12, 1960

52 / INDEPENDENT PRESIDENCY

The kind of America in which I believe . . . represents the kind of Presidency in which I believe—a great office that must neither be humbled by making it the instrument of any one religious group nor tarnished by arbitrarily withholding its occupancy from the members of any one religious group. I believe in a President whose religious views are his own private affair, neither imposed by him upon the nation or imposed by the nation upon him as a condition to holding that office.

Ibid.

53 / FULFILLMENT OF PRESIDENTIAL OATH

I want a Chief Executive whose public acts are responsible to all groups and obligated to none—who can attend any ceremony, service, or dinner his office may appropriately require of him—and whose fulfillment of his Presidential oath is not limited or conditioned by any religious oath, ritual, or obligation.

Ibid.

54 / REGARDLESS OF RACE OR CREED

I do not promise to consider race or religion in my appointments. . . . I promise only that I will not consider them.

Campaign address, Wittenberg College Stadium, Springfield, Ohio, Oct. 17, 1960

55 / LIBERTY OF CONSCIENCE

The Founding Fathers believed that liberty of conscience and freedom of worship should rest upon something stronger than inference or tradition. The necessary guarantee was therefore written into the first amendment.

They believed religious freedom would be strengthened if all faiths and creeds were guaranteed this protection, if no single church were permitted special privileges, and if every person felt secure in his right to his personal religious faith. This has proved to be the case.

> Campaign letter to Conference of the National Conference of Christians and Jews, Washington, D.C., Oct. 10, 1960

56 / PRAYER AT HOME

The Supreme Court has made its judgment. A good many people obviously will disagree with it; others will agree with it. But I think that it is important for us, if we're going to maintain our constitutional principle, that we support Supreme Court decisions even when we may not agree with them. In addition, we have in this case a very easy remedy, and that is to pray ourselves. And I think that it would be a welcome reminder to every American family that we can pray a good deal more at home, we can attend our churches with a good deal more fidelity, and we can make the true meaning of prayer much more important in the lives of all of our children.

> Reply to question on the Supreme Court's decision (June 25, 1962) banning official school prayers in New York State public schools, news conference, Washington, D.C., June 27, 1962

Political Extremism

57 / TWO EXTREMES

There are two groups of . . . frustrated citizens, far apart in their views yet very much alike in their approach. On the one hand are those who urge upon us what I regard to be the pathway to surrender—appeasing our enemies, compromising our commitments, purchasing peace at any price, disavowing our arms, our friends, our obligations. If their view had prevailed, the world of free choice would be smaller today.

On the other hand are those who urge upon us what I regard to be the pathway of war: equating negotiations with appeasement and substituting rigidity for firmness. If their view had prevailed, we would be at war today, and in more than one place.

It is a curious fact that each of these extreme opposites resembles the other. Each believes that we have only two choices: appeasement or war, suicide or surrender, humiliation or holocaust, to be either Red or dead. Each side sees only "hard" and "soft" nations, hard and soft policies, hard and soft men. Each believes that any departure from its own course inevitably leads to the other: one group believes that any peaceful solution means appeasement; the other believes that any arms build-up means war.

One group regards everyone else as warmongers, the other regards everyone else as appeasers. Neither side admits that its path will lead to disaster —but neither can tell us how or where to draw the line once we descend the slippery slopes of appeasement or constant intervention.

In short, while both extremes profess to be the true realists of our time, neither could be more unrealistic. While both claim to be doing the nation a service, they could do it no greater disservice. This kind of talk and easy solutions to difficult problems, if believed, could inspire a lack of confidence among our people when they must all—above all else—be united in recognizing the long and difficult days that lie ahead. It could inspire uncertainty among our allies when above all else they must be confident in us. And even more dangerously, it could, if believed, inspire doubt among our adversaries when they must above all be convinced that we will defend our vital interests.

The essential fact that both of these groups fail to grasp is that diplomacy and defense are not substitutes for one another. Either alone would fail. A willingness to resist force, unaccompanied by a willingness to talk, could provoke belligerence—while a willingness to talk, unaccompanied by a willingness to resist force, could invite disaster.

Address, University of Washington, Seattle, Nov. 16, 1961

58 / FRINGE FANATICS

In the most critical periods of our nation's history, there have always been those on the fringes of our society who have sought to escape their responsibility by finding a simple solution, an appealing slogan or a convenient scapegoat. Financial crises could be explained by the presence of too many immigrants or too few greenbacks.

War could be attributed to munitions makers or international bankers. Peace conferences failed because we were duped by the British, or tricked by the French, or deceived by the Russians. It was not the presence of Soviet troops in Eastern Europe that drove it to communism, it was the sell-out at Yalta. It was not a civil war that removed China from the Free World, it was treason in high places. At times these fanatics have achieved a temporary success among those who lack the will or the wisdom to face unpleasant facts or unsolved problems. But in time the basic good sense and stability of the great American consensus has always prevailed.

Address, Democratic Party dinner, Los Angeles, Nov. 18, 1961

59 / "NOW . . . AGAIN . . . VOICES OF EXTREMISM"

Now we are face to face once again with a period of heightened peril. The risks are great, the burdens heavy, the problems incapable of swift or lasting solution. And under the strains and frustrations imposed by constant tension and harassment, the discordant voices of extremism are once again heard in the land. Men who are unwilling to face up to the danger from without are convinced that the real danger is from within.

They look suspiciously at their neighbors and their leaders. They call for "a man on horseback" because they do not trust the people. They find treason in our churches, in our highest court, in our treatment of water. They equate the Democratic party with the welfare state, the welfare state with socialism, socialism with communism. They object quite rightly to politics intruding on the military—but they are very anxious for the military to engage in their kind of politics.

But you and I—most Americans, soldiers and civilians—take a different view of our peril. We know it comes from without, not within. It must be met by quiet preparedness, not provocative speeches. . . .

So let us not heed these counsels of fear and suspicion. Let us concentrate more on keeping enemy bombers and missiles away from our shores, and concentrate less on keeping neighbors away from our shelters. Let us devote more energy to organizing the free and friendly nations of the world, with common trade and strategic goals, and devote less energy to organizing armed bands of civilian guerrillas that are more likely to supply local vigilantes than national vigilance.

Let our patriotism be reflected in the creation of confidence in one another, rather than in crusades of suspicion. Let us prove we think our country great, by striving to make it greater.

Ibid.

60 / DOCTRINES OF UNREALITY

Today . . . voices are heard in the land—voices preaching doctrines wholly unrelated to reality, wholly unsuited to the sixties, doctrines which apparently assume that words will suffice without weapons, that vituperation is as good as victory and that peace is a sign of weakness.

Text of undelivered Dallas address, Nov. 22, 1963

10

Free Enterprise

Liberty's Way

1 / LABOR'S PROGRESS

You have shown that high living standards can be won within the context of freedom.

Campaign Labor Day message, Washington, D.C., Sept. 5, 1960

2 / FREEDOM FOR BUSINESS INITIATIVE

I believe in an America where the free enterprise system flourishes for all other systems to see and admire—where no businessman lacks either competition or credit—and where no monopoly, no racketeer, no government bureaucracy can put him out of business that he built up with his own initiative.

Campaign address, Convention Hall, Philadelphia, Oct. 31, 1960

3 / EFFICIENT ECONOMY

I believe in an America where every man, or woman, who wants to work can find work—a full week's work for a full week's pay; where every man or woman of talent can use those talents; where the waste of idle men and idle machines, of steel mills half shut down, and coal mines boarded up, of chronic recessions and slumps, can be limited; where a growing economy provides new jobs and new markets for a growing nation, without inflating the consumer's prices beyond the reach of their budgets and their families.

Ibid.

4 / ECONOMIC GOAL

We must show the world what a free economy can do—to reduce unemployment, to put unused capacity to work, to spur new productivity, and to foster higher economic growth within a range of sound fiscal policies and relative price stability.

> State of the Union Message, Jan. 30, 1961

5 / COLLECTIVE BARGAINING

Collective bargaining has always been the bedrock of the American labor movement. I hope that you will continue to anchor your movement to this foundation. Free collective bargaining is good for the entire nation. In my view, it is the only alternative to State regulation of wages and prices—a path which leads far down the grim road of totalitarianism. Those who would destroy or further limit the rights of organized labor —those who would cripple collective bargaining or prevent organization of the unorganized—do a disservice to the cause of democracy.

> Campaign Labor Day message, Washington, D.C., Sept. 5, 1960

6 / MUNITIONS FOR FREEDOM

The new frontiers at home . . . present the chance to make the plentiful products of our farms and factories the real munitions in the fight for freedom.

> *Ibid.*

Economic Policy

7 / GOALS

The unfinished business of economic policy includes (1) the achievement of full employment and sustained prosperity without inflation, (2) the acceleration of economic growth, (3) the extension of equality of opportunity, and (4) the restoration of balance of payments equilibrium.

> Economic report to Congress, Jan. 22, 1962

8 / ECONOMIC OBJECTIVES

As President, my interest is in an economy which will be strong enough to absorb the potential of a rapidly expanding population, steady enough to avert the wide swings which bring grief to so many of our people, and non-inflationary enough to persuade investors that this country holds a steady promise of growth and stability.

Address, U.S. Chamber of Commerce, Washington, D.C., April 30, 1962

9 / ECONOMIC STABILITY

The task of economic stabilization does not end with the achievement of full recovery. There remains the problem of keeping the economy from straying too far above or below the path of steady high employment. One way lies inflation, and the other way lies recession. Flexible and vigilant fiscal and monetary policies will allow us to hold the narrow middle course.

Economic report to Congress, Jan. 22, 1962

10 / ACHIEVING PRICE STABILITY

We seek . . . an economic climate in which an expanding concept of business and labor responsibility, and increasing awareness of world commerce and the free forces of domestic competition will keep the price level stable and keep the Government out of price-setting.

Address, U.S. Chamber of Commerce, Washington, D.C., April 30, 1962

11 / ECONOMIC DELUSIONS

We must not as a nation come to accept the proposition that reasonable price stability can be achieved only by tolerating a slack economy, chronic unemployment, and a creeping rate of growth. Neither will we seek to buy short-run economic gains by paying the price of excessive increases in the cost of living. Always a cruel tax upon the weak, inflation is now the certain road to a balance-of-payments crisis and the disruption of the international economy of the Western World.

Message to Congress on the economy, Feb. 2, 1961

12 / INFLATION

Inflation too often follows in the shadow of growth while price stability is made easy by stagnation or control. But we mean to maintain both stability and growth in a climate of freedom.

State of the Union Message, Jan. 11, 1962

13 / NEED FOR HARD THOUGHT

The national interest lies in high employment and steady expansion of output and stable prices and a strong dollar. The declaration of such an objective is easy. The attainment in an intricate and interdependent economy and world is a little more difficult. To attain them we require not some automatic response but hard thought.

Commencement address, Yale University, New Haven, June 11, 1962

14 / STRONG DOLLAR NEEDED

We are the principal banker of the free world and any potential weakness in our dollar spells trouble, not only for us but also for our friends and allies who rely on the dollar to finance a substantial portion of their trade.

Message to Congress on gold and balance-of-payments deficit, Feb. 6, 1961

15 / MAINTAINING DOLLAR STRENGTH

The real wealth of a nation resides in its farms and factories and the people who man them. A dynamic economy producing goods competitively priced in world markets will maintain the strength of the dollar.

Ibid.

16 / BASIC AIMS

We have two tasks in economic policy—to create demand, so that we will have a market for all we can produce, and to avoid inflation. To return to a policy of halting inflation by curbing demand would be self-defeating. But to expand the forces of demand by feeding the fires of inflation would be equally dangerous and delusive.

Address, United Auto Workers Convention, Atlantic City, N.J., May 8, 1962

17 / REAL WAGES

In general a wage policy which seeks its gains out of the fruits of technology, instead of the pockets of the consumers, is the one basic approach that can help every segment of the economy. . . . It is a simple, inescapable economic truth that increases in productivity, in output per man-hour, set the outer limits of our economic progress.

This country has the world's highest real wages and living standard simply because our output per man-hour is the highest in the world. No financial sleight of hand can raise real wages and profits faster than productivity without defeating their own purpose through inflation.

Ibid.

18 / OPPORTUNITY TO WORK

Whether they work in organized labor or whether they are teachers or doctors or nurses, whatever they may be, the chance to work at decent wages must be a basic, fundamental premise upon which our society must be based.

Campaign address, Portland, Ore., Sept. 7, 1960

19 / PROFIT: ESSENTIAL ELEMENT

We want prosperity and in a free enterprise system there can be no prosperity without profit. We want a growing economy, and there can be no growth without the investment that is inspired and financed by profit. We want to maintain our national security and other essential programs and we will have little revenue to finance them unless there is profit. We want to improve our balance of payments without reducing our commitments abroad, and we cannot increase our export surplus, which we must, without modernizing our plants through profit. We can help through new trade policies that increase the business man's access to foreign markets, particularly in the expanding markets of 200,000,000 people which we will have in Western Europe.

Address, U.S. Chamber of Commerce, Washington, D.C., April 30, 1962

20 / MEETING FOREIGN COMPETITION

If our own goods are to compete with foreign goods in price and quality, both at home and abroad, we shall need the most efficient plant and equipment.

Message to Congress on taxes, April 20, 1961

21 / BALANCE OF PAYMENTS

There is proper concern about our balance of payments and the recent drain of gold. It is vital that we keep our exports well ahead of our imports in order to cover our commitments abroad—our military forces around the world, our diplomatic obligations, our military aid, and our assistance to underdeveloped nations.

Campaign address, Associated Business Publications Conference, New York City, Oct. 12, 1960

22 / BALANCE-OF-PAYMENTS DEFICIT PERSISTS

This nation continues to be concerned about its balance-of-payments deficit, which, despite its decline, remains a stubborn and troublesome problem.

State of the Union Message, Jan. 14, 1963

23 / BALANCE-OF-PAYMENTS EQUILIBRIUM

Our commercial trade surplus—the excess of our exports of goods and services over imports must rise substantially to assure that we will reach balance of payments equilibrium within a reasonable period.

Economic report to Congress, Jan. 21, 1963

Economic Growth

24 / UTILIZING PRODUCTIVE CAPACITY

Our growing labor force and steadily rising productivity raise our capacity to produce by more than $20 billion a year. We need to run just to keep pace and run swiftly to gain ground in our race to full utilization.
Ibid.

25 / PACE STILL TOO SLOW

For all its advances, the nation is still falling substantially short of its economic potential—a potential we must fulfill both to raise our standards of well-being at home and to serve the cause of freedom abroad.
Ibid.

26 / ECONOMIC INITIATIVE

The nation cannot—and will not—be satisfied with economic decline and slack. The United States cannot afford, in this time of national need and world crisis, to dissipate its opportunities for economic growth.

Message to Congress on the economy, Feb. 2, 1961

27 / GEARING THE ECONOMY TO FULL CAPACITY

Employment, income, profit, construction and investment must all move up more quickly. . . . And the greater wages and profits which full capacity could bring to all of our American citizens must soon replace the most extravagant waste, which is to have men searching for jobs which they cannot find in factories which have a percentage of their machines unused.

Address to the nation on the economy, Washington, D.C., Aug. 13, 1962

28 / HUMAN ASPECTS OF ECONOMIC GROWTH

Economic growth is not a technical term. It goes to the kind of profit which businessmen make. It goes to the question of whether our children

will get jobs. It goes to the question of whether there will be full employment. . . . We have to provide 25,000 new jobs every week for the next
10 years if we are going to maintain full employment in the country and
we are going to have to do it at a time when machines are taking the jobs
of men. This is a tremendously difficult challenge for us all.

> Campaign address, Rotary Club luncheon, Dayton, Ohio, Oct. 17, 1960

29 / THE PRIMARY CHALLENGE

Our primary challenge is not how to divide the economic pie, but how to
enlarge it. To fight now over large slices of the existing pie, by seeking
higher margins on lower volume, or higher wages ahead of productivity,
can only weaken our effort to expand the economy of the United States.

> Address, U.S. Chamber of Commerce, Washington, D.C., April 30, 1962

30 / ECONOMIC OBJECTIVE

We want an economic growth second to none.

> Campaign address via telephone to AMVET Convention, Miami Beach, Aug. 26,
> 1960

31 / SHORT OF PRODUCTIVE CAPACITY

The failure to use our full capacity is the urgent economic problem of
the day.

> Message to Congress on the economy, Feb. 2, 1961

32 / ECONOMIC GROWTH AND EMPLOYMENT

Only by developing economic policies which encourage the growth of
the United States can we hope to maintain full employment in the United
States.

> Campaign address, Portland, Ore., Sept. 7, 1960

33 / CONSTRUCTIVE BUDGET DEFICIT

Our practical choice is not between deficit and surplus, but between two
kinds of deficits: between deficits born of waste and weakness and deficits
incurred as we build our future strength. . . . As the economy returns
to full employment, the budget will return to constructive balance.

> Message to Congress on the economy, Jan. 21, 1963

34 / INCENTIVE FOR REINVESTMENT

We want to provide opportunities for plant reinvestment. One of the
matters which is of concern in maintaining our economy now is the fact

that we do not have as much reinvestment in our plants as we did, for example, in '55, '56, and '57. And we want this economy and this rise to be continuous. And I believe that we have to give as much incentive as is possible to provide reinvestment in plants which makes work and will keep our economy moving ahead.

Address, AFL-CIO Convention, Miami, Dec. 7, 1961

35 / NATIONAL ECONOMIC GROWTH RATE

Our post-war economic growth—though a step ahead of our record for the last half-century—has been slowing down. We have not in recent years maintained the 4 to 4½ percent growth rate which characterized the early post-war period. We should not settle for less than the achievement of a long-term growth rate matching the early post-war record. Increasing our growth rate to 4½ percent a year lies within the range of our capabilities during the Nineteen Sixties. It will lay the groundwork for meeting both our domestic needs and our world responsibilities.

Economic report to Congress, Jan. 22, 1962

36 / CORNERSTONE

A prosperous and expanding economy is the cornerstone of our free enterprise system and vital to the maintenance of America's strength, as leader of the free world.

Campaign statement on views of businessmen, Washington, D.C., Sept. 26, 1960

Federal Tax Policy: Factor in
Growth and Prosperity

37 / CRUCIAL NEED

The most urgent task facing our nation at home today is to end the tragic waste of unemployment and unused resources, to step up the growth and vigor of our national economy, to increase job and investment opportunities, to improve our productivity, and thereby to strengthen our nation's ability to meet its worldwide commitments for the defense and growth of freedom. The revision of our Federal tax system on an equitable basis is crucial to the achievement of these goals.

Message to Congress on taxes, Jan. 24, 1963

38 / FEDERAL TAXES AND THE ECONOMY

The single most important fiscal weapon available to strengthen the national economy is the Federal tax policy. The right kind of tax cut at the right time is the most effective measure that this Government could take to spur our economy forward. For the facts of the matter are that our present tax system is a drag on economic recovery and economic growth, biting heavily into the purchasing power of every taxpayer and every consumer.

> Address to the nation on the economy, Washington, D.C., Aug. 13, 1962

39 / INORDINATE TAX RATES

Our tax rates . . . are so high as to weaken the very essence of the progress of a free society—the incentive for additional return for additional effort.

> *Ibid.*

40 / "THE CHECKREIN . . . MUST BE LOOSENED"

We must not allow the progress of the last two years to blunt the recognition that our economy can produce both more jobs and greater abundance than it is now doing. . . . The checkrein of taxes on private spending and productive incentives must be loosened if our economy is to perform at maximum efficiency.

> Annual budget message to Congress, Jan. 17, 1963

41 / DRAG ON ECONOMIC GROWTH

Our present tax system exerts too heavy a drag on growth. . . . It siphons out of the private economy too large a share of personal and business purchasing power. . . . It reduces the financial incentives for personal effort, investment and risk-taking.

> Address, Economic Club of New York, New York City, Dec. 14, 1962

42 / BLOCK TO EMPLOYMENT

The main block to full employment is an unrealistically heavy burden of taxation. The time has come to remove it.

> Economic report to Congress, Jan. 21, 1963

43 / LEEWAY FOR TAX REDUCTION

Idle men and machines allow plenty of room for decreased taxes and increased demand without the risk of inflation.

> Address, Florida Chamber of Commerce, Tampa, Nov. 18, 1963

44 / THE CASE FOR TAX REDUCTION

It is not the fear of recession but the fact of five years of excessive unemployment, unused capacity and slack profits—and the consequent hobbling of our growth rate—that constitutes the urgent case for tax reduction and reform.

> Economic report to Congress, Jan. 21, 1963

45 / SPURRING ECONOMIC GROWTH

In my opinion, it will be stepped up only by lightening the repressive rate of wartime tax rates which put a damper on private purchasing power and profits.

> Remarks, American Bankers Association, symposium on economic growth, Washington, D.C., Feb. 25, 1963

46 / SHARING OF BENEFITS AND BURDENS

Tax reduction is urgently needed to spur the growth of our economy—but both the fruits of growth and the burdens of the resulting new tax structure should be fairly shared by all. For the present patchwork of special provisions lightens the load on some by placing a heavier burden on others.

> Message to Congress on taxes, Jan. 24, 1963

47 / PRIORITY OF TAX REVISION

The most urgent economic business before the nation is a prompt and substantial reduction and revision of Federal income taxes in order to speed up our economic growth and wipe out our present excessive unemployment.

> News conference, Washington, D.C., July 17, 1963

American Labor

48 / LABOR'S RESPONSIBILITY

The unfinished business of this country is your business. . . . The progress of this country will depend in a great measure on the sense of public responsibility of members of organized labor.

> Address, ILGWU cooperative houses dedication, New York City, May 19, 1962

49 / PUBLIC INTEREST

Our unions have fought for aid to education, better housing, further development of our rich natural resources, and to save the family-size farm. They speak not for narrow self-interest, but for the public interest and the people.

> Campaign Labor Day message, Washington, D.C., Sept. 5, 1960

50 / BASIC PROGRAM

I know that the American labor movement wants for America what I want for America: the elimination of poverty and unemployment, the reestablishment of America's position of leadership in the world, the end of racial discrimination everywhere in our society. I know the American labor movement opposes what I oppose: complacency, unemployment, economic stagnation and national insecurity.

> Campaign remarks via telephone to New York State AFL-CIO Convention, from Washington, D.C., Aug. 30, 1960

51 / IMMIGRANT PIONEERS IN LABOR'S CAUSE

Many of these . . . immigrant families produced the pioneers and builders of the American labor movement. They are the men who sweated in our shops, who struggled to create a union, who were driven by longing for education for their children and for their children's development. They went to night schools; they built their own future, their union's future, and their country's future, brick by brick, block by block, neighborhood by neighborhood, and now in their children's time, suburb by suburb.

> Acceptance speech, Liberal Party Convention, New York City, Sept. 14, 1960

52 / THE AMERICAN LABOR MOVEMENT

Fifty years or so ago the American labor movement was little more than a group of dreamers, and look at it now. Nearly 14 million men and women belong to unions affiliated with the AFL-CIO. From coast to coast, in factories, stores, warehouses, and business establishments of all kinds, industrial democracy is at work. Employees, represented by free and democratic trade unions of their own choosing, participate actively in determining their wages, hours, and working conditions. Their living standards are the highest in the world. Their job rights are protected by collective bargaining agreements. They have fringe benefits that were unheard of less than a generation ago. Is there any better monument to the unlimited ability of Americans to turn dreams to reality than the American labor movement?

> Campaign remarks via telephone to New York State AFL-CIO Convention, from Washington, D.C., Aug. 30, 1960

53 / LABOR AND FREEDOM

As long as the labor movement is strong and as long as it is committed to freedom, then I think the freedom of this country is strengthened. So I would hope that every American, whether he was on one side of the bargaining table or the other, or whether he was in a wholly different sphere of life, would recognize that the strength of a free American labor movement is vital to the maintenance of freedom in this country and all around the world.

> Address, AFL-CIO Convention, Miami, Dec. 7, 1961

54 / FREE LABOR, FREE COUNTRY

A free, active, progressive trade union movement stands for a free, active, progressive country.

> Address, International Association of Machinists, Washington, D.C., May 5, 1963

55 / UNITY IN FREEDOM

What unites labor, what unites this country is far more important than those things on which we may disagree.

> Address, AFL-CIO Convention, Miami, Dec. 7, 1961

56 / WORLDWIDE INFLUENCE

I believe . . . that one of the great assets that this country has is the influence which this labor movement can promote around the world in demonstrating what a free trade union can do.

> *Ibid.*

The Business Community

57 / BUSINESS ACHIEVEMENTS

I believe that the business community—and our basic economic system —have well served the American people. They have provided a very large proportion of our people with a very high and constantly improving standard of living. They have provided the sinew and sustenance to make us the first nation of the world. They have brought a wide array of modern goods within the income of most of our people.

Campaign address, Associated Business Publications Conference, New York City, Oct. 12, 1960

58 / BUSINESS AND GOVERNMENT, INTERDEPENDENT

. . . we are—in the National Government, and I know—a rather unpopular partner in every one of your businesses. Our revenues come from you. When you are making profits, then we are able to meet our bills. When you fail, then we fail. So for every reason, Government and business are completely interdependent and completely involved. And while we may differ on the policies which may bring this country prosperity, there is no disagreement, I am sure, on either side, about the tremendous importance of you gentlemen moving ahead, and prospering, and contributing to the growth of this country.

Address, National Association of Manufacturers, New York City, Dec. 6, 1961

59 / GOVERNMENT AND BUSINESS: NECESSARY ALLIES

The complaint has often been made in business circles that the Federal Government is a "silent partner" in every corporation—taking roughly half of all of your net earnings without risk to itself. But it should be also realized that this makes business a not always "silent partner" of the Federal Government—that our revenues and thus our success are dependent upon your profits and your success—and that, far from being natural enemies, Government and business are necessary allies.

Address, National Industrial Conference Board luncheon, Washington, D.C., Feb. 13, 1961

60 / BUSINESS PROSPERITY VITAL TO FREEDOM

We are committed to the defense of freedom around the world. When business does well in this country, we have full employment, and this country is moving ahead, then it strengthens our image as a prosperous and vital country in this great fight in which we are engaged. When you do well, the United States does well, and our policies abroad do well. And when you do badly, all suffer.

Address, National Association of Manufacturers, New York City, Dec. 6, 1961

61 / COMMON GOAL OF GOVERNMENT AND INDUSTRY

Whether we work in the White House or the State House, or in a house of industry or commerce, mankind is our business and if we work in harmony, if we understand the problems of each other and the responsibilities that each of us bears, then surely the business of mankind will prosper, and your children and mine will move ahead in a secure world, and one in which there is opportunity for them all.

Address, Florida Chamber of Commerce, Tampa, Nov. 18, 1963

62 / SMALL BUSINESSMEN

One of the great challenges of the sixties will be to strengthen the small independent businessman against the large business units which threaten to crowd him from the American economic scene—and to reverse the disastrous policies which are destroying this historic cornerstone of our free enterprise system.

Campaign statement on small business, Washington, D.C., Oct. 10, 1960

Management-Labor Relations

63 / ECONOMIC HARMONY

Our goals of economic growth and price stability are dependent upon the success of both . . . business and labor, and there can be no room on either side in this country . . . for any feelings of hostility or vindictiveness.

News conference, Washington, D.C., April 19, 1962

64 / WAGE AND PRICE STABILITY

The course of the American price level depends in substantial measure on wage and price decisions of labor and management. This dependence grows in importance as the economy moves toward full employment. All of us must now be conscious of the need for policies that enable American goods to compete successfully with foreign goods. We cannot afford unsound wage and price movements which push up costs, weaken our international competitive position, restrict job opportunities, and jeopardize the health of our domestic economy.

Message to Congress on the economy, Feb. 2, 1961

65 / PRICES AND WAGES, AND INFLATION

In those sectors where both companies and unions possess substantial market power, the interplay of price and wage decisions could set off a movement toward a higher price level. If this were to occur, the whole nation would be the victim.

I do not believe that American business or labor will allow this to happen. All of us have learned a great deal from the economic events of the past fifteen years. Among both businessmen and workers, there is growing recognition that the road to higher real profits and higher real wages is the road of increased productivity. When better plant and equipment enable the labor force to produce more in the same number of hours, there is more to share among all the contributors to the productive process—and this can happen with no increase in prices. Gains achieved in this manner endure, while gains achieved in one turn of the price-wage spiral vanish on the next.

The nation must rely on the good sense and public spirit of our business and labor leaders to hold the line on the price level in 1962. If labor leaders in our major industries will accept the productivity benchmark as a guide to wage objectives, and if management in these industries will practice equivalent restraint in their price decisions, the year ahead will be a brilliant chapter in the record of the responsible exercise of freedom.

Economic report to Congress, Jan. 22, 1962

66 / PRICE STABILITY

As long as wage rate increases stay within the bounds of productivity increases, as long as the push for higher margins through higher prices is restrained . . . the outlook for stable prices is excellent.

Economic report to Congress, Jan. 21, 1963

67 / WAGES AND INFLATION

What good is it to get an increase in wages if it is taken away by an increase in prices? What counts is the real increase in wages which comes from increased productivity and technology.

Address, United Auto Workers Convention, Atlantic City, N.J., May 8, 1962

68 / PROSPERITY THROUGH INCREASED PRODUCTIVITY

Unjustified wage demands which require price increases and then other demands and then other price increases are equally as contrary to the national interest as unjustified profit demands which require price increases. But when productivity has been raised by the skills of better management, the efficiency of labor and the modernization financed by investors, all three groups can reap the rewards of that productivity and still pass lower prices on to the consumer.

Ibid.

69 / THE GREAT PROBLEM

There can be no lasting increases in wages without industry making a profit. There can be no lasting profit on plants when they are producing less than capacity. And that has been the great problem of the American economy since the end of 1957.

Ibid.

70 / FOR STABILITY AND GROWTH

We can . . . help by creating a climate of collective bargaining in which increased wages are held within the approximate limits of rising productivity, a rising productivity that will also provide for investments in modernization, for profits, and even we hope lower prices, to stimulate increased purchasing.

Address, U.S. Chamber of Commerce, Washington, D.C., April 30, 1962

71 / PURSUIT OF PRICE STABILITY

I believe that reasonable stability in the price level is a vital goal of economic policy. By pursuing this goal we keep faith with those who save; we protect those who live on a fixed income; and we build world confidence in the soundness of the dollar. It is equally urgent that we do not achieve this kind of stability at the expense of any one group in the economy, such as farmers—or at the price of recessions, unemployment, and stagnation.

Campaign address, Associated Business Publications Conference, New York City, Oct. 12, 1960

72 / SHARE OF RESPONSIBILITY

Labor, too, has its responsibility for price stability.

Address, National Association of Manufacturers, New York City, Dec. 6, 1961

73 / FREEDOM DEMANDS RESPONSIBILITY

The simultaneous and identical actions of United States Steel and other leading steel corporations increasing steel prices by some $6 a ton constitute a wholly unjustifiable and irresponsible defiance of the public interest.

In this serious hour in our nation's history when we are confronted with grave crises in Berlin and Southeast Asia, when we are devoting our energies to economic recovery and stability, when we are asking Reservists to leave their homes and families months on end and service-men to risk their lives—and four were killed in the last two days in Vietnam—and asking union members to hold down their wage requests at a time when restraint and sacrifice are being asked of every citizen, the American people will find it hard, as I do, to accept a situation in which a tiny handful of steel executives whose pursuit of private power and profit exceeds their sense of public responsibility can show such utter contempt for the interest of 185,000,000 Americans.

If this rise in the cost of steel is imitated by the rest of the industry, instead of rescinded, it would increase the cost of homes, autos, appliances and most other items for every American family. It would increase the cost of machinery and tools to every American business man and farmer. It would seriously handicap our efforts to prevent an inflationary spiral from eating up the pensions of our older citizens and our new gains in purchasing power. It would add, Defense Secretary Robert S. McNamara informed me this morning, an estimated $1,000,000,000 to the cost of our defenses, at a time when every dollar is needed for national security and other purposes.

It will make it more difficult for American goods to compete in foreign markets, more difficult to withstand competition from foreign imports and thus more difficult to improve our balance-of-payments position and stem the flow of gold. And it is necessary to stem it for our national security if we're going to pay for our security commitments abroad.

And it would surely handicap our efforts to induce other industries and unions to adopt responsible price and wage policies.

The facts of the matter are that there is no justification for an increase in steel prices.

The recent settlement between the industry and the union, which does not even take place until July 1, was widely acknowledged to be non-inflationary, and the whole purpose and effect of this Administration's role, which both parties understood, was to achieve an agreement which would make unnecessary any increases in prices.

Steel output per man is rising so fast that labor costs per ton of steel can actually be expected to decline in the next twelve months. And, in fact, the Acting Commissioner of the Bureau of Labor Statistics informed me this morning that, and I quote, "employment costs per unit of steel output in 1961 were essentially the same as they were in 1958." The cost of major raw materials—steel scrap and coal—has also been declining.

And for an industry which has been generally operating at less than two-thirds capacity, its profit rate has been normal and can be expected to rise sharply this year in view of the reduction in idle capacity. Their lot has been easier than that of a hundred thousand steelworkers thrown out of work in the last three years.

The industry's cash dividends have exceeded $600,000,000 in each of the last five years; and earnings in the first quarter of this year were estimated in the Feb. 28 Wall Street Journal to be among the highest in history.

In short, at a time when they could be exploring how more efficiency and better prices could be obtained, reducing prices in this industry in recognition of lower costs, their unusually good labor contract, their foreign competition and their increase in production and profits which are coming this year, a few gigantic corporations have decided to increase prices in ruthless disregard of their public responsibility.

The Steelworkers Union can be proud that it abided by its responsibilities in this agreement. And this Government also has responsibilities which we intend to meet.

The Department of Justice and the Federal Trade Commission are examining the significance of this action in a free competitive economy.

The Department of Defense and other agencies are reviewing its impact on their policies of procurement.

And I am informed that steps are under way by those members of Congress who plan appropriate inquiries into how these price decisions are so quickly made and reached and what legislative safeguards may be needed to protect the public interest.

Price and wage decisions in this country, except for a very limited restriction in the case of monopolies and national emergency strikes, are and ought to be freely and privately made. But the American people have a right to expect, in return for that freedom, a higher sense of business responsibility for the welfare of their country than has been shown in the last two days.

Some time ago I asked each American to consider what he would do for his country, and I asked the steel companies. In the last twenty-four hours we had their answer.

> Statement on April 10 price increases by six major steel companies, news conference, Washington, D.C., April 11, 1962. The companies rescinded the increases on April 13

74 / ACROSS-THE-BOARD PRICE INCREASE IN STEEL IS OPPOSED

This Administration is watching closely the possibilities of a general across-the-board price increase in steel. I opposed such an increase last year—I oppose such an increase now.

This Administration is not interested in determining the appropriate price or profit levels of any particular industry. We are interested in protecting the American public—and it is the American public which would suffer most from a general increase in steel prices.

It would invite another inflationary spiral in place of the present wage-price stability. It would hamper our export expansion and increase import competition. It would adversely affect our balance-of-payment position on which our worldwide commitments depend. It would reduce the gains of our economic growth and reduce job opportunities in this country.

This Government in the past year has taken major steps to improve the economic position of the steel industry and assist in its modernization. Depreciation and investment tax benefits of some $100,000,000 were provided in 1962 to the steel industry alone; and its increased cash flow has made possible a planned increase in plant and equipment investment more than twice the national average. Additional tax gains will be realized in this year's tax reduction program.

I therefore strongly urge the leaders of the steel industry to refrain from any across-the-board price increases which will aggravate their competitive position and injure the public interest.

The steel industry, which has been hard hit from competition from lower-priced substitute products and foreign producers, has been operating far below capacity. What it needs is more business at competitive prices, not less business at higher prices.

I urge similar restraint on the steel workers' union. With over 100,000 steel workers still unemployed, there is a need for more jobs with job security, not fewer jobs at higher wages.

Across-the-board price increases could precipitate labor demands and unrest that would cause great difficulty for the country.

I realize that price and wage controls in this one industry while all others are unrestrained would be unfair and inconsistent with our free competitive market—that unlike last year the Government's good faith has not been engaged in talks with industry and union representatives—and that selected price adjustments, up or down as prompted by changes in supply and demand, as opposed to across-the-board increases, are not incompatible within a framework of general stability and steel price stability and are characteristic of any healthy economy.

In a free society both management and labor are free to do voluntarily what we are unwilling to impose by law, and I urge the steel industry and the steel union to avoid any action which would lead to a general across-the-board increase. I urge this in their own enlightened self-interest and in the public interest as well.

Statement on April 9 increase in steel prices by the Wheeling Steel Corporation, Washington, D.C., April 11, 1963

75 / SOME RESTRAINT

. . . selected price increases up or down seemed to me to be responsive to market situations. We've had selective price increases up; now it may be that we will have them down in the not too distant future. As to the general effect, of course, it represents about a 1 per cent price increase for steel products, which restores, really, the 1 per cent that's been lost . . . since 1959 in the price of steel. It is certainly our hope that this can be absorbed, particularly by the automobile companies who are making very high profits. The amount of increase of cost to them—we hope—will not be substantial enough to affect their price.

What I'm concerned about is not the actual effect, though that's important, but the psychological effect may cause a more general rise in prices, which may therefore be reflected in additional wage demands. I believe that price stability . . . is the best thing for the steel industry and wage stability is the best thing for the [United Steel Workers] union. . . . I know the steel industry, it seems to me, have acted with some restraint in this case, which I think is very useful. I'm hopeful that other companies, particularly in the oil industry, will act with similar restraint and that the union itself will guide its conduct in accordance with its long-range interest, which is the national interest.

Address, American Society of Newspaper Editors, Washington, D.C., April 19, 1963

76 / BEYOND "THE POINT OF PUBLIC TOLERATION"

The New York newspaper strike is now in its 75th day. The situation has long since passed the point of public toleration. The essence of free collective bargaining in this country is a sense of responsibility and restraint by both sides, not merely an effort by one side or the other to break those who sit across the bargaining table from them.

It is clear in the case of the New York newspaper strike that the Local of the International Typographical Union and its president, Bertram Powers, insofar as anyone can understand his position, are attempting to impose a settlement which could shut down several newspapers in New York and throw thousands out of work. Collective bargaining has failed. The most intensive mediation has failed. This is a situation which is bad for the union movement all over the country, bad for the newspaper managements and bad for the New York citizens, more than five million of them, who are newspaper readers.

In my view, one solution to this prolonged strike, if no immediate progress is made, would be for the striking printers, companies, and other involved unions, to submit their differences to independent determination of some kind. I cannot see any other alternative which at present would bring about a solution to this critical labor dispute which has already had a vital effect on the economic life of this great city of New York.

Comment on the 75th day of the 114-day New York City newspaper strike, news conference, Washington, D.C., Feb. 21, 1963

77 / LAST RESORT: ARBITRATION

I consider negotiated agreement infinitely superior to arbitration. But where private parties cannot negotiate successfully, arbitration is infinitely superior to a shutdown over a period of a vital segment of the nation's economy.

> Statement to railroad and operating rail union officials on impending shutdown of railroads, Washington, D.C., July 9, 1963

Employment—Automation

78 / NUMBER ONE ECONOMIC PROBLEM

Unemployment is our number one economic problem. It wastes the lives of men and women, depriving both them and the nation.

> Manpower report to Congress, March 11, 1963

79 / ATTENTION TO UNEMPLOYMENT

Anyone who honestly is seeking a job and can't find it deserves the attention of the United States Government and the people.

> News conference, Washington, D.C., April 12, 1961

80 / PROSPERITY BASIC TO EMPLOYMENT

We're unable to maintain the kind of high employment which we must maintain, unless you are making profits, and reinvesting, and producing; and therefore as we are committed to the goal—and we must all be in this country, of trying to make sure that everyone who wants a job will find it, then quite obviously we must make the system work, and the business community must prosper.

> Address, National Association of Manufacturers, New York City, Dec. 6, 1961

81 / INVOLUNTARY UNEMPLOYMENT

Involuntary unemployment is the most dramatic sign and disheartening consequence of underutilization of productive capacity. It translates into human terms what may otherwise seem merely an abstract statistic.

> Economic report to Congress, Washington, D.C., Jan. 22, 1962

82 / THE UNEMPLOYMENT ACT OF 1946

As a declaration of national purpose and as a recognition of Federal responsibility, the Act has few parallels in the nation's history. In passing the Act by heavy bipartisan majorities, the Congress registered the consensus of the American people that this nation will not countenance the suffering, frustration and injustice of unemployment, or let the vast potential of the world's leading economy run to waste in idle manpower, silent machinery and empty plants.

Ibid.

83 / RESOURCES WASTED

The resources that we need for the great contest of the 1960's to demonstrate that we are the most vital society are lost when we do not use our hands, when men are out of work and cannot find work, and when we have a lack of economic growth.

Campaign address, Zembo Mosque Temple, Harrisburg, Pa., Sept. 15, 1960

84 / UNEMPLOYED YOUTHS

Our youth are our greatest resource, and the social and economic implications of protracted unemployment among the one million young job seekers today and the many millions who will enter the labor force in the next few years demand immediate attention and action.

Statement on unemployment among youth, Washington, D.C., Nov. 15, 1961

85 / EXPERIENCE WASTED

Our older people must receive not only their earned reward for their contributions to America's past—they must be allowed to share in the great task of building America's future. Today too many of our older people who can work—who want to work—cannot find work. Their abilities and skills—their experience and wisdom and knowledge—are wastefully ignored, by a country which desperately needs their services.

We must embark on a great program to use the skills of older Americans—through changes in Government hiring policies—through expanded employment services—and through an intensive education of our nation's employers to the immense value of this great reservoir of unused talents.

Address, memorial program for Franklin D. Roosevelt, 25th anniversary of signing of Social Security Act, Hyde Park, N.Y., Aug. 14, 1960

86 / EMPLOYMENT PROBLEM INTENSIFIED BY AUTOMATION

One million five hundred thousand people will come into the labor movement every year in the 1960's and are going to have to find a job, and they come into the labor market at the very same time when automation is revolutionizing employment.

Campaign address, Portland, Ore., Sept. 7, 1960

87 / REPLACING MEN

A revolution of automation finds machines replacing men in the mines and mills of America without replacing their income or their training or their need to pay the family doctor, grocer and landlord.

Acceptance speech, Democratic National Convention, Los Angeles, July 15, 1960

88 / AUTOMATION: "MAJOR DOMESTIC CHALLENGE OF THE SIXTIES"

It is a fact that we have to find over a ten-year period 25,000 new jobs every week to take care of those who are displaced by machines and those who are coming into the labor market. So that this places a major burden upon our economy and on our society, and it's one to which we will have to give a good deal of attention in the next decade. I regard it as a very serious problem.

If our economy is moving forward, we can absorb this 1,800,000 even though, in particular industries, we may get special structural unemployment. We've seen that in steel, we've seen it in coal, we may see it in other industries. But if our economy is progressing as we hope it will, then we can absorb a good many of these men and women. But I regard it as the major domestic challenge of the Sixties—to maintain full employment at a time when automation is replacing men.

News conference, Washington, D.C., Feb. 14, 1962

89 / AUTOMATION: NATIONAL PROBLEM

We must recognize that the problem of automation is not a problem for a family or even for a company, or even for an industry. The problem of automation is a national problem.

Campaign address, Charleston, W. Va., Sept. 19, 1960

90 / TECHNOLOGICAL CHANGE: GOVERNMENT'S ROLE IN ADJUSTMENT

Rapid technological change is resulting in serious employment dislocations, which deny us the full stimulus to growth which advancing technology makes possible. Labor and industry have demonstrated cooperative initiative in working out solutions in specific plants and industries. Government action is also necessary, not only to maintain an environment favorable to economic growth, but also to deal with special problems in communities and industries suffering from economic dislocations and to help those who through unemployment are bearing an unfair share of the burden of technological change. . . . Government can help further by encouraging labor and management to find ways to smooth the adjustment to technological change and thus to maintain and reinforce the favorable attitude toward economic progress that characterizes American business and labor alike.

Message to Congress on the economy, Washington, D.C., Feb. 2, 1961

91 / RETRAINING

We need a program of retraining our unemployed workers. . . . We want to make sure that our workers are able to take advantage of the new jobs that must inevitably come as technology changes in the 1960's.

Address, AFL-CIO Convention, Miami, Dec. 7, 1961

92 / MANPOWER DISPLACEMENT

We cannot stop progress in technology or arrest economic change in transportation or any other industry—nor would we want to. For technological change has increased man's knowledge, income, convenience, leisure and comfort. It has reinforced this nation's leadership in scientific, economic, educational and military endeavors. It has saved lives as well as money, and enriched society as well as business. Our task as a nation . . . is simply to make sure that this public blessing is not a private curse. We cannot pretend that these changes will not occur, that some displacement will not result or that we are incapable of adapting our legislative tools to meet this problem.

While last year's Manpower Development and Training Act recognized the Federal Government's responsibility to help retrain and readjust workers who have been displaced by industrial change, as do this year's Vocational Education proposals, their scope is too limited to provide the full answer to a problem of this magnitude. The problems of manpower displacement, of which automation is only one cause, should not be settled primarily by the use of private economic power and pressure, or discussed only on the picket lines. They cut across many departments of Government, all types of occupations, all standards of income, all sections of the country. Their solution is of importance to the entire nation which now enjoys all the benefits of economic progress but, except when it is part of the employee group affected, now bears very little of its burdens.

Message to Congress on the railroad rules dispute, July 22, 1963

93 / THE HUMAN FACTOR

Modern machines and advanced technology are not enough, unless they are used by a labor force that is educated, skilled, and in good health.

Message to Congress on the economy, Feb. 2, 1961

94 / CHANGE IN MANPOWER REQUIREMENTS

Occupationally, the new technology has been altering manpower requirements in favor of occupations requiring more education and training.

Manpower report to Congress, March 11, 1963

Transportation

95 / TRANSPORTATION PROBLEMS

An efficient and dynamic transportation system is vital to our domestic economic growth, productivity and progress. Affecting the cost of every commodity we consume or export, it is equally vital to our ability to compete abroad. It influences both the cost and the flexibility of our defense preparedness, and both the business and recreational opportunities of our citizens. This nation has long enjoyed one of the most highly developed and diversified transportation systems in the world, and this system has helped us to achieve a highly efficient utilization of our manpower and resources. . . .

But pressing problems are burdening our national transportation system, jeopardizing the progress and security on which we depend. A chaotic patchwork of inconsistent and often obsolete legislation and regulation has evolved from a history of specific actions addressed to specific problems of specific industries at specific times. This patchwork does not fully reflect either the dramatic changes in technology of the past half-century or the parallel changes in the structure of competition.

Message to Congress on transportation problems, April 5, 1962

96 / FACING UP TO REALITIES

The troubles in our transportation system are deep; and no just and comprehensive set of goals—which meets all the needs of each mode of transportation as well as shippers, consumers, taxpayers and the general public —can be quickly or easily reached. But few areas of public concern are more basic to our progress as a nation. The Congress and all citizens, as well as all Federal agencies, have an increasing interest in and an increasing responsibility to be aware of the shortcomings of existing transportation policies. . . .

The difficulty and the complexity of these basic troubles will not correct themselves with the mere passage of time. On the contrary, we cannot afford to delay further. Facing up to the realities of the situation, we must begin to make the painful decisions necessary to providing the transportation system required by the United States of today and tomorrow.

Ibid.

97 / WAY TO IMPROVEMENT

Our economic health depends on having healthy transportation arteries; and I believe the way to a more modern economical choice of national transportation service is through increased competition and decreased regulation.

State of the Union Message, Jan. 14, 1963

98 / LOCAL MASS TRANSIT

Local mass transit . . . is as essential a community service as highways. Nearly three-fourths of our citizens live in urban areas, which occupy only 2 percent of our land, and if local transit is to survive and relieve the congestion of these cities it needs Federal stimulation and assistance.

Ibid.

Agriculture

99 / FARMING: LARGEST INDUSTRY

Farming remains our largest industry. It employs, in fact, more people than steel, automobiles, public utilities, and the transportation industry combined.

Message to Congress on agriculture, March 16, 1961

100 / GOALS

We seek continued production of food and fiber at reasonable prices in quantities sufficient to meet the needs of all Americans and to combat hunger and contribute to economic development throughout the free world.

Message to Congress on agriculture, Jan. 31, 1962

101 / CONTINUING OBJECTIVES

The benefits of our agricultural progress still need to be translated into improved income to farm families, lower prices to consumers for food and fiber, expanded exports, and reduced expenditures for price support programs.

Message to Congress on agriculture, Jan. 31, 1963

102 / EXPANSION OF EXPORTS

The American farmer is one of our best foreign exchange earners. It is our firm policy to maintain and expand these exports.
Ibid.

103 / THE FAMILY FARM

One of the great issues confronting agriculture and the nation is the economic survival of the family farm pattern of agriculture. . . . The family farm should remain the backbone of American agriculture.

Campaign statement: "Agricultural Policy for the New Frontier," Washington, D.C., Oct. 9, 1960

104 / PRESERVATION OF FAMILY FARMING

It is . . . our purpose to insure that the farm family that produced this wealth will have a parity in income and equality in opportunity with urban families—for the family farm should be protected and preserved as a basic American institution.

Message to Congress on agriculture, March 16, 1961

105 / "RURAL RENEWAL"

In some rural areas the general level of economic activity and family income is so low, and the lack of community facilities so acute, that a complete new development operation is the only sensible solution—a program of "rural renewal."

Message to Congress on agriculture, Jan. 31, 1962

106 / FAIR FARM INCOME

It must be our purpose to see that farm products return a fair income because they are fairly priced. No farm program should exploit the consumer. But neither can it subsidize the consumer at the cost of subnormal incomes to the farmer. We cannot tolerate substandard conditions on the farm any more than we can in industry. A fair return is a necessity for labor, capital, and management in industry. It is equally necessary for those who produce our food and fiber.

> Message to Congress on agriculture, March 16, 1961

107 / RETURNS TO FARMERS

The American farmer should receive for his managerial skills, his labor, and his capital investment returns that are similar to those received for comparable human talents and resources in other types of enterprise.

> Message to Congress on the economy, Feb. 2, 1961

108 / DOUBLE FREIGHT

The farmer is the only man in our economy who buys everything he buys at retail, sells everything he sells at wholesale, and pays the freight both ways.

> Campaign address, national plowing contest, Sioux Falls, S.D., Sept. 22, 1960

109 / INTERDEPENDENCE

I preach the doctrine of interdependence of the American economy, because this country cannot be prosperous unless the farmers and the workers are prosperous together.

> Campaign remarks, Michigan State Fair, Detroit, Sept. 5, 1960

110 / LESSON OF THE TWENTIES

The economy of the United States is interconnected. It is interdependent. It is interrelated. When there is a recession on the farm, sooner or later —and the twenties taught us it was sooner—there is a recession in the cities.

> Campaign remarks, Sioux City, Iowa, Sept. 21, 1960

111 / MUTUAL INTEREST

My people [in Massachusetts] cannot manufacture textiles or sell fish or make television sets and sell them to the Middle West unless you have the income to buy them. And you cannot prosper on the farms unless our cities move ahead.

> Campaign address, national plowing contest, Sioux Falls, S.D., Sept. 22, 1960

112 / RURAL PROSPERITY

Small town and rural America is dependent for prosperity upon the farmer. An improvement in his standard of living and in his income is immediately reflected in an improvement in the economy of the small urban center in his community.

Message to Congress on agriculture, Jan. 31, 1962

113 / THE FARMER AS CONSUMER

The farmer is a consumer as well as a producer, and other economic groups are affected by the continued drop in farm purchasing power. Some $40 billion is spent each year for production goods and services needed on our farms and for the consumer goods used by farm families. Six million people are employed in the manufacture and distribution of the supplies that farmers use. Each year farm families spend from $2.5 to $3 billion for new automobiles, trucks, tractors and other farm machinery; and $3.5 billion for fuel, lubricants, and maintenance of motor vehicles and machinery. It is deeply in the interest of all Americans that our agriculture be not only progressive but prosperous.

Message to Congress on agriculture, March 16, 1961

114 / FIGHTING INFLATION

Should farmers receive low prices to offset inflationary pressures in other sectors of the economy? My answer is "No." Inflation is something for all of us to combat. It is not fair for one economic group to bear the cost alone for the benefit of others.

Campaign statement: "Agricultural Policy for the New Frontier," Washington, D.C., Oct. 9, 1960

115 / AGRICULTURAL REVOLUTION

A technological revolution on the farm has led to an output explosion— but we have not yet learned to harness that explosion usefully, while protecting our farmers' right to full parity income.

Acceptance speech, Democratic National Convention, Los Angeles, July 15, 1960

116 / IMPACT OF AUTOMATION

Automation has hit the farmers much harder than it has hit any other element in our community, and their production is growing faster than our consumption.

News conference, Washington, D.C., May 22, 1963

117 / PARADOX

Abundant production has filled our bins and warehouses, but 1 out of 10 American households have diets so inadequate that they fall below two-thirds of the standard nutrition requirements.

Message to Congress on agriculture, March 16, 1961

118 / PROPER CHANNELING

The solution lies not so much in severe restriction upon our talent to produce as upon proper channeling of our abundance into more effective and expanded uses. American agricultural abundance can be forged into both a significant instrument of foreign policy and a weapon against domestic hardship and hunger.

Ibid.

119 / UNIQUE OPPORTUNITY

Our rapidly growing capacity to produce far outruns the growth of our domestic and foreign demand for food and fiber. This offers us an opportunity to manage abundance, rather than scarcity, an opportunity that is unique among nations of the world. It is relatively new even for the United States.

Message to Congress on agriculture, Jan. 31, 1962

120 / MANAGING AGRICULTURAL ABUNDANCE

. . . there are . . . revolutions going on around the world—populations growing faster than food supplies—new nations in need of assistance—underdeveloped nations in need of food for capital. These are fast-changing, fast-moving times. . . . We must harness these revolutions. We must ride these waves of change. We must learn to manage our abundance—to bring the great productive capacity of American agriculture into balance with total needs at home and abroad, at prices that will yield to our farmers a fair return on their capital and labor.

Campaign remarks at Farm Conference, Des Moines, Iowa, Aug. 21, 1960

121 / USES OF AGRICULTURAL ABUNDANCE

Our agricultural resources can advance the cause of peace and freedom throughout the world; they assure Americans of a high standard of living; they can be an important weapon against poverty and disease.

Message to Congress on agriculture, Jan. 31, 1962

122 / A BLESSING

Around the world, when we and the Soviet Union are engaged in a great competition to see whether the world will be free or slave, we continue to persist in regarding the production of food from the ground as a problem, as a surplus, as a burden, when it is a blessing from the Lord.

Campaign address, national plowing contest, Sioux Falls, S.D., Sept. 22. 1960

123 / FOOD FOR FREEDOM

I do not regard the distribution of food around the world as a great burden upon us. I regard it as an opportunity, to use our assets in a way which will attract people to the cause of freedom. I am glad that this is our problem and not starvation. I am glad, for we are our brother's keeper, and if we have great assets in this country, I believe we should hold out the hand of friendship. When hundreds of millions of people stagger through their lives searching for food, and we have it, and we are trying to determine which way the world will go, I would rather see our food used in an imaginative way.

Ibid.

124 / SOURCE OF PRIDE

Our task is to master and turn to fully fruitful ends the magnificent productivity of our farms and farmers. The revolution on our own countryside stands in the sharpest contrast to the repeated farm failures of the Communist nations and is a source of pride to us all.

State of the Union Message, Jan. 11, 1962

125 / SALE OF SURPLUS WHEAT TO RUSSIA A HOPEFUL SIGN

This transaction advertises to the world, as nothing else could, the success of free American agriculture.

It demonstrates our willingness to relieve food shortages, to reduce tensions and to improve relations with all countries, and it shows that peaceful agreements with the United States which serve the interests of both sides are a far more worthwhile course than a course of isolation and hostility.

For this Government to tell our grain traders that they cannot accept these offers, on the other hand, would accomplish little or nothing. The Soviets would continue to buy wheat and flour elsewhere, including wheat flour from those nations which buy our wheat.

Moreover, having for many years sold them farm products which are not in surplus, it would make no sense to refuse to sell those products on which we must otherwise pay the cost of storage.

In short, this particular decision with respect to sales to the Soviet Union, which is not inconsistent with many smaller transactions over a long period of time, does not represent a new Soviet-American trade policy. That must await the settlement of many matters.

But it does represent one more hopeful sign that a more peaceful world is both possible and beneficial to us all.

Statement on authorizing $250-million wheat sale to the Soviet Union, news conference, Washington, D.C., Oct. 9, 1963

The Consumer

126 / VOICELESS GROUP

Consumers, by definition, include us all. They are the largest economic group in the economy, affecting and affected by almost every public and private economic decision. Two-thirds of all spending in the economy is by consumers. But they are the only important group in the economy who are not effectively organized, whose views are often not heard.

Message to Congress on protecting the consumer interest, March 15, 1962

127 / THE FEDERAL GOVERNMENT'S OBLIGATION

The Federal Government—by nature the highest spokesman for all the people—has a special obligation to be alert to the consumer's needs and to advance the consumer's interests.

Ibid.

128 / GUARDING AGAINST WASTE IN CONSUMPTION

Fortunate as we are, we nevertheless cannot afford waste in consumption any more than we can afford inefficiency in business or Government. If consumers are offered inferior products, if prices are exorbitant, if drugs are unsafe or worthless, if the consumer is unable to choose on an informed basis, then his dollar is wasted, his health and safety may be threatened, and the national interest suffers. On the other hand, increased efforts to make the best possible use of their incomes can contribute more to the well-being of most families than equivalent efforts to raise their incomes.

Ibid.

129 / CONSUMER PERPLEXITIES

Many of the new products used every day in the home are highly complex. The housewife is called upon to be an amateur electrician, mechanic, chemist, toxicologist, dietitian and mathematician—but she is rarely furnished the information she needs to perform these tasks proficiently.

Marketing is increasingly impersonal. Consumer choice is influenced by mass advertising utilizing highly developed arts of persuasion. The consumer typically cannot know whether drug preparations meet minimum standards of safety, quality and efficacy. He usually does not know how much he pays for consumer credit; whether one prepared food has more nutritional value than another; whether the performance of a product will in fact meet his needs; or whether the "large economy size" is really a bargain.

Ibid.

130 / GOVERNMENT MUST STRENGTHEN CONSUMER RIGHTS

Additional legislative and administrative action is required . . . if the Federal Government is to meet its responsibility to consumers in the exercise of their rights.

Ibid.

II

Civil Liberties

To Strengthen Basic Rights

1 / AUGMENTING FREEDOM

In giving rights to others which belong to them, we give rights to ourselves and to our country.

> Message on the 100th anniversary of the Emancipation Proclamation, Washington, D.C., Sept. 22, 1962

2 / RACIAL DISCRIMINATION

Equality before the law has not always meant equal treatment and opportunity. And the harmful, wasteful, and wrongful results of racial discrimination and segregation still appear in virtually every aspect of national life, in virtually every part of the nation.

> Message to Congress on civil rights, Feb. 28, 1963

3 / "IT IS WRONG"

Race discrimination hampers our economic growth by preventing the maximum development and utilization of our manpower. It hampers our world leadership by contradicting at home the message we preach abroad. It mars the atmosphere of a united and classless society in which this nation rose to greatness. It increases the costs of public welfare, crime, delinquency, and disorder. Above all, it is wrong. Therefore, let it be clear, in our own hearts and minds, that it is not merely because of the economic waste of discrimination, that we are committed to achieving true equality of opportunity. The basic reason is because it is right.

Ibid.

4 / SHARING FREEDOM'S BENEFITS

We are the privileged. And it should be the ambition of every free citizen to express and expand that privilege so that all of our countrymen and women share it.

Commencement address, San Diego State College, June 6, 1963

5 / HUMAN RIGHTS

America stands for progress in human rights as well as economic affairs, and a strong America requires the assurance of full and equal rights to all its citizens, of any race or of any color.

State of the Union Message, Jan. 11, 1962

6 / A MORAL ISSUE

We are confronted primarily with a moral issue. It is as old as the Scriptures and is as clear as the American Constitution. The heart of the question is whether all Americans are to be afforded equal rights and equal opportunities; whether we are going to treat our fellow Americans as we want to be treated.

Address to the nation on the racial crisis, Washington, D.C., June 11, 1963

7 / MOMENT OF DECISION

It is clear to me that the time for token moves and talk is past, that these rights are going to be won, and that our responsibility, yours and mine, is to see that they are won in a peaceful and constructive manner.

Address, National Conference of Mayors, Honolulu, June 9, 1963

8 / DOMESTIC PEACE AND FREEDOM

Peace and freedom walk together. In too many of our cities today, the peace is not secure because freedom is incomplete.

Commencement address, American University, Washington, D.C., June 10, 1963

9 / UNIVERSAL VALUES

When the universal values of human dignity, truth, and justice under law have been guaranteed to all men—we will have created an enduring peace for ourselves, our children, and the priceless institutions of our way of life.

> Message to Archbishop Iakovos, Conference of Greek Orthodox Church, Buffalo, N.Y., Sept. 17, 1960

10 / CITIZENSHIP

In America there must be only citizens, not divided by grade, first and second, but citizens, east, west, north, and south.

> Campaign address, National Conference on Constitutional Rights and American Freedom, New York City, Oct. 12, 1960

11 / CITIZEN RESPONSIBILITY

It is the responsibility of all citizens in all sections of this country to respect the rights of others and respect the law of the land.

> Commencement address, American University, Washington, D.C., June 10, 1963

12 / BASIC SOLUTION: THE GOLDEN RULE

Legislation cannot solve this problem alone. It must be solved in the homes of every American in every community across the country.

> Address to the nation on the racial crisis, Washington, D.C., June 11, 1963

13 / "A SENSE OF JUSTICE"

I ask you to look into your hearts—not in search of charity, for the Negro neither wants nor needs condescension—but for the one plain, proud and priceless quality that unites us all as Americans: a sense of justice.

> Message to Congress on civil rights, June 19, 1963

14 / EQUAL SACRIFICES, EQUAL RIGHTS

No one has been barred on account of his race from fighting or dying for America—there are no "white" or "colored" signs on the foxholes or graveyards of battle. Surely, in 1963, 100 years after Emancipation, it should not be necessary for any American citizen to demonstrate in the streets for the opportunity to stop at a hotel, or to eat at a lunch counter in the very department store in which he is shopping, or to enter a motion picture house, on the same terms as any other customer.

> *Ibid.*

15 / NATIONWIDE ISSUE

This is not a sectional issue. Difficulties over segregation and discrimination exist in every city, in every state of the Union, producing in many cities a rising tide of discontent that threatens the public safety.

Address to the nation on the racial crisis, Washington, D.C., June 11, 1963

16 / AN AMERICAN'S RIGHTS

We hold the view that every American, regardless of his religion or his race is entitled to his constitutional rights.

Campaign remarks, rally, Greensboro, N.C., Sept. 17, 1960

17 / AMERICAN FAITH

I believe in an America . . . where every citizen is free to think and speak as he pleases and write and worship as he pleases—and where every citizen is free to vote as he pleases, without instructions from anyone, his employer, the union leader or his clergyman.

Campaign address, Convention Hall, Philadelphia, Oct. 31, 1960

18 / INDIVIDUAL FREEDOM

I want every American free to stand up for his rights, even if sometimes he has to sit down for them.

Campaign address, Detroit, Sept. 5, 1960

19 / NONPARTISAN UNITY

I would hope that on questions of constitutional rights and freedom, as in matters affecting our national security, there is a fundamental unity among us that will survive partisan debate over particular issues.

Message to Congress on civil rights, Feb. 28, 1963

20 / ECONOMIC FACTOR

To provide equal rights for all requires that we respect the liberties of speech and belief and assembly, guaranteed by the Constitution, and these liberties in turn are hollow mockeries unless they are maintained also by a decent economic life. . . . Those who are too poor, uninformed, too uneducated to enjoy their constitutional freedoms of choice, do not really possess those freedoms.

Campaign address, National Conference on Constitutional Rights and American Freedom, New York City, Oct. 12, 1960

21 / FRACTIONAL OPPORTUNITIES

The Negro baby born in America today—regardless of the section or State in which he is born—has about one-half as much chance of completing high school as a white baby born in the same place on the same day, one-third as much chance of completing college, one-third as much chance of becoming a professional man, twice as much chance of becoming unemployed, about one-seventh as much chance of earning $10,000 per year, a life expectancy which is 7 years less, and the prospects of earning only half as much.

Message to Congress on civil rights, Feb. 28, 1963

22 / UNEQUAL EDUCATIONAL OPPORTUNITY

Nearly three-quarters of the young population of the United States have graduated from high school, but only about two-fifths of our non-white population has done the same.

Commencement address, San Diego State College, June 6, 1963

23 / EQUAL CHANCE

I do not say that all men are equal in their ability, character and motivation. I do say that every American should be given a fair chance to develop all the talents they may have.

Address, National Conference of Mayors, Honolulu, June 9, 1963

24 / ABOVE ALL, INTEGRITY

In this year of the Emancipation centennial, justice requires us to insure the blessings of liberty for all Americans and their posterity—not merely for reasons of economic efficiency, world diplomacy and domestic tranquility—but, above all, because it is right.

Message to Congress on civil rights, June 19, 1963

25 / RACIAL DISCRIMINATION—A CONTINUING DEBATE

This nation is now engaged in a continuing debate about the rights of a portion of its citizens. That will go on and those rights will expand until the standard first forged by the nation's founders has been reached—and all Americans enjoy equal opportunity and liberty under the law.

Address, Vanderbilt University, Nashville, Tenn., May 18, 1963

26 / UNCONFINED DISEASE

The cruel disease of discrimination knows no sectional or State boundaries. The continuing attack on this problem must be equally broad. It must be both private and public, it must be conducted at National, State, and local levels; and it must include both legislative and executive action.

> Message to Congress on civil rights, Feb. 28, 1963

27 / LOCAL ACTION IMPERATIVE

Justice cannot await too many meetings. It cannot await the action of the Congress or even the courts. We face a moment of moral and constitutional crisis, and men of generosity and vision must make themselves heard in every part of the land.

> Address, National Conference of Mayors, Honolulu, June 9, 1963

28 / VOLUNTARY ACTION

Progress in race relations, while it cannot be delayed, can be more solidly and more peacefully accomplished to the extent that legislation can be buttressed by voluntary action.

> Message to Congress on civil rights, June 19, 1963

29 / PRIVATE AND LOCAL EFFORTS FOR EQUALITY

It is important . . . for private citizens and local governments to support the State Department's effort to end the discriminatory treatment suffered by too many foreign diplomats, students, and visitors to this country. But it is not enough to treat those from other lands with equality and dignity—the same treatment must be afforded to every American citizen.

> Message to Congress on civil rights, Feb. 28, 1963

Governmental Concern and Responsibility

30 / PROTECTION OF LIBERTIES

. . . it is the duty of Government to concern itself with protecting the opportunity to enjoy . . . basic liberties.

> Letter to the National Conference of Christians and Jews, Washington, D.C., Oct. 10, 1960

31 / EXECUTIVE RESPONSIBILITY

It is the responsibility of the executive branch at all levels of government —local, state, and national—to provide and protect . . . freedom for all of our citizens by all means within our authority.

Commencement address, American University, Washington, D.C., June 10, 1963

32 / "TO SECURE . . . CONSTITUTIONAL RIGHTS"

This Administration has shown as never before how much could be done through the full use of Executive powers—through persuasion, negotiation, litigation, to secure the constitutional rights of all: the right to vote, the right to travel without hindrance across state lines and the right to free public education.

I issued last March a comprehensive order to guarantee the right to equal employment opportunity in all Federal agencies and contractors. The Vice President's committee thus created has done much, including the voluntary Plans for Progress which, in all sections of the country, are achieving a quiet but striking success in opening up to all races new professional, supervisory and other job opportunities.

But there is much more to be done—by the Executive, by the courts, and by the Congress.

State of the Union Message, Jan. 11, 1962

33 / EXECUTIVE DRIVE AGAINST DISCRIMINATION

The executive branch of the Federal Government, under this administration and in all of its activities, now stands squarely behind the principle of equal opportunity, without segregation or discrimination, in the employment of Federal funds, facilities, and personnel. All officials at every level are charged with the responsibility of implementing this principle; and a formal interdepartmental action group, under White House chairmanship, oversees this effort and follows through on each directive. For the first time, the full force of Federal executive authority is being exerted in the battle against race discrimination.

Message to Congress on civil rights, Feb. 28, 1963

34 / "EQUAL OPPORTUNITY FOR ALL"

It is neither proper nor equitable that Americans should be denied the benefits of housing owned by the Federal Government or financed through the Federal assistance on the basis of their race, color, creed, or national origin. Our national policy is equal opportunity for all, and the

Federal Government will continue to take such legal and proper steps as it may to achieve the realization of this goal.

News conference statement on executive order prohibiting discrimination in federally aided housing, Washington, D.C., Nov. 20, 1962

35 / THE OBLIGATION OF CONGRESS

Pride in our progress must not give way to relaxation of our effort. Nor does progress in the executive branch enable the legislative branch to escape its own obligations. On the contrary, it is in the light of this nationwide progress, and in the belief that Congress will wish once again to meet its responsibilities in this matter, that I stress in the . . . agenda of existing and prospective action important legislation as well as administrative measures.

Message to Congress on civil rights, Feb. 28, 1963

36 / CONGRESS MUST ACT

Federal action must lead the way, providing both the nation's standard and a nationwide solution. . . . The time has come for the Congress of the United States to join with the executive and judicial branches in making it clear to all that race has no place in American life or law.

Message to Congress on civil rights, June 19, 1963

37 / DESEGREGATION OF PUBLIC FACILITIES

This provision will open doors in every part of the country which never should have been closed. Its enactment will hasten the end to practices which have no place in a free and united nation.

Ibid.

38 / STRENGTHENING EXECUTIVE AUTHORITY TO PROTECT CIVIL LIBERTIES

It is the responsibility of the legislative branch at all levels, wherever the authority is not now adequate, to make it adequate.

Commencement address, American University, Washington, D.C., June 10, 1963

39 / IMPRUDENT NEGLECT

The events in Birmingham and elsewhere have so increased the cries for equality that no city or state or legislative body can prudently choose to ignore them.

Address to the nation on the racial crisis, Washington, D.C., June 11, 1963

40 / IN COMMEMORATION OF EMANCIPATION

As we approach the 100th anniversary next January of the Emancipation Proclamation, let the acts of every branch of the Government—and every citizen—portray that "righteousness that exalteth a nation."

State of the Union Message, Jan. 11, 1962

The Right to Vote

41 / PRECIOUS RIGHT

The right to vote in a free American election is the most powerful and precious right in the world—and it must not be denied on the grounds of race or color. It is a potent key to achieving other rights of citizenship.

Message to Congress on civil rights, Feb. 28, 1963

42 / BASIC RIGHT

The right to vote is very basic. If we're going to neglect that right, then all of our talk about freedom is hollow, and therefore we shall give every protection that we can to anybody seeking to vote.

News conference, Washington, D.C., Sept. 13, 1962

43 / DENIAL OF SUFFRAGE BY ARBITRARY DEVICES

The right to vote . . . should no longer be denied through such arbitrary devices on a local level, sometimes abused, as literacy tests and poll taxes.

State of the Union Message, Jan. 11, 1962

44 / POLL TAX

The right to vote in Federal elections should not be denied or abridged because of failure to pay a poll tax or to meet a property qualification.

Letter to Sen. Spessard L. Holland on proposal of a constitutional amendment to abolish the poll tax, Washington, D.C., March 6, 1962

45 / THE ABOLITION OF POLL TAXES

The 87th Congress—after 20 years of effort—passed and referred to the States for ratification a constitutional amendment to prohibit the levying of poll taxes as a condition to voting. Already 13 States have ratified the proposed amendment and in 3 more one body of the legislature has acted. I urge every State legislature to take prompt action on this matter and to outlaw the poll tax—which has too long been an outmoded and arbitrary bar to voting participation by minority groups and others—as the 24th amendment to the Constitution. This measure received bipartisan sponsorship and endorsement in the Congress and I shall continue to work with Governors and legislative leaders of both parties in securing adoption of the anti-poll-tax amendment.

> Message to Congress on civil rights, Feb. 28, 1963. The anti-poll-tax amendment was certified as the 24th constitutional amendment on Feb. 4, 1964

46 / FAIRNESS IN QUALIFYING VOTERS

Uniformity of treatment is required by the dictates of both the Constitution and fair play.

> *Ibid.*

47 / INJUSTICE THROUGH DISCRIMINATORY ADMINISTRATION OF VOTER TESTS

No one can rightfully contend that any voting registrar should be permitted to deny the vote to any qualified citizen, anywhere in this country, through discriminatory administration of qualifying tests, or upon the basis of minor errors in filling out a complicated form which seeks only information.

> *Ibid.*

48 / UNIFORM VOTING STANDARDS IN FEDERAL ELECTIONS

The law should specifically prohibit the application of different tests, standards, practices, or procedures for different applicants seeking to register and vote in Federal elections. Under present law, the courts can ultimately deal with the various forms of racial discrimination practiced by local registrars. But the task of litigation, and the time consumed in preparation and proof, should be lightened in every possible fashion.

> *Ibid.*

49 / PRESUMPTION OF LITERACY

Completion of the sixth grade should, with respect to Federal elections, constitute a presumption that the applicant is literate. Literacy tests pose especially difficult problems in determining voter qualification. The essentially subjective judgment involved in each individual case, and the difficulty of challenging that judgment, have made literacy tests one of the cruelest and most abused of all voter qualification tests. The incidence of such abuse can be eliminated, or at least drastically curtailed, by the proposed legislation providing that proof of completion of the sixth grade constitutes a presumption that the applicant is literate.

Ibid.

50 / INTERIM RELIEF IN VOTING CASES

To provide for interim relief while voting suits are proceeding through the courts in areas of demonstrated need, temporary Federal voting referees should be appointed to determine the qualifications of applicants for registration and voting during the pendency of a lawsuit in any county in which fewer than 15 percent of the eligible number of persons of any race claimed to be discriminated against are registered to vote. Existing Federal law provides for the appointment of voting referees to receive and act upon applications for voting registration upon a court finding that a pattern or practice of discrimination exists. But to prevent a successful case from becoming an empty victory, insofar as the particular election is concerned, the proposed legislation would provide that, within these prescribed limits, temporary voting referees would be appointed to serve from the inception to the conclusion of the Federal voting suit, applying, however, only State law and State regulations. As officers of the court, their decisions would be subject to court scrutiny and review.

Ibid.

51 / VOTING CASES IN FEDERAL COURTS

Voting suits brought under the Federal civil rights statutes should be accorded expedited treatment in the Federal courts, just as in many State courts election suits are given preference on the dockets on the sensible premise that, unless the right to vote can be exercised at a specific election, it is, to the extent of that election, lost forever.

Ibid.

Discrimination in Employment

52 / UNFAIR EMPLOYMENT PRACTICES

Racial discrimination in employment is especially injurious both to its victims and to the national economy. It results in a great waste of human resources and creates serious community problems. It is, moreover, inconsistent with the democratic principle that no man should be denied employment commensurate with his abilities because of his race or creed or ancestry.

Ibid.

53 / MINORITY CITIZENS

All of you know the statistics of those who are first discharged and the last to be rehired too often are among those who are members of our minority groups. We want everyone to have a chance, regardless of their race or color, to have an opportunity to make a life for themselves and their families, to get a decent education so they have a fair chance to compete, and then be judged on what's in here and not what's on the outside.

Address, AFL-CIO Convention, Miami, Dec. 7, 1961

54 / ELIMINATION OF BARRIERS

We cannot be satisfied until all racial and religious barriers to employment have been destroyed in the nation.

Address, Democratic Party dinner, Los Angeles, Nov. 18, 1961

55 / "MEN WHO SERVED TOGETHER CAN WORK TOGETHER"

Racial discrimination in employment must be eliminated. Denial of the right to work is unfair, regardless of its victim. It is doubly unfair to throw its burden on an individual because of his race or color. Men who served side by side with each other on the field of battle should have no difficulty working side by side on an assembly line or construction project.

Message to Congress on civil rights, June 19, 1963

56 / ANTI-DISCRIMINATION IN FEDERAL CONTRACTS

We are making a great effort to make sure that all those who secure Federal contracts—and there are billions of dollars spent each year by the Federal Government—will give fair opportunity to all of our citizens to participate in that work.

Address, AFL-CIO Convention, Miami, Dec. 7, 1961

Desegregation of Public Facilities

57 / EQUAL TREATMENT, TENET OF DEMOCRACY

No act is more contrary to the spirit of our democracy and Constitution

—or more rightfully resented by a Negro citizen who seeks only equal treatment—than the barring of that citizen from restaurants, hotels, theaters, recreational areas, and other public accommodations and facilities.

Message to Congress on civil rights, Feb. 28, 1963

58 / PROPERTY RIGHTS AND HUMAN RIGHTS

There is an age-old saying that "property has its duties as well as its rights"; and no property owner who holds those premises for the purpose of serving at a profit the American public at large can claim any inherent right to exclude a part of that public on grounds of race or color.

Message to Congress on civil rights, June 19, 1963

59 / URGENCY OF PROPOSED LEGISLATION

Its enactment will . . . help move this potentially dangerous problem from the streets to the courts.

Ibid.

60 / SOME ADVANCES

Systematic segregation in interstate transportation has virtually ceased to exist. No doubt isolated instances of discrimination in transportation terminals, restaurants, restrooms, and other facilities will continue to crop up, but any such discrimination will be dealt with promptly. In addition, restaurants and public facilities in buildings leased by the Federal Government have been opened up to all Federal employees in areas where previously they had been segregated. The General Services Administration no longer contracts for the lease of space in office buildings unless such facilities are available to all Federal employees without regard to race. . . . National parks, forests, and other recreation areas—and the District of Columbia Stadium—are open to all without regard to race. Meetings sponsored by the Federal Government or addressed by Federal appointees are held in hotels and halls which do not practice discrimination or segregation.

Message to Congress on civil rights, Feb. 28, 1963

Desegregation of Public Schools

61 / PUPIL SEGREGATION—NORTH AND SOUTH

We must recognize that segregation in education—and I mean *de facto* segregation in the North as well as the proclaimed segregation in the

South—brings with it serious handicaps to a large proportion of the population.

Commencement address, San Diego State College, June 6, 1963

62 / EDUCATIONAL INEQUALITY: TWO REASONS

American children today do not yet enjoy equal educational opportunities for two primary reasons: One is economic, and the other is racial.

Ibid.

63 / NONWHITE ILLITERACY

In some states almost 40 percent of the nonwhite population has completed less than five years of school, contrasted with 7 percent of the white population.

Ibid.

64 / RECOMMENDATION OF FEDERAL AID FOR AREAS WISHING TO DESEGREGATE THEIR PUBLIC SCHOOLS

. . . progress toward primary and secondary school desegregation has still been too slow, often painfully so. Those children who are being denied their constitutional rights are suffering a loss which can never be regained, and which will leave scars which can never be fully healed. I have in the past expressed my belief that the full authority of the Federal Government should be placed behind the achievement of school desegregation, in accordance with the command of the Constitution. One obvious area of Federal action is to help facilitate the transition to desegregation in those areas which are conforming or wish to conform their practices to the law.

Many of these communities lack the resources necessary to eliminate segregation in their public schools while at the same time assuring that educational standards will be maintained and improved. The problem has been compounded by the fact that the climate of mistrust in many communities has left many school officials with no qualified source to turn to for information and advice. There is a need for technical assistance by the Office of Education to assist local communities in preparing and carrying out desegregation plans, including the supplying of information on means which have been employed to desegregate other schools successfully. There is also need for financial assistance to enable those communities which desire and need such assistance to employ specialized personnel to cope with problems occasioned by desegregation and to train school personnel to facilitate the transition to desegregation. While some facilities for providing this kind of assistance are presently available in the Office of Education, they are not adequate to the task.

I recommend, therefore, a program of Federal technical and financial assistance to aid school districts in the process of desegregation in compliance with the Constitution.

Message to Congress on civil rights, Feb. 28, 1963

65 / FOR LEGAL AID IN SCHOOL DESEGREGATION CASES

It is unfair and unrealistic to expect that the burden of initiating cases can be wholly borne by private litigants. Too often those entitled to bring suit on behalf of their children lack the economic means for instituting and maintaining such cases or the ability to withstand the personal, physical and economic harassment which sometimes descends upon those who do institute them. The same is true of students wishing to attend the college of their choice but unable to assume the burden of litigation. . . . I recommend that . . . authority . . . be given the Attorney General to initiate in the Federal District Courts appropriate legal proceeding against local public school boards or public institutions of higher learning—or to intervene in [certain] existing cases.

Message to Congress on civil rights, June 19, 1963

66 / RECOMMENDATION THAT "SEPARATE BUT EQUAL" BE DELETED FROM FEDERAL STATUTES

It is obvious that the unconstitutional and outmoded concept of "separate but equal" does not belong in the Federal statute books. This is particularly true with respect to higher education, where peaceful desegregation has been underway in practically every state for some time. I repeat, therefore, this administration's recommendation of last year that this phrase be eliminated from the Morrill Land Grant College Act.

Message to Congress on civil rights, Feb. 28, 1963

67 / PLEA TO PRIVATE SCHOOLS AND COLLEGES

I strongly urge them to live up to their responsibilities and to recognize no arbitrary bar of race or color—for such bars have no place in any institution, least of all one devoted to the truth and the improvement of all mankind.

Message to Congress on civil rights, June 19, 1963

The Mississippi Crisis

68 / APPEAL FOR LAW AND FREEDOM

Let us preserve both the law and the peace, and then healing those wounds that are within, we can turn to the greater crises that are without and stand united as one people in our pledge to man's freedom.

> Appeal for an end to rioting and for peaceful compliance with Federal court order for admission of Negro James H. Meredith to the University of Mississippi, television address, Sept. 30, 1962

69 / SAFEGUARD OF LIBERTY

Our nation is founded on the principle that observance of the law is the eternal safeguard of liberty and defiance of the law is the surest road to tyranny.

> *Ibid.*

70 / RESPECT FOR LAW

Even among law-abiding men few laws are universally loved. But they are uniformly respected and not resisted.

> *Ibid.*

71 / OBEDIENCE TO THE LAW

Americans are free . . . to disagree with the law, but not to disobey it. For in a government of laws and not of men, no man, however prominent or powerful, and no mob, however unruly, or boisterous, is entitled to defy a court of law. If this country should ever reach the point where any man or group of men, by force or threat of force, could long deny the commands of our courts and our Constitution, then no law would stand free from doubt, no judge would be sure of his writ, and no citizen would be safe from his neighbors.

> *Ibid.*

72 / PROGRESSIVE SOUTHERNERS

This nation is proud of the many instances in which governors, educators, and everyday citizens from the South have shown to the world the gains that can be made by persuasion and goodwill in a society ruled by law.

> *Ibid.*

73 / SOUTHERN MATURITY

The shameful violence which accompanied but did not prevent the end of segregation at the University of Mississippi was an exception. State-supported universities in Georgia and South Carolina met this test in recent years with calm and maturity, as did the State-supported universities of Virginia, North Carolina, Florida, Texas, Louisiana, Tennessee, Arkansas, and Kentucky in earlier years. In addition, progress toward the desegregation of education at all levels has made other notable and peaceful strides.

Message to Congress on civil rights, Feb. 28, 1963

Crises in Alabama

74 / FEDERAL EFFORTS TO ENCOURAGE RACIAL PEACE IN BIRMINGHAM

I am gratified to note the progress in the efforts by white and Negro citizens [in talks initiated by Department of Justice representatives] to end an ugly situation in Birmingham, Alabama.

I have made it clear since assuming the Presidency that I would use all available means to protect human rights and uphold the law of the land.

Through mediation and persuasion, and when that effort has failed, through lawsuits and court actions, we have attempted to meet our responsibilities in this most difficult field where Federal orders have been circumvented, ignored or violated.

We have committed all the power of the Federal Government to insure respect and obedience of court decisions and the law of the land.

In the City of Birmingham the Department of Justice some time ago instituted an investigation into voting discrimination. It supported in the Supreme Court an attack on the city's segregation ordinances.

We have, in addition, been watching the present controversy to detect any violations of the Federal statutes. In the absence of such violations, or any other Federal jurisdiction, our efforts have been focused on getting both sides together to settle in a peaceful fashion the very real abuses too long inflicted on the Negro citizens of that community.

Assistant Attorney General Burke Marshall, representing the Attorney General and myself on the scene, has made every possible effort to halt a spectacle which was seriously damaging the reputation of both Birmingham and the country.

Today, as the result of responsible efforts on the part of both white and Negro leaders over the last 72 hours, the business community of

Birmingham has responded in a constructive and commendable fashion, and pledged that substantial steps would begin to meet the justifiable needs of the Negro community.

Negro leaders have announced [5.8.63] suspension of their demonstrations.

Statement on disorders in Birmingham following start of antisegregation campaign of passive resistance under leadership of Rev. Dr. Martin Luther King, Jr., news conference, Washington, D.C., May 8, 1963

75 / THE LESSON OF BIRMINGHAM'S PLIGHT

I have attempted to make clear my strong view that there is an important moral issue involved of equality for all of our citizens, and that until you give it to them, they are going to have these difficulties, as we have had this week in Birmingham. The time to give it to them is before the disasters come, and not afterwards.

Ibid.

76 / REMINDER OF URGENCY FOR REMOVAL OF BARS TO EQUAL RIGHTS

While much remains to be settled before the situation can be termed satisfactory, we can hope that tensions will ease, and that this case history, which has so far only narrowly avoided widespread violence and fatalities, will remind every state, every community and every citizen how urgent it is that all bars to equal opportunity and treatment be removed as promptly as possible.

Ibid.

77 / FEDERAL GOVERNMENT'S OBLIGATION TO UPHOLD THE LAW

I am deeply concerned about the events which occurred in Birmingham, Alabama, last night. The home of Rev. A. D. King was bombed and badly damaged. Shortly thereafter the A. G. Gaston motel was also bombed.

These occurrences led to rioting, personal injuries, property damage and various reports of violence and brutality. This Government will do whatever must be done to preserve order, to protect the lives of its citizens and to uphold the law of the land. I am certain that the vast majority of the citizens of Birmingham, both white and Negro—particularly those who labored so hard to achieve the peaceful, constructive settlement of last week—can feel nothing but dismay at the efforts of those who would replace conciliation and good will with violence and hate.

The Birmingham agreement was and is a fair and just accord. It recognized the fundamental right of all citizens to be accorded equal treatment and opportunity. It was a tribute to the process of peaceful negotiation and to the good faith of both parties. The Federal Government will not permit it to be sabotaged by a few extremists on either side who think they can defy both the law and the wishes of responsible citizens by inciting or inviting violence.

I call upon all the citizens of Birmingham, both Negro and white, to live up to the standards their responsible leaders set in reaching the agreement of last week, to realize that violence only breeds more violence and that good will and good faith are most important now to restore the atmosphere in which last week's agreement can be carried out. There must be no repetition of last night's incidents by any group. To make certain that this Government is prepared to carry out its statutory and constitutional obligations, I have ordered the following three initial steps:

1. I am sending Assistant Attorney General Burke Marshall to Birmingham this evening to consult with local citizens. He will join Assistant Deputy Attorney General Joseph F. Dolan and other Justice Department officials who were sent back to Birmingham this morning.

2. I have instructed Secretary of Defense McNamara to alert units of the armed forces trained in riot control and to dispatch selected units to military bases in the vicinity of Birmingham.

3. Finally I have directed that the necessary preliminary steps to calling the Alabama National Guard into the Federal service be taken now so that units of the guard will be promptly available should their services be required.

It is my hope, however, that the citizens of Birmingham themselves maintain standards of responsible conduct that will make outside intervention unnecessary and permit the city, the state and the country to move ahead in protecting the lives and the interests of those citizens and the welfare of our country.

Statement on renewed outbreak of racial violence in Birmingham, Washington, D.C., May 12, 1963

78 / FEDERAL TROOPS NOT TO BE SENT INTO BIRMINGHAM IF RACIAL PEACE PREVAILS

In response to the question raised in your telegram last night, Federal troops would be sent into Birmingham, if necessary, under the authority of Title 10, Section 333, Paragraph 1 of the United States Code relating to the suppression of domestic violence.

Under this section, which has been invoked by my immediate predecessor and other Presidents as well as myself on previous occasions, the Congress entrusts to the President all determinations as to (1) the necessity for action; (2) the means to be employed; and (3) the adequacy or inadequacy of the protection afforded by state authorities to the citizens of that state.

As yet, no final action has been taken under this section with respect to Birmingham inasmuch as it continues to be my hope, as stated last night, "that the citizens of Birmingham themselves will maintain standards of responsible conduct that will make outside intervention unnecessary."

Also, as I said last Wednesday [news conference, 5.8.63], in the absence of any violation of Federal statutes or court orders or other grounds for Federal intervention, our efforts will continue to be focused on helping local citizens to achieve and maintain a peaceful, reasonable settlement.

The community leaders who worked out this agreement [on a plan for desegregation and the elimination of discriminatory employment practices, consummated 5.10.63] with a great sense of justice and foresight deserve to see it implemented in an atmosphere of law and order. I trust that we can count on your constructive cooperation in maintaining such an atmosphere; but I would be derelict in my duty if I did not take preliminary steps announced last night that will enable this Government, if required, to meet its obligations without delay.

> Telegram replying to appeal by Alabama's Governor George C. Wallace that the Birmingham situation be left to state and local handling, Washington, D.C., May 13, 1963

79 / PRESIDENTIAL OBLIGATION

I am obligated to carry out the court order—that is part of our constitutional system. . . . We are a people of laws and we have to obey them.

> Statement on Governor George C. Wallace's announced determination to defy a Federal court order that desegregation of the University of Alabama begin on June 10, 1963, news conference, Washington, D.C., May 22, 1963

80 / EVERY AMERICAN CITIZEN'S RIGHTS

This afternoon, following a series of threats and defiant statements, the presence of Alabama National Guardsmen was required on the University of Alabama to carry out the final and unequivocal order of the United States District Court of the Northern District of Alabama.

That order called for the admission of two clearly qualified young Alabama residents [Miss Vivian Malone and Mr. James Hood] who happened to have been born Negro.

That they were admitted peacefully on the campus is due in good measure to the conduct of the students of the University of Alabama who met their responsibilities in a constructive way.

I hope that every American, regardless of where he lives, will stop and examine his conscience about this and other related incidents.

This nation was founded by men of many nations and backgrounds. It was founded on the principle that all men are created equal, and that the rights of every man are diminished when the rights of one man are threatened.

Today we are committed to a worldwide struggle to promote and protect the rights of all who wish to be free. And when Americans are sent to Vietnam or West Berlin we do not ask for whites only.

It ought to be possible, therefore, for American students of any color to attend any public institution they select without having to be backed up by troops. It ought to be possible for American consumers of any color to receive equal service in places of public accommodation, such as hotels and restaurants, and theaters and retail stores without being forced to resort to demonstrations in the street.

And it ought to be possible for American citizens of any color to register and vote in a free election without interference or fear of reprisal.

It ought to be possible, in short, for every American to enjoy the privileges of being American without regard to his race or color.

Address to the nation on the racial crisis, Washington, D.C., June 11, 1963

81 / THE GOVERNOR'S INTRANSIGENCY

It should be clear that United States Government action regarding the Alabama schools will come only if Governor Wallace compels it.

In 144 school districts in 11 Southern and border states desegregation was carried out for the first time this month in an orderly and peaceful manner.

Parents, students, citizens, school officials and public officials of these areas met their responsibilities in a dignified law-abiding way. It was not necessary for the Federal Government to become involved in any of those states.

In the State of Alabama, however, where local authorities repeatedly stated they were prepared to carry out court directives and maintain public peace, Governor Wallace has refused to respect either the law or the authority of local officials. For his own personal and political reasons—so that he may later charge Federal interference—he is desperately anxious to have the Federal Government intervene in a situation in which we have no desire to intervene.

The Governor knows that the United States Government is obligated to carry out the orders of the United States courts. He knows that the great majority of the citizens in Birmingham, Mobile, Tuskegee and

Huntsville were willing to face this difficult transition with the same courage and respect for the law as did the communities in neighboring states. And he knows that there was and is no reason or necessity for intervention by the Federal Government unless he wishes and forces that result.

This Government will do whatever must be done to see that the orders of the court are implemented—but I am hopeful that Governor Wallace will enable the local officials and communities to meet their responsibilities in this regard; as they are willing to do.

> Statement on Governor George C. Wallace's attempt to block public school desegregation in Tuskegee, Birmingham, Mobile, and Huntsville, Alabama, Washington, D.C., Sept. 9, 1963

82 / RACIAL FOLLY

I know I speak on behalf of all Americans in expressing a deep sense of outrage and grief over the killing of the children yesterday in Birmingham, Alabama. It is regrettable that public disparagement of law and order has encouraged violence which has fallen on the innocent. If these cruel and tragic events can only awaken that city and State—if they can only awaken this entire nation—to a realization of the folly of racial injustice and hatred and violence, then it is not too late for all concerned to unite in steps toward peaceful progress before more lives are lost. . . .

This nation is committed to a course of domestic justice and tranquility—and I call upon every citizen, white and Negro, North and South, to put passions and prejudices aside and join in this effort.

> Statement on bombing of Birmingham's 16th Street Baptist Church, Washington, D.C., Sept. 16, 1963

Some Thoughts on Recent
Racial Disorders and Crises

83 / SMOLDERING RESENTMENTS

The fires of frustration and discord are burning in every city, North and South. Where legal remedies are not at hand, redress is sought in the streets in demonstrations, parades and protests, which create tensions and threaten violence—and threaten lives.

> Address to the nation on the racial crisis, Washington, D.C., June 11, 1963

84 / TIME FOR ACTION

We face a moral crisis as a country and a people. It cannot be met by repressive police action. It cannot be left to increased demonstrations in the streets. It cannot be quieted by token moves or by talk. It is a time to act in the Congress, in your state and local legislative body, and, above all, in all of our daily lives.

Ibid.

85 / MUTUAL RESPONSIBILITIES

We have a right to expect that the Negro community will be responsible, will uphold the law. But they have a right to expect the law will be fair, that the Constitution will be color blind, as Justice Harlan said at the turn of the century.

Ibid.

86 / RIOTOUS DEMONSTRATIONS RETARD JUSTICE

I'm concerned about those demonstrations. I think they go beyond information—they go beyond protest and they get into a very bad situation where you get violence, and I think the cause of advancing equal opportunities only loses.

News conference, Washington, D.C., July 17, 1963

87 / REASONING TOGETHER

Dialogue and discussion are always better than violence.

Message to Congress on civil rights, June 19, 1963

88 / TO SOLVE THE CIVIL RIGHTS PROBLEM

The way to make the problem go away, in my opinion, is to provide for redress of grievances.

News conference, Washington, D.C., July 17, 1963

89 / A TWO-WAY STREET

I would hope that, along with a cessation of the kinds of demonstrations that would lead to rioting, the people would also do something about the grievances. You just can't tell people, "Don't protest," but, on the other hand, "We're not going to let you come into a store, or restaurant." It seems to me it's a two-way street.

Ibid.

90 / THE EDUCATED CITIZEN'S SPECIAL RESPONSIBILITY

The educated citizen has an obligation to uphold the law. This is the obligation of every citizen in a free and peaceful society—but the educated citizen has a special responsibility by the virtue of his greater understanding. For, whether he has ever studied history or current events, ethics or civics, the rules of a profession or the tools of a trade, he knows that only a respect for the law makes it possible for free men to dwell together in peace and progress.

He knows that law is the adhesive force of the cement of society, creating order out of chaos and coherence in place of anarchy. He knows that for one man to defy a law or court order he does not like is to invite others to defy those which they do not like, leading to a breakdown of all justice and all order.

He knows, too, that every fellow man is entitled to be regarded with decency and treated with dignity. Any educated citizen who seeks to subvert the law, to suppress freedom, or to subject other human beings to acts that are less than human, degrades his inheritance, ignores his learning and betrays his obligations.

Certain other societies may respect the rule of force—we respect the rule of law. . . .

In these moments of tragic disorder, a special burden rests on the educated men and women of our country—to reject the temptations of prejudice and violence, and to reaffirm the values of freedom and law on which our free society depends.

Address, Vanderbilt University, Nashville, Tenn., May 18, 1963

The March on Washington

91 / MARCH ON WASHINGTON

I think that the way that the Washington march has now developed, which is a peaceful assembly calling for a redress of grievances—the cooperation with the police, every evidence that it's going to be peaceful—they're going to the Washington Monument, they're going to express their strong views—I think that's in the great tradition.

News conference, Washington, D.C., July 17, 1963

92 / "CONTRIBUTION TO ALL MANKIND"

We have witnessed today in Washington tens of thousands of Americans —both Negro and white—exercising their right to assemble peaceably and direct the widest possible attention to a great national issue. Efforts to secure equal treatment and equal opportunity for all without regard to race, color, creed or nationality are neither novel nor difficult to understand. What is different today is the intensified and widespread public awareness of the need to move forward in achieving these objectives—objectives which are older than this nation.

Although this summer has seen remarkable progress in translating civil rights from principles into practices, we have a very long way yet to travel. One cannot help but be impressed with the deep fervor and the quiet dignity that characterizes the thousands who have gathered in the nation's capital from across the country to demonstrate their faith and confidence in our democratic form of government. History has seen many demonstrations—of widely varying character and for a whole host of reasons. As our thoughts travel to other demonstrations that have occurred in different parts of the world, this nation can properly be proud of the demonstration that has occurred here today. The leaders of the organizations sponsoring the march and all who have participated in it deserve our appreciation for the detailed preparations that made it possible and for the orderly manner in which it has been conducted.

The executive branch of the Federal Government will continue its efforts to obtain increased employment and to eliminate discrimination in employment practices, two of the prime goals of the march. In addition, our efforts to secure enactment of the legislative proposals made to the Congress will be maintained including not only the civil rights bill, but also proposals to broaden and strengthen the manpower development and training program, the youth employment bill, amendments to the vocational education program, the establishment of a work-study program for high-school-age youth, strengthening of the adult basic education provisions in the Administration's education program and the amendments proposed to the public welfare work-relief and training program. This nation can afford to achieve the goals of a full employment policy—it cannot afford to permit the potential skills and educational capacity of its citizens to be unrealized.

The cause of 20,000,000 Negroes has been advanced by the program conducted so appropriately before the nation's shrine to the Great Emancipator, but even more significant is the contribution to all mankind.

Statement on the march on Washington, Washington, D.C., Aug. 28, 1963

The Struggle for Equality

93 / SLOW STRUGGLE

The Emancipation Proclamation was not an end. It was a beginning. The century since has seen the struggle to convert freedom from rhetoric to reality. It has been in many respects a somber story. For many years progress toward the realization of equal rights was very slow. . . . And the task is not finished. Much remains to be done to eradicate the vestiges of discrimination and segregation, to make equal rights a reality for all our people, to fulfill finally the promises of the Declaration of Independence. Like the proclamation we celebrate, this observance must be regarded not as an end, but as a beginning.

> Message on the 100th anniversary of the Emancipation Proclamation, Washington, D.C., Sept. 22, 1962

94 / CELEBRATION OF THE EMANCIPATION PROCLAMATION

The centennial of the issuance of the Emancipation Proclamation is an occasion for celebration, for a sober assessment of our failures, and for rededication to the goals of freedom. Surely there could be no more meaningful observance of the centennial than the enactment of effective civil rights legislation and the continuation of effective Executive action.

> Message to Congress on civil rights, Feb. 28, 1963

95 / TRIBUTE TO THE NEGRO'S LOYALTY AND INITIATIVE

. . . despite humiliation and deprivation, the Negro retained his loyalty to the United States and to democratic institutions. He showed this loyalty by brave service in two world wars, by the rejection of extreme or violent policies, by a quiet and proud determination to work for long-denied rights within the framework of the American Constitution. . . . despite deprivation and humiliation, the Negro never stopped working for his own salvation. There is no more impressive chapter in our history than the one in which our Negro fellow citizens sought better education for themselves and their children, built better schools and better housing, carved out their own economic opportunity, enlarged their press, fostered their arts, and clarified and strengthened their purpose as a people. . . . It can be said, I believe, that Abraham Lincoln emancipated the slaves, but that, in this century since, our Negro citizens have emancipated themselves.

> Message on the 100th anniversary of the Emancipation Proclamation, Washington, D.C., Sept. 22, 1962

12

Education

A National Concern

1 / THE HUMAN MIND

The human mind is our fundamental resource.
>   Message to Congress on education, Feb. 20, 1961

2 / EDUCATION AND NATIONAL PROGRESS

Our progress as a nation can be no swifter than our progress in education.
>   *Ibid.*

3 / A BENEFIT OF FREEDOM

The education of our people is a national investment. It yields tangible returns in economic growth, an improved citizenry and higher standards of living. But even more importantly, free men and women value education as a personal experience and opportunity—as a basic benefit of a free and democratic civilization. It is our responsibility to do whatever needs to be done to make this opportunity available to all and to make it of the highest possible quality.
>   Message to Congress on education, Feb. 6, 1962

4 / KEYSTONE

Education is the keystone in the arch of freedom and progress. Nothing has contributed more to the enlargement of this nation's strength and opportunities than our traditional system of free, universal elementary and secondary education, coupled with widespread availability of college education.

Message to Congress on education, Jan. 29, 1963

5 / INDIVIDUAL DEVELOPMENT FOR NATIONAL BENEFIT

Let us not think of education only in terms of its costs, but rather in terms of the infinite potential of the human mind that can be realized through education. Let us think of education as the means of developing our greatest abilities, because in each of us there is a private hope and dream which, fulfilled, can be translated into benefit for everyone and greater strength for our nation.

Presidential proclamation of American Education Week, July 25, 1961

6 / DEMOCRACY AND EDUCATION

Unless we have a good and increasing educational system, we are not going to have a strong democratic society.

Campaign remarks, Eugene, Ore., Sept. 7, 1960

7 / FOUNDATION OF DEMOCRACY

Education is both the foundation and the unifying force of our democratic way of life. It is the mainspring of our economic and social progress. It is the highest expression of achievement in our society, ennobling and enriching human life. In short, it is at the same time the most profitable investment society can make and the richest reward it can confer.

Message to Congress on education, Feb. 6, 1962

8 / FOR FREEDOM

In order to maintain a free society, in order that we can maintain our independence in the coming years, we have to have the best educated citizens in the world.

Campaign remarks, Carpentersville, Ill., Oct. 25, 1960

9 / THE DANGER OF IGNORANCE

The ignorance of one voter in a democracy impairs the security of all.

Address, Vanderbilt University, Nashville, Tenn., May 18, 1963

10 / TRADITIONAL CONCEPT

The concept that every American deserves the opportunity to attain the highest level of education of which he is capable is not new to this Administration—it is a traditional ideal of democracy.

Message to Congress on education, Feb. 6, 1962

11 / THE RACE

There is an old saying that the course of civilization is a race between catastrophe and education. In a democracy such as ours, we must make sure that education wins the race.

Campaign address, Valley Forge, Pa., Oct. 29, 1960

12 / NATIONAL STATURE

The issue of education is clearly bound up with our national stature; one cannot and has not through American history been achieved without the other.

Campaign letter to National Association of Broadcasters, Washington, D.C., Oct. 14, 1960

13 / ADEQUATE OPPORTUNITY

I am not satisfied if my particular community has a good school. I want to make sure that every child in this country has an adequate opportunity for a good education.

Address, AFL-CIO Convention, Miami, Dec. 7, 1961

14 / NECESSITY

A quality education is a necessity for all American children, not merely those who by good fortune live in a district covered by [a partial Federal school-aid] program.

Statement on signing Federal school-aid bill, Washington, D.C., Oct. 3, 1961

15 / INVESTMENT

I believe we must invest in our youth.

Address, AFL-CIO Convention, Miami, Dec. 7, 1961

16 / BASIC EDUCATION

Elementary and secondary schools are the foundation of our educational system. There is little value in our efforts to broaden and improve our higher education, or increase our supply of such skills as science and engineering, without a greater effort for excellence at this basic level of education. With our mobile population and demanding needs, this is not a matter of local or state action alone—this is a national concern.

Message to Congress on education, Feb. 6, 1962

17 / NATIONAL LOSS

Children whose education suffers from overcrowded classrooms or underpaid teachers can never gain back what they have lost—and it is the nation's loss as well as theirs.

Campaign address, Louisville, Ky., Oct. 5, 1960

18 / THE MISEDUCATED

A child miseducated is a child lost.

State of the Union Message, Jan. 11, 1962

19 / CHAIN ILLITERACY

An uneducated American child makes an uneducated parent who produces, in many cases, another uneducated American child.

Commencement address, San Diego State College, June 6, 1963

20 / URGENT NECESSITY

The [educational] problems . . . would require solution whether or not we were confronted with a massive threat to freedom. The existence of that threat lends urgency to their solution—to the accomplishment of those objectives which, in any case, would be necessary for the realization of our highest hopes and those of our children.

Message to Congress on education, Feb. 6, 1962

21 / A NATIONAL PROBLEM

Today our schools are overcrowded and our teachers ill paid. Yet our advanced technological society depends on the resources of the mind for scientific advances, the development of new industries and increased productivity. This problem is a national problem—and the National Government must act to meet it.

Campaign address, Charleston, W. Va., Sept. 19, 1960

22 / EDUCATION AND ECONOMIC GROWTH

The increasing complexity of modern industry requires the best talent and skills which America has to offer. The history of American economic growth has, in large measure, been the history of the developing skills of our labor force, and the imagination and creativity of our businessmen and scientists. To assure continued growth we must invest in better school systems, in vocational training programs for unemployed workers, and in scholarship programs which will make higher education available to all young men and women of intellect and ability.

Campaign statement on balance of payments, Philadelphia, Oct. 31, 1960

23 / NATIONAL INTEREST

For the nation, increasing the quality and availability of education is vital to both our national security and our domestic well-being. A free nation can rise no higher than the standard of excellence set in its schools and colleges. Ignorance and illiteracy, unskilled workers and school dropouts —these and other failures of our educational system breed failures of our social and economic system: delinquency, unemployment, chronic dependence, a waste of human resources, a loss of productive power and purchasing power, and an increase in tax-supported benefits. The loss of only 1 year's income due to unemployment is more than the total cost of 12 years of education through high school. Failure to improve educational performance is thus not only poor social policy, it is poor economics.

Message to Congress on education, Jan. 29, 1963

24 / DEFENSE

If we are to defend ourselves effectively in a world of international tension and move ahead, we must rely no less upon the strength of our educational system than upon the strength of our Military Establishment.

Campaign letter to National Association of Broadcasters, Washington, D.C., Oct. 14, 1960

25 / COLD WAR NECESSITY

The twisting course of the cold war requires a citizenry that understands our principles and problems. It requires skilled manpower and brainpower to match the power of totalitarian discipline. It requires a scientific effort which demonstrates the superiority of freedom. And it requires an electorate in every State with sufficiently broad horizons and sufficient maturity of judgment to guide this nation safely through whatever lies ahead.

Message to Congress on education, Jan. 29, 1963

Goals and Standards

26 / TWIN GOALS

Our twin goals must be: a new standard of excellence in education—and the availability of such excellence to all who are willing and able to pursue it.

Message to Congress on education, Feb. 20, 1961

27 / AT THE START

Excellence in education must begin at the elementary level.

State of the Union Message, Jan. 11, 1962

28 / CAPACITY

I believe in an America where every child is educated not according to his means or his race, but according to his capacity.

Campaign address, Convention Hall, Philadelphia, Oct. 31, 1960

29 / INDIVIDUAL DEVELOPMENT

Our requirements for world leadership, our hopes for economic growth, and the demands of citizenship itself in an era such as this all require the maximum development of every young American's capacity.

Message to Congress on education, Feb. 20, 1961

30 / REALIZING POTENTIALS

We want . . . an educational system that turns out the brightest of hardworking boys and girls in the world.

Campaign address via telephone to AMVET Convention, Miami Beach, Aug. 26, 1960

31 / PREPARATION FOR RESPONSIBILITIES

If the boys and girls of this country are going to meet their responsibilities as Americans, if they are going to find employment and decent wages, if they are going to maintain the freedoms of this country, we are going to have to have the best educational system in the world.

Campaign remarks, Kalamazoo, Mich., Oct. 14, 1960

32 / VALUABLE RESOURCE

A good education is the most valuable resource that you can pass on to your children.

> Campaign remarks, Carpentersville, Ill., Oct. 25, 1960

33 / DOORS TO WELL-BEING

For the individual, the doors to the schoolhouse, to the library, and to the college lead to the richest treasures of our open society: to the power of knowledge—to the training and skills necessary for productive employment—to the wisdom, the ideals, and the culture which enrich life—and to the creative, self-disciplined understanding of society needed for good citizenship in today's changing and challenging world.

> Message to Congress on education, Jan. 29, 1963

34 / INDIVIDUAL NEED

Today only the well-educated man or woman is equipped to work in an age of technology or to be a good citizen in an age of complexity.

> Address, American Society of Newspaper Editors, Washington, D.C., April 19, 1963

35 / ECONOMIC ADVANTAGE

Those with higher educational achievement have a higher average salary as well as a lower rate of unemployment.

> *Ibid.*

36 / STIMULATION OF INTEREST

We must stimulate interest in learning in order to reduce the alarming number of students who now drop out of school or who do not continue into higher levels of education.

> Message to Congress on education, Jan. 29, 1963

37 / EDUCATION AND ECONOMIC GROWTH

Growth requires that we have the best trained and best educated labor force in the world. Investment in manpower is just as important as investment in facilities. Yet today we waste precious resources when the bright youngster, who should have been a skilled draftsman or able scientist or engineer must remain a pick-and-shovel worker because he never had a chance to develop his talents. It is time we geared our educational systems to meet the increased demand of modern industry—strengthening our public schools, our colleges, and our vocational programs for retraining unemployed workers.

Campaign address, Associated Business Publications Conference, New York City, Oct. 12, 1960

38 / THE NEW AGE

In the new age of science and space, improved education is essential to give new meaning to our national purpose and power. In the last 20 years, mankind has acquired more scientific information than in all of previous history. Ninety percent of all the scientists that ever lived are alive and working today. Vast stretches of the unknown are being explored every day for military, medical, commercial, and other reasons.

Message to Congress on education, Jan. 29, 1963

Educational Deficiencies and Needs

39 / LAGGING PACE

To be sure, Americans are still the best-educated and best-trained people in the world. But our educational system has failed to keep pace with the problems and needs of our complex technological society. Too many are illiterate or untrained, and thus either unemployed or underemployed. Too many receive an education diminished in quality in thousands of districts which cannot or do not support modern and adequate facilities, well-paid and well-trained teachers, or even a sufficiently long school year.

Message to Congress on education, Feb. 6, 1962

40 / PRESENT ACTION REQUIRED

An educational system which is inadequate today will be worse tomorrow, unless we act now to improve it.

Ibid.

41 / NEEDS OF THE IMMEDIATE FUTURE

We must provide facilities for 14,000,000 more elementary, secondary school and college students by 1970, an increase of 30 percent. College enrollments alone will nearly double, requiring approximately twice as many facilities to serve nearly 7,000,000 students by 1970. We must find the means of financing a 75 percent increase in the total cost of education —another $20,000,000,000 a year for expansion and improvement— particularly in facilities and instruction which must be of the highest quality if our nation is to achieve its highest goals.

Ibid.

42 / INADEQUATE FACILITIES

Our classrooms contain 2 million more children than they properly have room for, taught by 90,000 teachers not properly qualified to teach.

State of the Union Message, Jan. 30, 1961

43 / NEED FOR CLASSROOMS

To meet current needs and accommodate increasing enrollments— increasing by nearly one million elementary and secondary pupils a year in the Sixties—and to provide every child with the opportunity to receive a full-day education in an adequate classroom, a total of 600,000 classrooms must be constructed during this decade. The states report an immediate shortage today of more than 127,000 classrooms and a rate of construction which, combined with heavily increasing enrollments, is not likely to fill their needs for ten years. Already over half a million pupils are in curtailed or half-day sessions. Unless the present rate of construction is accelerated and Federal resources made available to supplement state and local resources that are already strained in many areas, few families and communities in the nation will be free from the ill effects of overcrowded or inadequate facilities in our public schools.

Message to Congress on education, Feb. 6, 1962

44 / INSUFFICIENT EDUCATIONAL PROGRAM

Too many—an estimated one million a year—leave school before completing high school—the bare minimum for a fair start in modern-day life. Too many high school graduates with talent—numbering in the hundreds of thousands—fail to go on to college; and 40 per cent of those who enter college drop out before graduation. And too few, finally, are going on to the graduate studies that modern society requires in increasing number. The total number of graduates receiving doctorate degrees has increased only about one-third in ten years; in 1960 they numbered less than 10,000, including only 3,000 in mathematics, physical sciences and engineering.

Ibid.

45 / DROPOUT PROBLEM

We must give special attention to the problem of our younger people . . . the problem of those who drop out of school before they finish because of hardships in their home, inadequate motivation or counseling or whatever it may be, and then drift without being able to find a decent job. And this falls particularly heavily upon the young men and women who are in our minority groups. . . .

Millions . . . leave school early, destined to fall for life into a pattern of being untrained, unskilled and frequently unemployed. It's for this reason that I have asked the Congress to pass a Youth Employment Opportunities Act to guide these hands so that they can make a life for themselves.

Address, AFL-CIO Convention, Miami, Dec. 7, 1961

46 / INADEQUATE TRAINING PROGRAMS; DROPOUTS

We know that 5,000,000 jobs will open up in this decade for skilled workers, and yet, at the present time, the number of youth being trained for these jobs is totally inadequate. In light of our national need for a better-prepared work force, it is tragic indeed to be reminded of the estimate that 7,500,000 boys and girls will fail to complete high school during the decade of the Nineteen Sixties, unless we, as a nation, take positive steps to prevent it.

This situation is tragic, not only because it represents a great loss to our society in undeveloped talent and potential, but also because the outlook for these young people is black indeed.

Labor Day message to the youth of the nation, Newport, R.I., Sept. 3, 1962

47 / AN EMERGENCY PROGRAM

The end of this summer of 1963 will be an especially critical time for 400,000 young Americans who, according to the experience of earlier years, will not return to school when the summer is ended. Moreover, without a special effort to reverse this trend, another 700,000 students will return to school in September, but will fail to complete the school year. The greatest growth in labor demand today is for highly trained professional workers with 16 or more years of education. The second fastest growing demand is for technical and semiprofessional workers with 1 to 3 years of post high school education. Jobs filled by high school graduates rose 30 percent, while jobs for those with no secondary education decreased 25 percent in the last decade.

We must therefore combat, intensify our efforts to meet this problem. We are now talking about the lives of a million young American boys and girls who will fail to meet their educational requirements in the next few months unless we do something about it.

This is a serious national problem. A boy or girl has only a limited time in their life in which to get an education, and yet it will shape their whole lives and the lives of their children. So I am asking all American parents to urge their children to go back to school in September, to assist them in every way to stay in school. I am asking school principals, clergymen, trade union leaders, business leaders, everyone in this country, to concern themselves. Here is something that all of us can do in a practical way in the month of August and in the months to come.

One of the things which we are going to do here is to provide, out of the Presidential emergency fund, $250,000 on an emergency basis for guidance counselors in the month of August to see if we can get some of these boys and girls back to school. They will appreciate any effort we make for the rest of their lives.

News conference, Washington, D.C., Aug. 1, 1963

48 / FINANCIAL HANDICAP

One-third of our most promising high school graduates are financially unable to continue development of their talents.

State of the Union Message, Jan. 30, 1961

49 / INTELLECTUAL WASTE

Today, more than at any other time in our history, we need to develop our intellectual resources to the fullest. But the facts of the matter are that many thousands of our young people are not educated to their maximum capacity—and they are not, therefore, making the maximum contribution of which they are capable to themselves, their families, their communities and the nation. Their talents lie wasted—their lives are frequently pale and blighted—and their contribution to our economy and culture are lamentably below the levels of their potential skills, knowledge and creative ability.

Message to Congress on education, Feb. 6, 1962

50 / COSTS OF EDUCATIONAL INADEQUACY

Educational failures breed delinquency, despair and dependence. They increase the costs of unemployment and public welfare. They cut our potential national economic output by billions. They deny the benefits of our society to large segments of our people. They undermine our capabil-

ity as a nation to discharge world obligations. All this we cannot afford
—better schools we can afford.

　　Ibid.

51 / AID TO HANDICAPPED CHILDREN

[A] long-standing national concern has been the provision of specially
trained teachers to meet the educational needs of children afflicted with
physical and mental disabilities. The existing program providing Federal
assistance to higher education institutions and to state education agencies
for training teachers and supervisory personnel for mentally retarded
children was supplemented last year to provide temporarily for training
teachers of the deaf. I recommend broadening the basic program to include assistance for the special training needed to help all our children
afflicted with the entire range of physical and mental handicaps.

　　Ibid.

52 / MIGRANT WORKERS

The neglected educational needs of America's one million migrant agricultural workers and their families constitute one of the gravest re-
proaches to our nation.

　　Ibid.

Federal Aid

53 / NATIONAL COMMITMENT

Education, quite rightly, is the responsibility of the state and the local
community. But from the beginning of our country's history . . . it has
been recognized that there must be a national commitment and that the
national government must play its role in stimulating a system of excellence which can serve the great national purpose of a free society.

　　Commencement address, San Diego State College, June 6, 1963

54 / FEDERAL AID DOES NOT WEAKEN LOCAL CONTROL

The control and operation of education in America must remain the responsibility of state and local governments and private institutions. This
tradition assures our educational system of the freedom, the diversity and
the vitality necessary to serve our free society fully. But the Congress has
long recognized the responsibility of the nation as a whole—the additional resources, meaningful encouragement and vigorous leadership that

must be added to the total effort by the Federal Government if we are to meet the task before us. For education in this country is the right—the necessity—and the responsibility—of all. Its advancement is essential to national objectives and dependent on the greater financial resources available at the national level.

Let us put to rest the unfounded fears that "Federal money means Federal control." From the Northwest Ordinance of 1787, originally conceived by Thomas Jefferson, through the Morrill Act of 1862, establishing the still-important and still-independent land-grant college system, to the National Defense Education Act of 1958, the Congress repeatedly recognized its responsibility to strengthen our educational system without weakening local responsibility. Since the end of the Korean War, Federal funds for constructing and operating schools in districts affected by Federal installations have gone directly to over 5,500 districts without any sign or complaint of interference or dictation from Washington. In the last decade, over $5,000,000,000 of Federal funds have been channeled to aid higher education without in any way undermining local administration.

Message to Congress on education, Feb. 6, 1962

55 / MORE INDEPENDENCE

Federal aid will enable our schools, colleges, and universities to be more stable financially and therefore more independent.

Message to Congress on education, Jan. 29, 1963

56 / FEDERAL AID URGENTLY NEEDED

The war babies of the 1940's, who overcrowded our schools in the 1950's, are now descending in the 1960's upon our colleges—with two college students for every one 10 years from now—and our colleges are ill prepared. We lack the scientists, the engineers, and the teachers our world obligations require. We have neglected oceanography, saline water conversion, and the basic research that lies at the root of all technological progress. Federal grants for both higher and public school education can no longer be delayed.

State of the Union Message, Jan. 30, 1961

Teachers

57 / "TRUSTEES OF OUR CHILDREN'S MINDS"

We entrust to our teachers our most valuable possession—our children—for a very large share of their waking hours during the most formative years of their life. We make certain that those to whom we entrust our financial assets are individuals of the highest competence and character—we dare not do less for the trustees of our children's minds.

Message to Congress on education, Feb. 6, 1962

58 / WELL-TRAINED TEACHERS

Democracy demands more of us than any other system of education, character, self-restraint, self-discipline. How are we going to get the best education in the world? One of the ways is to have the best-trained teachers.

Campaign remarks, Moline, Ill., Oct. 24, 1960

59 / TEACHER QUALIFICATIONS

The key to educational quality is the teaching profession. About one out of every five of the nearly 1,600,000 teachers in our elementary and secondary schools fails to meet full certification standards for teaching or has not completed four years of college work. Our immediate concern should be to afford them every possible opportunity to improve their professional skills and their command of the subjects they teach.

Message to Congress on education, Feb. 6, 1962

60 / LEAVE FOR STUDY

Many elementary and secondary school teachers would profit from a full year of full time study in their subject-matter fields. Very few can afford to do so. Yet the benefits of such a year could be shared by outstanding teachers with others in their schools and school systems as well as with countless students. We should begin to make such opportunities available to the elementary and secondary school teachers of this country and thereby accord to this profession the support, prestige and recognition it deserves.

Ibid.

61 / TEACHERS' SALARIES

In no other sector of our national economy do we find such a glaring discrepancy between the importance of one's work to society and the financial reward society offers. Can any able and industrious student, unless unusually motivated, be expected to elect a career that pays more poorly than almost any other craft, trade, or profession? Until the situation can be dramatically improved—unless the states and localities can be assisted and stimulated in bringing about salary levels which will make the teaching profession competitive with other professions which require the same length of training and ability—we cannot hope to succeed in our efforts to improve the quality of our children's instruction and to meet the need for more teachers.

Ibid.

62 / DISPROPORTIONATE VALUES OF MODERN CYNICS AND SKEPTICS

They see no harm in paying those to whom they entrust the minds of their children a smaller wage than is paid to those to whom they entrust the care of their plumbing.

Address, Vanderbilt University, Nashville, Tenn., May 18, 1963

63 / INSUFFICIENT INCENTIVE

Without sufficient incentive to make teaching a lifetime career, teachers with valuable training and experience but heavy family responsibilities too often become frustrated and drop out of the profession.

Message to Congress on education, Jan. 29, 1963

Higher Education

64 / EQUAL OPPORTUNITY

In our democracy every young person should have an equal opportunity to obtain a higher education, regardless of his station in life or financial means.

Message to Congress on education, Feb. 6, 1962

65 / FOR NATIONAL STRENGTH

If this nation is to grow in wisdom and strength, then every able-bodied high school graduate should have the opportunity to develop his talents.

State of the Union Message, Jan. 11, 1962

66 / REGRETTABLE LOSS

It is . . . a regrettable fact that here in the richest country on earth 150,-000 of our brightest students are unable to go to college every year because they cannot afford it.

Campaign remarks, Eugene, Ore., Sept. 7, 1960

67 / ENTRANCE REQUIREMENT

A student's ability—not his parents' income—should determine whether he has the opportunity to enter medicine or dentistry.

Message to Congress on education, Feb. 6, 1962

68 / NEED FOR MORE SCIENTISTS AND ENGINEERS

Our economic, scientific and military strength increasingly requires that we have sufficient numbers of scientists and engineers to cope with the fast-changing needs of our time.

Ibid.

69 / TECHNICAL TRAINING

Many once-familiar occupations have declined or disappeared and wholly new industries and jobs have emerged from economic growth and change. The complexities of modern science and technology require training at a higher level than ever before.

Message to Congress on education, Jan. 29, 1963

70 / FOR DEFENSE AND PROSPERITY

Expansion of high quality graduate education and research in all fields is essential to national security and economic growth.

Ibid.

71 / FINANCIAL AID NEEDED

There will be twice as many college students in 1970 as there were in 1960. Without outside financial help, our colleges must either raise their rate of tuition or turn new students away.

Address, American Society of Newspaper Editors, Washington, D.C., April 19, 1963

72 / INADEQUATE COLLEGE FACILITIES

The opportunity for a college education is severely limited for hundreds of thousands of young people because there is no college in their own community. . . . A demonstrated method of meeting this particular problem effectively is the creation of 2-year community colleges—a program that should be undertaken without delay and which will require Federal assistance for the construction of adequate facilities.

Message to Congress on education, Jan. 29, 1963

73 / WORLD ORDER AND THE UNIVERSITY

As we press forward on every front to realize a flexible world order, the role of the university becomes ever more important, both as a reservoir of ideas and as a repository of the long view of the shore dimly seen.

Address, Berkeley Division of the University of California, March 23, 1962

74 / LIBERTY AND LEARNING

Liberty and learning will be and must be the touchstones of . . . any free university in this country or the world. I say two touchstones—yet they are almost inseparable if not indistinguishable. For liberty without learning is always in peril, and learning without liberty is always in vain.

Address, Vanderbilt University, Nashville, Tenn., May 18, 1963

75 / ROLE OF UNIVERSITIES IN THE WORLD STRUGGLE

If we are to move forward, we shall need all the calm and thoughtful citizens our great universities can produce, all the light they can shed, all the wisdom they can bring to bear.

Address, University of Washington, Seattle, Nov. 16, 1961

76 / SPECIAL OBLIGATION OF THE UNIVERSITY

We live in an age of movement and change, both evolutionary and revolutionary, both good and evil—and in such an age a university has a special obligation to hold fast to the best of the past and move fast to the best of the future.

Address, Vanderbilt University, Nashville, Tenn., May 18, 1963

77 / LIBERAL TRADITION

I want to emphasize in the great concentration which we now place upon scientists and engineers how much we still need the men and women educated in the liberal tradition . . . who attempt to make an honest judgment on difficult events.

Address, University of North Carolina, Chapel Hill, Oct. 12, 1961

78 / THE EDUCATED MUST DEFEND LEARNING

If the pursuit of learning is not defended by the educated citizen, it will not be defended at all. For there will always be those who scoff at intellectuals, who cry out against research, who seek to limit our educational system.

Address, Vanderbilt University, Nashville, Tenn., May 18, 1963

79 / EDUCATION AND POLITICS

From the beginning of this country . . . there has been the closest link between educated men and women and politics and government. . . . Our nation's first great leaders were also our first great scholars.

Address, University of North Carolina, Chapel Hill, Oct. 12, 1961

Adult Education

80 / ADULT ILLITERACY

Eight million adult Americans are classified as functionally illiterate. This is a disturbing figure reflected in Selective Service rejection rates, reflected in welfare rolls and crime rates.

State of the Union Message, Jan. 11, 1962

81 / ADULT EDUCATION TO REDUCE ILLITERACY

Adult education must be pursued aggressively. Over eight million American citizens aged 25 or above have attended school for less than five years, and more than a third of these completely lack the ability to read and write. The economic result of this lack of schooling is often chronic unemployment, dependency or delinquency, with all the consequences this entails for these individuals, their families, their communities and the nation. The twin tragedies of illiteracy and dependency are often passed on from generation to generation.

There is no need for this. Many nations—including our own—have shown that this problem can be attacked and virtually wiped out. Unfortunately, our state school systems—overburdened in recent years by the increasing demands of growing populations and the increasing handicaps of insufficient revenues—have been unable to give adequate attention to this problem.

Message to Congress on education, Feb. 6, 1962

82 / NEED FOR ADULT PROGRAMS

Despite our high level of educational opportunity and attainment, nearly 23 million adult Americans lack an eighth grade education.

Message to Congress on education, Jan. 29, 1963

83 / CONTINUING EDUCATION

We must . . . recognize that a free society today demands that we keep on learning or face the threat of national deterioration.

Campaign statement to the Adult Education Association of the U.S.A., Denver, Oct. 14, 1960

84 / A LIFELONG PROCESS

The education of our people should be a lifelong process by which we continue to feed new vigor into the lifestream of the nation through intelligent, reasoned decisions.

Presidential proclamation of American Education Week, July 25, 1961

85 / MEETING OUR COMPLEX PROBLEMS

I believe that an America that understands the importance of "lifelong learning" will be able to deal with those problems more wisely and more vigorously.

Campaign statement to the Adult Education Association of the U.S.A., Denver, Oct. 14, 1960

86 / PREPARATION FOR AN UNPREDICTABLE FUTURE

We must educate people today for a future in which the choices to be faced cannot be anticipated by even the wisest now among us.

Ibid.

87 / RETRAINING

It is . . . necessary to provide training or retraining for the millions of workers who need to learn new skills or whose skills and technical knowledge must be updated.

Message to Congress on education, Jan. 29, 1963

88 / INADEQUATE LIBRARY FACILITIES

The public library is . . . an important resource for continuing education. But 18 million people in this nation still have no access to any local library service and over 110 million more have only inadequate service.
Ibid.

Educational Television

89 / POTENTIALITIES

The use of television for education purposes—particularly for adult education—offers great potentialities.
Message to Congress on education, Feb. 6, 1962

90 / EDUCATIONAL AID

Television, a device which has the potential to teach more things to more people in less time than anything yet devised, seems a providential instrument to come to education's aid. Educational television has already proved it can be a valuable supplement to formal education and a direct medium for nonformal education.
Campaign letter to National Association of Broadcasters, Washington, D.C., Oct. 14, 1960

91 / FEDERAL ASSISTANCE FOR EDUCATIONAL TELEVISION

Since education is a matter of national concern, the Federal Government should assist in expediting and accelerating the use of television, as a tested aid to education in the schools and colleges of the nation and as a means of meeting the needs of adult education.
Ibid.

Federal Encouragement of the Arts

92 / ADVANCEMENT OF CULTURE

Our nation has a rich and diverse cultural heritage. We are justly proud of the vitality, the creativity and the variety of the contemporary contributions our citizens can offer to the world of the arts. If we are to be among the leaders of the world in every sense of the word this sector of our national life cannot be neglected or treated with indifference. Yet, almost alone among the Governments of the world, our Government has displayed little interest in fostering cultural development. Just as the Federal Government has not, would not, and will not undertake to control the subject matter taught in local schools, so its efforts should be confined to broad encouragement of the arts. While this area is too new for hasty action, the proper contribution that should and can be made to the advancement of the arts by the Federal Government—many of them outlined by the Secretary of Labor in his decision settling the Metropolitan Opera labor dispute—deserve thorough and sympathetic consideration. . . . I urge approval of . . . a measure establishing a Federal Advisory Council on the arts to undertake these studies.

Message to Congress on education, Feb. 6, 1961

13

Social Welfare

Health and Physical Fitness

1 / BASIC RESOURCE

The basic resource of a nation is its people. Its strength can be no greater than the health and vitality of its population. Preventable sickness, disability and physical or mental incapacity are matters of both individual and national concern.

Message to Congress on the nation's health needs, Feb. 27, 1962

2 / FOR NATIONAL STRENGTH

Good health for all our people is a continuing goal. In a democratic society where every human life is precious, we can aspire to no less. Healthy people build a stronger nation, and make a maximum contribution to its growth and development.

Message to Congress on a health program, Feb. 7, 1963

3 / KEY TO FUTURE

The health of our nation is a key to its future—to its economic vitality, to the morale and efficiency of its citizens, to our success in achieving our own goals and demonstrating to others the benefits of a free society. Ill health and its harsh consequences are not confined to any State or region, to any race, age, or sex or to any occupation or economic level. This is a matter of national concern.

Message to Congress on a health program, Feb. 9, 1961

4 / MUCH TO BE DONE

We can take justifiable pride in our achievements in the field of medicine. . . . But measured against the scope of the problems that remain and the opportunities to be seized, this nation still falls far short of its responsibility.

> Message to Congress on the nation's health needs, Feb. 27, 1962

5 / FEDERAL GOVERNMENT SHARES RESPONSIBILITY

Basically, health care is a responsibility of individuals and families, of communities and voluntary agencies, of local and state governments. But the Federal Government shares this responsibility by providing leadership, guidance and support in areas of national concern.

> *Ibid.*

6 / MEETING HEALTH NEEDS

Good health is a prerequisite to the enjoyment of "pursuit of happiness." Whenever the miracles of modern medicine are beyond the reach of any group of Americans, for whatever reason—economic, geographic, occupational or other—we must find a way to meet their needs and fulfill their hopes. For one true measure of a nation is its success in fulfilling the promise of a better life for each of its members. Let this be the measure of our nation.

> *Ibid.*

7 / CHILDREN'S NEEDS

The nation's children—now 40 percent of our population—have urgent needs which must be met. Many still die in infancy. Many are not immunized against diseases which can be prevented, have inadequate diets, or unnecessarily endure physical and emotional problems.

> Message to Congress on a health program, Feb. 9, 1961

8 / THE UNDERPRIVILEGED

The dramatic results of new medicines and new methods—opening the way to a fuller and more useful life—are too often beyond the reach of those who need them most. Financial inability, absence of community resources, and shortages of trained personnel keep too many people from getting what medical knowledge can obtain for them.

> *Ibid.*

9 / SHORTAGE OF TRAINED HEALTH MANPOWER

Perhaps the most threatening breach in our health defenses is the shortage of trained health manpower. Our health can be no better than the knowledge and skills of the physicians, dentists, nurses, and others to whom we entrust it. It is essential that we always have a sufficient supply of such talent, drawn from the best and most gifted men and women in the land. But the harsh fact of the matter is that we are already hard hit by a critical shortage in our supply of professional health personnel, with the situation threatening to become even more critical in the years immediately ahead. . . . I urgently recommend enactment of legislation authorizing (1) Federal matching grants for the construction of new, and the expansion or rehabilitation of existing, teaching facilities for the medical, dental, and other health professions; and (2) Federal financial assistance for students of medicine, dentistry and osteopathy. . . . To meet [our] goals [in nurses' education], and generally to improve the quality of nursing services . . . the Federal Government should (1) provide financial assistance to expand teaching facilities for nurses' training; (2) provide financial assistance to students of nursing, many of whom cannot afford an education beyond high school; (3) initiate new and improved programs for the support of graduate nursing education, to provide more teachers of nursing; and (4) initiate new programs and expand current programs of research which are directed toward improved utilization of nursing personnel.

Message to Congress on a health program, Feb. 7, 1963

10 / INADEQUATE COMMUNITY SERVICES

The ability to afford adequate health care is to no avail without adequate health facilities. . . . Our communities need additional help to provide those services where everybody can use them.

Message to Congress on a health program, Feb. 9, 1961

11 / SHORTAGE OF HEALTH FACILITIES

Significant progress has been made in reducing the deficit of general hospital beds throughout the country, especially in rural areas. Nevertheless, shortage areas remain and their needs should be met. Indeed, rapid population growth alone requires a constantly expanding hospital system.

Message to Congress on a health program, Feb. 7, 1963

12 / COMMUNITY HEALTH PROTECTION

Substantial advances have been made during the past year in protecting the American people against contamination of food, air, and water, and the hazards associated with drugs. . . . But much remains to be done. We need to broaden our surveillance and control of pollution in the air we breathe, the water we drink, and the food we eat. We need to intensify our research effort in this area, to define the precise damages done to our health by various contaminants, and to develop more effective and economical means of controlling or eliminating them. We need to step up our training of scientific manpower in the many disciplines related to the maintenance of a healthy environment. We need to continue our support and stimulation of vigorous control programs in States and communities.

Ibid.

13 / HEALTH RESEARCH

This nation has made impressive strides in its search for knowledge to combat disease and, as a result of a deliberate national effort, a bold and far-reaching program is moving well. . . . But this effort is unending; new breakthroughs lie ahead; major problems are unsolved. This country must invest in a further expansion of essential and high-quality research and related activities.

Ibid.

14 / THE UNFINISHED TASK

The health of the American people must ever be safeguarded; it must ever be improved. As long as people are stricken by a disease which we have the ability to prevent, as long as people are chained by a disability which can be reversed, as long as needless death takes its toll, then American health will be unfinished business. It is to the unfinished business in health—which affects every person and home and community in this land—that we must now direct our best efforts.

Message to Congress on a health program, Feb. 9, 1961

15 / PHYSICAL FITNESS TO PURSUE INDIVIDUAL GOALS

Good physical fitness is essential to good physical and mental health. If our young men and women are to attain the social, scientific, and economic goals of which they are capable, they must all possess the strength, the energy and the good health to pursue them vigorously.

Message to Congress on the nation's youth, Feb. 14, 1963

16 / NEED FOR BROAD SPORTS PROGRAMS

We are under-exercised as a nation; we look instead of play; we ride instead of walk. Our existence deprives us of the minimum of physical activity essential for healthy living. And the remedy, in my judgment, lies in one direction—that is in developing programs for broad participation in exercise by all of our young men and women, all of our boys and girls.

> Address, National Football Foundation dinner, New York City, Dec. 5, 1961

17 / INADEQUATE EXERCISE

There is nothing, I think, more unfortunate than to have soft, chubby, fat-looking children who go to watch their school play basketball every Saturday and regard that as their week's exercise.

> Address at 50th birthday ceremonies for the U.S. Children's Bureau, Washington, D.C., April 9, 1962

18 / GOAL IN SPORTS

There are more important goals than winning contests, and that is to improve on a broad level the health and vitality of all of our people.

> Address, National Football Foundation dinner, New York City, Dec. 5, 1961

19 / URGENT NEED TO AUGMENT PHYSICAL EDUCATION PROGRAMS

I strongly urge those schools which do not provide adequate time and facilities for physical activity programs to do so. . . . All who can participate in the active life should do so, for their individual benefit and for the nation's.

> Message to Congress on the nation's youth, Feb. 14, 1963

20 / TO RAISE NATIONAL LEVELS OF PHYSICAL FITNESS

We must . . . change the physical habits of millions of Americans. And that is far more difficult than changing their tastes, their fashions, or even their politics.

> Address, National Football Foundation dinner, New York City, Dec. 5, 1961

21 / REMEDIABLE DEFECTS

About one-fifth of American youth currently examined by selective service were rejected for conditions which might have been remedied had timely attention been provided. School health programs can play an effective role in identifying and correcting these problems.

> Message to Congress on the nation's youth, Feb. 14, 1963

22 / MENTAL ILLNESS AND MENTAL RETARDATION: CRITICAL PROBLEMS

Two health problems—because they are of such critical size and tragic impact, and because their susceptibility to public action is so much greater than the attention they have received—are deserving of a wholly new national approach. . . . These twin problems are mental illness and mental retardation. . . . Mental illness and mental retardation are among our most critical health problems. They occur more frequently, affect more people, require more prolonged treatment, cause more suffering by the families of the afflicted, waste more of our human resources, and constitute more financial drain upon both the public treasury and the personal finances of the individual families than any other single condition.

Message to Congress on mental health, Feb. 5, 1963

23 / PRIMARY AIM: PREVENTION

We must seek out the causes of mental illness and of mental retardation and eradicate them. Here, more than in any other area, "an ounce of prevention is worth more than a pound of cure." For prevention is far more desirable for all concerned. It is far more economical and it is far more likely to be successful. Prevention will require both selected specific programs directed especially at known causes, and the general strengthening of our fundamental community, social welfare, and educational programs which can do much to eliminate or correct the harsh environmental conditions which often are associated with mental retardation and mental illness.

Ibid.

24 / NEED FOR GREATER KNOWLEDGE AND INCREASE OF PROFESSIONAL PERSONNEL

We must strengthen the underlying resources of knowledge and, above all, of skilled manpower which are necessary to mount and sustain our attack on mental disability for many years to come. Personnel from many of the same professions serve both the mentally ill and the mentally retarded. We must increase our existing training programs and launch new ones; for our efforts cannot succeed unless we increase by severalfold in the next decade the number of professional and subprofessional personnel who work in these fields. . . . We must also expand our research efforts, if we are to learn more about how to prevent and treat the crippling or malfunction of the mind.

Ibid.

25 / STRENGTHENING MENTAL HEALTH PROGRAMS

We must strengthen and improve the programs and facilities serving the mentally ill and the mentally retarded. The emphasis should be upon timely and intensive diagnosis, treatment, training, and rehabilitation so that the mentally afflicted can be cured or their functions restored to the extent possible.

Ibid.

26 / INEFFICIENT AND INADEQUATE CARE: GOVERNMENTAL AND PRIVATE RESPONSIBILITIES

There are now about 800,000 . . . patients in this nation's institutions —600,000 for mental illness and over 200,000 for mental retardation. Every year nearly 1,500,000 people receive treatment in institutions for the mentally ill and mentally retarded. Most of them are confined and compressed within an antiquated, vastly overcrowded, chain of custodial State institutions. The average amount expended on their care is only $4 a day—too little to do much good for the individual, but too much if measured in terms of efficient use of our mental health dollars. In some States the average is less than $2 a day. . . .

This situation has been tolerated far too long. It has troubled our national conscience, but only as a problem unpleasant to mention, easy to postpone, and despairing of solution. The Federal Government, despite the nationwide impact of the problem, has largely left the solutions up to the States. The States have depended on custodial hospitals and homes. Many such hospitals and homes have been shamefully understaffed, overcrowded, unpleasant institutions from which death too often provided the only firm hope of release.

The time has come for a bold new approach. New medical, scientific, and social tools and insights are now available. A series of comprehensive studies initiated by the Congress, the executive branch and interested private groups have been completed and all point in the same direction.

Governments at every level—Federal, State, and local—private foundations and individual citizens must all face up to their responsibilities in this area.

Ibid.

27 / FEDERAL AID

. . . I am proposing a new approach to mental illness and to mental retardation. This approach is designed, in large measure, to use Federal resources to stimulate State, local, and private action. When carried out, reliance on the cold mercy of custodial isolation will be supplanted by the open warmth of community concern and capability. Emphasis on prevention, treatment, and rehabilitation will be substituted for a desultory interest in confining patients in an institution to wither away.

Ibid.

28 / COMMUNITY-BASED SERVICES

Services to both the mentally ill and to the mentally retarded must be community based and provide a range of services to meet community needs.

Ibid.

29 / FURTHER PROCRASTINATION UNJUSTIFIED

We cannot afford to postpone any longer a reversal in our approach to mental affliction. For too long the shabby treatment of the many millions of the mentally disabled in custodial institutions and many millions more now in communities needing help has been justified on grounds of inadequate funds, further studies and future promises. We can procrastinate no more. The national mental health program and the national program to combat mental retardation herein proposed warrant prompt congressional attention.

Ibid.

30 / AN IMPORTANT LANDMARK

It gives me great pleasure to approve this bill, the Mills-Ribicoff bill, which strengthens our maternal and child health and crippled children services. It will initiate a new program of comprehensive maternity and infant care, aimed directly at preventing mental retardation. It will help to arouse local communities to a major attack on the problems of mental retardation. . . . Studies indicate that much of this suffering is preventable—that we can prevent what cannot afterwards be cured. Infants born prematurely are 10 times more likely to be mentally retarded. Mothers who have not received adequate prenatal care are two to three times more likely to give birth to premature babies. Yet, in 132 large cities, studies have shown that an estimated 455,000 mothers are unable to pay for health care during pregnancy and after birth. This bill will help insure that no child need be born retarded for such reasons, which are wholly in our control. . . . Enactment of this legislation is, therefore, an important landmark in our drive to eliminate one of the major health hazards affecting mankind. We can say with some assurance that, although children may be the victims of fate, they will not be the victims of our neglect.

Remarks on signing the maternal and child health and mental retardation planning bill, Oct. 24, 1963

Problems of the Aged

31 / CARE OF THE ELDERLY: OUR GROWING PROBLEM

On the basis of his study of the world's civilizations, the historian Toynbee concluded that a society's quality and durability can best be measured "by the respect and care given its elderly citizens." Never before in our history have we had so many "senior citizens." There are present today in our population 17½ million people aged 65 years or over, nearly one-tenth of our population—and their number increases by 1,000 every day. By 1980, they will number nearly 25 million. Today there are already 25 million people aged 60 and over, nearly 6 million aged 75 and over, and more than 10,000 over the age of 100.

> Message to Congress on problems of the aged, Feb. 21, 1963

32 / INSECURITY

A medical revolution has extended the life of our elder citizens without providing the dignity and security those later years deserve.

> Acceptance speech, Democratic National Convention, Los Angeles, July 15, 1960

33 / HARDSHIP

Prolonged and costly illness in later years robs too many of our elder citizens of pride, purpose and savings.

> Message to Congress on the nation's health needs, Feb. 27, 1962

34 / COST OF MEDICAL CARE

No costs have increased more rapidly in the last decade than the cost of medical care. And no group of Americans has felt the impact of these skyrocketing costs more than our older citizens.

> Address, Franklin D. Roosevelt memorial program on 25th anniversary of signing of Social Security Act, Hyde Park, N.Y., Aug. 14, 1960

35 / A SIGNIFICANT GAP IN SOCIAL SECURITY

Twenty-six years ago this nation adopted the principle that every member of the labor force and his family should be insured against the haunting fear of loss of income caused by retirement, death, or unemployment. To that we have added insurance against the economic loss caused by disability. But there remains a significant gap that denies to all but those with the highest incomes a full measure of security—the high cost of ill health in old age.

Message to Congress on a health program, Feb. 9, 1961

36 / PROPOSAL TO ADD SENIOR-CITIZEN HEALTH INSURANCE TO THE SOCIAL SECURITY SYSTEM

A proud and resourceful nation can no longer ask its older people to live in constant fear of a serious illness for which adequate funds are not available. We owe them the right of dignity in sickness as well as in health. We can achieve this by adding health insurance—primarily hospitalization insurance—to our successful social security system. Hospital insurance for our older citizens on social security offers a reasonable and practical solution to a critical problem. It is the logical extension of a principle established 28 years ago in the social security system and confirmed many times since by both Congress and the American voters. It is based on the fundamental premise that contributions during the working years, matched by employers' contributions, would enable people to prepay and build earned rights and benefits to safeguard them in their old age.

Message to Congress on problems of the aged, Feb. 21, 1963

37 / SUBSTANDARD INCOMES

This is not 1935—or 1945. This is 1960—and today there are 16 million Americans past the age of 65; 3 out of every 5 of these—more than 9½ million people—must struggle to survive on an income of less than $1,000 a year; 3 million receive less than $2,000 from all sources combined; and those who draw social security receive an average check of $72 a month which—in 1960 dollars—does not begin to do the job. With the cost of living continually spiraling upward, with the cost of basic items continually rising—$72 a month or $1,000 a year cannot pay for even the most basic rudiments of a decent and dignified old age. And, even worse, the substandard incomes—the poverty and neglect—dissipate and destroy the morale, the self-respect, the personal pride of our older citizens.

Address, Franklin D. Roosevelt memorial program on 25th anniversary of signing of Social Security Act, Hyde Park, N.Y., Aug. 14, 1960

38 / IMPROVING SOCIAL SECURITY INSURANCE

The OASDI * system is the basic income maintenance program for our older people. It serves a vital purpose. But it must be kept up to date.

Message to Congress on problems of the aged, Feb. 21, 1963

* Old-age Survivors and Disability Insurance.

39 / NEED OF BETTER DIET

Too many elderly people with small incomes skimp on food at a time when their health requires greater quantity, variety, and balance in their diets. The pilot food stamp program recommended in my farm message [1.31.63] could improve their nutrition and health.

Ibid.

40 / FOOD AND DRUG PROTECTION

Measures which safeguard consumers against both actual danger and monetary loss resulting from frauds in sales of unnecessary or worthless dietary preparations, devices, and nostrums are especially important to the elderly. It has been estimated that consumers waste $500 million a year on medical quackery and another $500 million dollars annually on some "health foods" which have no beneficial effect. The health of the aged is in jeopardy from harmful and useless products and they are unable to bear the financial loss from worthless products. Unnecessary deaths, injuries, and financial loss to our senior citizens can be expected to continue until the law requires adequate testing for safety and efficacy of products and devices before they are made available to consumers. I therefore . . . urge that the Congress extend the provisions of the Food, Drug, and Cosmetic Act of 1938 to include testing of the safety and effectiveness of therapeutic devices, to extend existing requirements for label warnings to include household articles which are subject to the Food, Drug, and Cosmetic Act, and to extend adequate factory inspection to foods, over-the-counter drugs, devices, and cosmetics.

Ibid.

41 / NEED OF BETTER MENTAL CARE

Too many senior citizens are wasting away in obsolete mental institutions without adequate treatment or care. The mental health program previously recommended [5.5.63] can help restore many of them to their communities and homes.

Ibid.

42 / SPECIAL HOUSING NEEDS: PROPOSAL OF ADDITIONAL AID

The elderly have special needs for housing designed to sustain their independence even when disability occurs, and to promote dignity, self-respect, and usefulness in later years. Yet millions of older people are forced to live in inferior homes because they cannot find or afford better. Nearly half of our people 65 and older, it has been estimated, live in substandard housing or in housing unsuited to their special needs.

Ibid.

43 / PARTICULAR HOUSING ACCOMODATIONS REQUIRED

The housing problem of the elderly is attributable only in part to low incomes—many have physical infirmities limiting their activities; many need access to special community services. Special equipment and apartment designs can make their home life safer and more comfortable.

Message to Congress on housing and community development, March 9, 1961

44 / LIMITED OPPORTUNITIES FOR OLDER WORKERS

Retirement . . . should be through choice, not through compulsion due to the lack of employment opportunities. For many of our aged, social security and retirement benefits are not a satisfactory substitute for a pay check. Many of those who are able to work need to work and want to work. But, often knowingly and sometimes unwittingly, industrialization and related social and economic trends have progressively limited the possibilities for gainful employment of our older citizens.

Message to Congress on problems of the aged, Feb. 21, 1963

45 / ECONOMIC WASTE OF EXPERIENCE

Denial of employment opportunity to older persons is a personal tragedy. It is also a national extravagance, wasteful of human resources. No economy can reach its maximum productivity while failing to use the skills, talents, and experience of willing workers.

Ibid.

46 / EFFICIENCY OF OLDER WORKERS

Rules of employment that are based on the calendar rather than upon ability are not good rules, nor are they realistic. Studies of the Department of Labor show that large numbers of older workers can exceed the average performance of younger workers, and with added steadiness, loyalty, and dependability.

Ibid.

47 / EDUCATIONAL OPPORTUNITY

Of the more than 17½ million persons aged 65 and over, about 14 million did not finish high school, some 6 million of these did not finish grade school, and over 1 million received no education at all. The comprehensive education program previously recommended [1.29.63] would encourage Federal-State programs of general university extension for those previously unable to take college courses, and adult basic education for those who are considered to be functionally illiterate. The largest percentage of illiteracy still existing in this country is found among men and women 65 and over. To gain the ability to read and write could bring them a new vision of the world in their later years. Increased library services provided under this program would also be of particular interest to older people.

Ibid.

48 / COMMUNITY ACTION

The heart of our program for the elderly must be opportunity for and actual service to our older citizens in their home communities. The loneliness or apathy which exists among many of our aged is heightened by the wall of inertia which often exists between them and their community. We must remove this wall by planned, comprehensive action to stimulate or provide not only opportunities for employment and community services by our older citizens but the full range of the various facilities and services which aged individuals need for comfortable and meaningful life. I believe that in each State government specific responsibility should be clearly assigned for stimulating and coordinating programs on aging; and that every locality of 25,000 population or above should make similar provision, possibly in the form of a community health and welfare council with a strong section on aging. The Federal Government can assume a significant leadership role in stimulating such actions. To do this, I recommend a 5-year program of assistance to State and local agencies and voluntary organizations for planning and developing services; for research, demonstration, and training projects leading to new or improved programs to aid older people; and for construction, renovation, and equipment of public and nonprofit multipurpose activity and recreational centers for the elderly.

Ibid.

49 / ROOM FOR IMPROVEMENT

Our national record in providing for our aged is a proud and hopeful one. But it can and must improve. We can continue to move forward by building needed Federal programs, by developing means for comprehensive action in our communities, and by doing all we can, as a nation and as individuals, to enable our senior citizens to achieve both a better standard of life and a more active, useful and meaningful role in a society that owes them much and can still learn much from them.

Ibid.

Youth

50 / AMERICA'S DESTINY

The future promise of any nation can be directly measured by the present prospects of its youth. This nation—facing increasingly complex economic, social and international challenges—is increasingly dependent on the opportunities, capabilities, and vitality of those who are soon to bear its chief responsibilities.

Message to Congress on the nation's youth, Feb. 14, 1963

51 / YOUTH'S OPPORTUNITIES

This is still the greatest nation in the world in which a child can be born and raised. His freedom, his security, his opportunity, his prospects for a full and happy life are greater here than any place on earth. We do not conceal the problems and imperfections which still confront our youth —but they are in large part a reflection of the growing number of youth in this country today.

Ibid.

52 / GAINFUL INVESTMENT

To the extent that the nation is called upon to promote and protect the interests of our younger citizens, it is an investment certain to bring a high return, not only in basic human values but in social and economic terms.

Ibid.

53 / PRIORITY

The needs of children should not be made to wait.

Ibid.

54 / SERVING POSTERITY

If we serve them better now, they will serve their nation better when the burdens are theirs alone.

Ibid.

55 / PRIMARY INFLUENCE: HOME AND FAMILY

A child's opportunity and development are shaped first and most by the strength or weakness of his home and family situation.

Ibid.

56 / THE GROUNDWORK

When the youngest child alive today has grown to the cares of manhood, our position in the world will be determined first of all by what provisions we make today—for his education, his health, his opportunities for a good home and a good job and a good life.

State of the Union Message, Jan. 11, 1962

57 / ATTENTION TO YOUNG PEOPLE

We must start, in America, to pay a good deal more attention to our young people. We must start to plan much more systematically to open up the channels and to provide greater opportunities for each young American to develop his own God-given talents to the fullest of his capacity and his initiative. Above all we must provide the kind of leadership which will challenge the very best that is within our young people, and will guide them to the execution of the vital tasks which the common welfare of men on earth demands.

Campaign message to the nation's new voters, Washington, D.C., Oct. 5, 1960

58 / LACK OF OPPORTUNITY: BASIC CAUSE OF JUVENILE INFRACTIONS

A common subject of discussion in midcentury America is assigning the blame for our mounting juvenile delinquency—to parents, schools, courts, communities, and others, including the children themselves. There is no single answer—and no single cause or cure. But surely the place to begin is the malady which underlies so much of youthful frustration, rebellion and idleness; and that malady is a lack of opportunity. This lack cannot be cured without a more perfect educational and vocational training system, a more prosperous full employment economy, the removal of racial barriers, and the elimination of slum housing and dilapidated neighborhoods.

Message to Congress on the nation's youth, Feb. 14, 1963

59 / ECONOMICALLY UNDERPRIVILEGED CHILDREN

Some 16 million children live in families with incomes so low that Federal income tax reduction is of no direct benefit because they are not required to pay taxes now.

Ibid.

60 / DISADVANTAGED CHILDREN

At least one out of eight children is affected by divorce, desertion, or mental illness in the family.

Ibid.

61 / FEDERAL CONCERN

Juvenile delinquency is of direct national concern. . . . The Federal Government should mobilize its resources to provide leadership and direction in a national effort (*a*) to strengthen and correlate, at all levels of government, existing juvenile and youth services; (*b*) to train more personnel for juvenile and youth programs; and (*c*) to encourage research and planning for more effective measures for the prevention, treatment and control of juvenile delinquency.

Ibid.

62 / PROPOSED YOUTH EMPLOYMENT ACT

First, a Youth Conservation Corps would be established, putting young men to work improving our forests and recreation areas. This would initially provide useful training and work for 15,000 youths. Second, the Federal Government will provide half the wages and related costs for young persons employed on local projects that offer useful work experience in nonprofit community services—such as hospitals, schools, parks, and settlement houses. Forty thousand youths can be employed in the first year in this part of the program.

This bill is a measure of the first priority. The effects of unemployment are nowhere more depressing and disheartening than among the young. Common sense and justice compel establishment of this program, which will give many thousands of currently unemployed young persons a chance to find employment, to be paid for their services, and to acquire skills and work experience that will give them a solid start in their working lives.

Ibid.

Poverty in the Midst of Prosperity

63 / AMERICAN HUMANITARIANISM

Few nations do more than the United States to assist their least fortunate citizens—to make certain that no child, no elderly or handicapped citizen, no family in any circumstances in any state, is left without the essential needs for a decent and healthy existence. In too few nations, I might add, are the people aware of the progressive strides this country has taken in demonstrating the humanitarian side of freedom. Our record is a proud one—and it sharply refutes those who accuse us of thinking only in the materialistic terms of cash registers and calculating machines.

Message to Congress on welfare programs, Feb. 1, 1962

64 / BASIC OBLIGATION

If a free society cannot help the many who are poor, it cannot save the few who are rich.

Inaugural address, Jan. 20, 1961

65 / INHERITED POVERTY

There is inherited wealth in this country and also inherited poverty.

Address, Amherst College, Mass., Oct. 26, 1963

66 / SPIRITUAL NEEDS

The quality of American life must keep pace with the quantity of American goods. This country cannot afford to be materially rich and spiritually desperately poor.

State of the Union Message, Jan. 14, 1963

67 / FOR ALL

Our concern is a better life for all Americans.

Campaign address, Billings, Mont., Sept. 22, 1960

68 / ENDLESS STRUGGLE

The war against poverty and degradation is not yet over.

Address, Franklin D. Roosevelt memorial program on 25th anniversary of signing of Social Security Act, Hyde Park, N.Y., Aug. 14, 1960

69 / CONTINUING FIGHT

The fight to eliminate poverty and human exploitation goes on in our day.

> Acceptance speech, Liberal Party Convention, New York City, Sept. 14, 1960

70 / DIFFICULT OBJECTIVE

The conquest of poverty is as difficult as the conquest of outer space.

> Address, reception for Latin American diplomats, Washington, D.C., March 13, 1962

71 / MATTERS OF CONSCIENCE

We can no longer tolerate growing patches of poverty and injustice in America—substandard wages, unemployment, city slums, inadequate medical care, inferior education, and the sad plight of migratory workers.

> Senate address on fair labor standards, Aug. 10, 1960

72 / CONSIDERATION FOR VICTIMS OF UNEMPLOYMENT

We have long since decided as a nation that we will not turn our backs upon workers and their families undergoing the hardships of unemployment.

> Message to Congress on the economy, Feb. 2, 1961

73 / FREEDOM'S WORK

Our concern is with the improvement of free institutions.

> Campaign address, Billings, Mont., Sept. 22, 1960

74 / FOR SOME, THE PROMISE UNFULFILLED

For some of our people, the promise of the revolution is not yet known —poverty, illiteracy and racial prejudice block its fulfillment in their lives.

> Message to the 72nd Continental Congress of the Daughters of the American Revolution, Washington, D.C., April 15, 1963

75 / UNFINISHED BUSINESS

As long as there are 15 million American homes in the United States substandard, as long as there are 5 million American homes in the cities of the

United States which lack plumbing of any kind, as long as 17 million Americans live on inadequate assistance when they get older, then I think we have unfinished business in this country.

Campaign remarks, Niagara Falls, N.Y., Sept. 28, 1960

76 / SOCIAL GOAL

The policy of this Administration is to give to the individual the opportunity to realize his own highest possibilities. Our program is to open to all the opportunity for steady and productive employment, to remove from all the handicap of arbitrary or irrational exclusion, to offer to all the facilities for education and health and welfare, to make society the servant of the individual and the individual the source of progress, and thus to realize for all the full promise of American life.

State of the Union Message, Jan. 11, 1962

77 / PURPOSE OF NATIONAL WEALTH

A strong America cannot neglect the aspirations of its citizens—the welfare of the needy, the health care of the elderly, the education of the young. For we are not developing the nation's wealth for its own sake. Wealth is the means and people are the ends. All our material riches will avail us little if we do not use them to expand the opportunities of our people.

Ibid.

78 / SHARING PROSPERITY

Increasingly in our lifetime, American prosperity has been widely shared and it must continue so. The spread of primary, secondary and higher education, the wider availability of medical services, and the improved post-war performance of our economy have bettered the economic status of the poorest families and individuals.

But prosperity has not wiped out poverty. In 1960, seven million families and individuals had personal incomes lower than $2,000. In part, our failure to overcome poverty is a consequence of our failure to operate the economy at potential. The incidence of unemployment is always uneven, and increases in unemployment tend to inflict the greatest income loss on those least able to afford it. But there is a claim on our conscience from others, whose poverty is barely touched by cyclical improvements in general economic activity. To an increasing extent, the poorest families in America are those headed by women, the elderly, non-

whites, migratory workers, and the physically or mentally handicapped
—people who are short-changed even in time of prosperity.

Economic report to Congress, Jan. 22, 1962

79 / PRESENT-DAY CAUSES OF POVERTY

At the time [1935] the Social Security Act established our present basic
framework for public aid, the major cause of poverty was unemployment
and economic depression. Today, in a year of relative prosperity and high
employment, we are more concerned about the poverty that persists in
the midst of abundance.

The reasons are often more social than economic, more often subtle
than simple. Some are in need because they are untrained for work—some
because they cannot work, because they are too young or too old, blind
or crippled. Some are in need because they are discriminated against for
reasons they cannot help. Responding to their ills with scorn or suspicion
is inconsistent with our moral precepts and inconsistent with their nearly
universal preference to be independent. But merely responding with a
"relief check" to complicated social or personal problems—such as ill
health, faulty education, domestic discord, racial discrimination, or inadequate skills—is not likely to provide a lasting solution. Such a check must
be supplemented. Or in some cases made unnecessary, by positive services
and solutions, offering the total resources of the community to meet the
total needs of the family to help our less fortunate citizens help themselves.

Message to Congress on welfare programs, Feb. 1, 1962

80 / PUBLIC WELFARE GOALS

The goals of our public welfare programs must be positive and constructive—to create economic and social opportunities for the less fortunate—
to help them find productive, happy and independent lives. It must stress
the integrity and preservation of the family unit. It must contribute to
the attack on dependency, juvenile delinquency, family breakdown, ille-
gitimacy, ill health and disability. It must reduce the incidence of these
problems, prevent their occurrence and recurrence, and strengthen and
protect the vulnerable in a highly competitive world.

Ibid.

81 / MORE THAN SALVAGE

Public welfare . . . must be more than a salvage operation, picking up
the debris from the wreckage of human lives. Its emphasis must be di-

rected increasingly toward prevention and rehabilitation—on reducing not only the long-range cost in budgetary terms but the long-range cost in human terms as well. Poverty weakens individuals and nations. Sounder public welfare policies will benefit the nation, its economy, its morale, and, most importantly, its people.

    Ibid.

82 / CARE OF DEPENDENT CHILDREN

The prevention of future adult poverty and dependency must begin with the care of dependent children—those who must receive public welfare by virtue of a parent's death, disability, desertion or unemployment. Our society not only refuses to leave such children hungry, cold, and devoid of opportunity—we are insistent that such children not be community liabilities throughout their lives. Yet children who grow up in deprivation, without adequate protection, may be poorly equipped to meet adult responsibilities.

    Ibid.

83 / NEED FOR MORE VOLUNTEER SERVICE

Through the years millions of Americans have served their communities through the willing donation of their time and skill to voluntary private service organizations. But in a population growing in numbers, urbanization, and the recognition of social problems, we need not only more professional personnel—more doctors, nurses, teachers, and social workers—but an even greater number of dedicated volunteers to support the professional in every area of service.

    Message to Congress on the nation's youth, Feb. 14, 1963

84 / THE OPPORTUNITIES FOR SERVICE

Although the United States is the wealthiest nation the world has ever known, the poverty of millions of our people, and the need for training, assistance, and encouragement in numerous corners of our country—from teeming slum areas to those depressed rural areas virtually bypassed by technological and economic progress—provide fertile fields for those citizens with the desire and the ability to be of assistance.

    Ibid.

85 / RECOMMENDATION FOR A NATIONAL SERVICE CORPS

I . . . recommend legislation to establish a National Service Corps—a small carefully selected volunteer corps of men and women of all ages working under local direction with professional personnel and part-time local volunteers to help provide urgently needed services in mental health centers and hospitals, on Indian reservations, to the families of migrant workers, and in the educational and social institutions of hard-hit slum or rural poverty areas. This small task force of men and women will work in locally planned and initiated projects, at the invitation of community institutions, and under local supervision. The community's chief goal should properly be the development of the project to the point where local volunteers or paid staff workers could take over permanently the tasks initially undertaken by the corpsmen; and it is to be hoped that the example of men and women rendering this kind of full-time voluntary service would motivate many more Americans to participate on a part-time basis. This is not . . . a constructive channel for youthful energy and idealism only. Many of our senior citizens indicated their willingness to participate in this endeavor.

Ibid.

86 / POTENTIAL PERSONNEL

The National Service Corps . . . is designed for those citizens of every age, young and old, who wish to be of help, whose present skills, jobs, or aptitudes enable them to serve their community in meeting its most critical needs, and whose idealism and situation in life enable them to undertake such an assignment on a volunteer basis.

Ibid.

87 / SPIRIT OF IDEALISM

The National Service Corps—which will not be limited to young people —will add to and make use of this nation's wealth of idealism and strengthen its spirit.

Ibid.

Immigration

88 / QUOTA SYSTEM OF IMMIGRATION OUT OF DATE

The use of a national origins system is without basis in either logic or reason. It neither satisfies a national need nor accomplishes an international purpose. In an age of interdependence among nations, such a system is an anachronism, for it discriminates among applicants for admission into the United States on the basis of accident of birth.

Message to Congress on revising the immigration laws, July 23, 1963

89 / PURPOSE OF PROPOSALS TO LIBERALIZE IMMIGRATION STATUTES

The enactment of this legislation will . . . provide a sound basis upon which we can build in developing an immigration law that serves the national interest and reflects in every detail the principles of equality and human dignity to which our nation subscribes.

Ibid.

90 / PROPOSED FORMULA FOR REVISION OF THE IMMIGRATION LAWS

I recommend that there be substituted for the national origins system a formula governing immigration to the United States which takes into account (1) the skills of the immigrant and their relationships to our needs, (2) the family relationship between immigrants and persons already here, so that the reuniting of families is encouraged, and (3) the priority of registration. Present law . . . should be modified so that those with the greatest ability to add to the national welfare, no matter where they are born, are granted the highest priority. The next priority should go to those who seek to be reunited with their relatives. As between applicants with equal claims the earliest registrant should be the first admitted.

Ibid.

91 / ASIAN BAR SHOULD BE REMOVED

A special discriminatory formula is now used to regulate the immigration of persons who are attributable by their ancestry to an area called the Asia-Pacific triangle. This area embraces all countries from Pakistan to Japan and the Pacific islands north of Australia and New Zealand. Usually, the quota under which a prospective immigrant must enter is determined by his place of birth. However, if as much as one half of an immigrant's ancestors came from nations in the Asia-Pacific triangle, he must rely upon the small quota assigned to the country of his ancestry, regardless of where he was born. This provision of the law should be repealed.

Ibid.

Urban Affairs and Housing

92 / CENTERS OF POPULATION

Urban and suburban areas now contain the overwhelming majority of our population, and preponderance of our industrial, commercial, and educational resources.

Message to Congress on housing and community development, March 9, 1961

93 / URBAN POPULATION EXPLOSION

An urban population revolution has overcrowded our schools, cluttered up our suburbs, and increased the squalor of our slums.

> Acceptance speech, Democratic National Convention, Los Angeles, July 15, 1960

94 / CITY LIFE

The good life is still just a dream for too many of the people who live in cities.

> Campaign address, Urban Affairs Conference, Pittsburgh, Oct. 10, 1960

95 / URBAN BLIGHT

Today there are more people in the United States living in slums than on farms.

> Campaign message to the Urban Problems Press Conference, Washington, D.C., Sept. 9, 1960

96 / EFFORTS FOR IMPROVEMENT

A strong America depends on its cities—America's glory and sometimes America's shame. To substitute sunlight for congestion and progress for decay, we have stepped up existing urban renewal and housing programs and launched new ones; redoubled the attacks on water pollution, speeded aid to airports, hospitals, highways and our declining mass transit system, and secured new weapons to combat organized crime, racketeering, and youth delinquency, assisted by the coordinated and hard-hitting efforts of our investigative services: the F.B.I., the Internal Revenue Service, the Bureau of Narcotics and many others.

> State of the Union Message, Jan. 11, 1962

97 / PLANNING FOR URBAN AREAS

During the 1960's, we must have the energy and vision to lay sound foundations for meeting the problems which will result from the steady growth of our urban areas through the balance of this century.

> Message to Congress on the economy, Feb. 2, 1961

98 / PREPARATION FOR THE EXPANSION OF URBAN LIVING

In a few short decades we have passed from a rural to an urban way of life; in a few short decades more, we shall be a nation of vastly expanded population, living in expanded urban areas in housing that does not now exist, served by community facilities that do not now exist, moving about by means of systems of urban transportation that do not now exist. The challenge is great, and the time is short. I propose to act now to strengthen and improve the machinery through which, in large part, the Federal Government must act to carry out its proper role of encouragement and assistance to states and local governments, to voluntary efforts and to private enterprise, in the solution of these problems.

> Message to Congress recommending establishment of Department of Urban Affairs and Housing, Jan. 30, 1962

99 / ORDERLY DEVELOPMENT OF URBAN AREAS

The present and future problems of our cities are as complex as they are manifold. There must be expansion: but orderly and planned expansion, not explosion and sprawl. Basic public facilities must be extended ever further into the areas surrounding urban centers: but they must be planned and coordinated so as to favor rather than hamper the sound growth of our communities. The scourge of blight must be overcome, and the central core areas of our cities, with all their great richness of economic and cultural wealth, must be restored to lasting vitality. New values must be created to provide a more efficient local economy and provide revenues to support essential local services. Sound old housing must be conserved and improved, and new housing created, to serve better all income groups in our population and to move ever closer to the goal of a decent home in a suitable living environment for every American family. We will neglect our cities at our peril, for in neglecting them we neglect the nation.

> *Ibid.*

100 / ADEQUATE VOICE FOR CITY PEOPLE: PROPOSAL OF A DEPARTMENT OF URBAN AFFAIRS AND HOUSING OF CABINET RANK

Our cities and the people who live in and near them need and deserve an adequate voice in the highest councils of government. The Executive branch and the Congress need an adequate instrument to assist them in the formulation and execution of policy concerning urban affairs and housing. States and local governing bodies urgently need an agency at the departmental level to assist them in formulating and carrying out their local programs for dealing with these problems. All these needs can best be met through the establishment of the department provided for in this reorganization plan.

> *Ibid.*

101 / STAKE OF SMALLER CITIES IN PROPOSED FEDERAL DEPARTMENT

Hundreds of smaller cities and towns are located on or near the fringes of rapidly growing urban areas. The problems of the cities affect them today, and will be theirs tomorrow. Hundreds of other smaller towns and cities not now affected will be so situated a few short years hence. Thus, the smaller towns and cities have a stake in this proposal as vital as, and only a little less immediate than, that of our large urban centers.

Ibid.

102 / STATE RESPONSIBLITIES UNDIMINISHED BY PLAN FOR FEDERAL DEPARTMENT

The establishment of this department does not connote any bypassing or reduction of the constitutional powers and responsibilities of the states under our Federal system of government. Rather, the states must assume additional leadership in the future in dealing with problems of urban areas, and the department will maintain close working and consultative relationships with them.

Ibid.

103 / HAPHAZARD SUBURBAN EXPANSION

Land adjoining urban centers has been engulfed by urban development at the astounding rate of about 1 million acres a year. But the result has been haphazard and inefficient suburban expansion, and continued setbacks in the central cities' desperate struggle against blight and decay. Their social and economic base has been eroded by the movement of middle and upper income families to the suburbs, by the attendant loss of retail sales, and by the preference of many industrial firms for outlying locations.

Message to Congress on housing and community development, March 9, 1961

104 / NEED FOR PLANNED SUBURBAN DEVELOPMENT

Land is the most precious resource of the metropolitan area. The present patterns of haphazard suburban development are contributing to a tragic waste in the use of a vital resource now being consumed at an alarming rate. Open space must be reserved to provide parks and recreation, conserve water and other natural resources, prevent building in undesirable locations, prevent erosion and floods, and avoid the wasteful extension of public services. Open land is also needed to provide reserves for future residential development, to protect against undue speculation, and to make it possible for State and regional bodies to control the rate and character of community development.

Ibid.

105 / RESEARCH IN COMMUNITY DEVELOPMENT

As we proceed in developing a comprehensive housing and community development program we must constantly widen our knowledge of the complex forces which shape our urban way of life. Since the beginning of the century the proportion of our people who live in urban and suburban areas has mounted rapidly. Yet we have lagged badly in mobilizing the intellectual resources needed to understand and improve this important sector of our civilization. The problems related to the development and renewal of our cities and their environs have received comparatively little attention in research and teaching.

Ibid.

106 / OUR COMMUNITIES

Our communities are what we make them. We as a nation have before us the opportunity—and the responsibility—to remold our cities, to improve our patterns of community development, and provide for the housing needs of all segments of our population.

Ibid.

107 / DECENT LIVING ACCOMMODATIONS

I believe in an America where every family can live in a decent home in a decent neighborhood; where children can play safely; where no home is unsafe or unsanitary.

Campaign address, Convention Hall, Philadelphia, Oct. 31, 1960

108 / THE GOAL

One of the greatest challenges of the next decade is the challenge to provide a decent home in a decent neighborhood for every American.

Campaign message to the Urban Problems Press Conference, Washington, D.C., Sept. 9, 1960

109 / SQUALOR

Our cities are being engulfed in squalor. Twelve long years after Congress declared our goal to be "a decent home and a suitable environment for every American family," we still have 25,000,000 Americans living in substandard homes.

State of the Union Message, Jan. 30, 1961

110 / HOUSING POLICY

In 1949 the Congress, with great vision, announced our national housing policy of "a decent home and a suitable living environment for every American family." We have progressed since that time; but we must still redeem this pledge to the 14 million American families who currently live in substandard or deteriorating homes, and protect the other 39 million American families from the encroachment of blight and slums.

An equal challenge is the tremendous urban growth that lies ahead. Within 15 years our population will rise to 235 million and by the year 2,000 to 300 million people. Most of this increase will occur in and around urban areas. We must begin now to lay the foundation for livable, efficient, and attractive communities of the future.

Message to Congress on housing and community development, March 9, 1961

111 / THREE OBJECTIVES

Our policy for housing and community development must be directed toward the accomplishment of three basic national objectives: First, to renew our cities and assure sound growth of our rapidly expanding metropolitan areas. Second, to provide decent housing for all of our people. Third, to encourage a prosperous and efficient construction industry as an essential component of general economic prosperity and growth.

Ibid.

112 / LOW-RENT HOUSING

Government housing subsidies are required for families with very low incomes. Public housing is the only housing they can afford; yet public housing is too often unavailable. Unless we increase the supply of low-rent housing, our communities cannot rid themselves of slums, provide adequate community facilities, and rehouse low-income families displaced by clearance operations.

Ibid.

14

Natural Resources

Conservation

1 / CARE OF MOTHER EARTH

The earth can be an abundant mother if we learn to use her with skill and wisdom—to tend her wounds, replenish her vitality, and utilize her potentialities.

> Address, centennial meeting of the National Academy of Sciences, Washington, D.C., Oct. 22, 1963

2 / FOR POSTERITY

Since we seek abundance for our children as well as for ourselves, we must conserve and use wisely our resources of land and water.

> Message to Congress on agriculture, Jan. 31, 1962

3 / BASIC IMPORTANCE

Our entire society rests upon—and is dependent upon—our water, our land, our forests, and our minerals. How we use these resources influences our health, security, economy, and well-being.

> Message to Congress on natural resources, Feb. 23, 1961

4 / FORTUNATE NATION

From the beginning of civilization, every nation's basic wealth and progress has stemmed in large measure from its natural resources. This nation has been, and is now, especially fortunate in the blessings we have inherited.

Ibid.

5 / NEED FOR PLANNED CONSERVATION

If we fail to chart a proper course of conservation and development—if we fail to use these blessings prudently—we will be in trouble within a short time. In the resource field, predictions of future use have been consistently understated. But even under conservative projections, we face a future of critical shortages and handicaps. By the year 2,000, a U.S. population of 300 million—nearly doubled in 40 years—will need far greater supplies of farm products, timber, water, minerals, fuels, energy, and opportunities for outdoor recreation. Present projections tell us that our water use will double in the next 20 years; that we are harvesting our supply of high-grade timber more rapidly than the development of new growth; that too much of our fertile topsoil is being washed away; that our minerals are being exhausted at increasing rates; and that the nation's remaining undeveloped areas of great natural beauty are being rapidly preempted for other uses.

Ibid.

6 / FORESIGHT AND ACTION

Actions deferred are all too often opportunities lost, particularly in safeguarding our natural resources.

Letter to the President of the Senate, Lyndon B. Johnson, and the Speaker of the House of Representatives, John W. McCormack, on the expansion of outdoor recreation resources, Washington, D.C., Feb. 14, 1963

7 / MAKE TIME OUR FRIEND

In the work of conservation, time should be made our friend, not our adversary. . . . And in terms of financial outlay, dollars invested today will yield great benefits in the years to come.

Message to Congress on conservation, March 1, 1962

8 / BASIC FACTOR

Implicit in the conservation thesis of wise use, improvement, preservation and restoration of our resources is the basic requirement of greater scientific knowledge and improved resources management.

Ibid.

9 / PRACTICE OF CONSERVATION

We depend on our natural resources to sustain us, but in turn their continued availability must depend on our using them prudently, improving them wisely, and where possible, restoring them promptly. We must reaffirm our dedication to the sound practices of conservation, which can be defined as the wise use of our natural environment; it is, in the final analysis, the highest form of national thrift—the prevention of waste and despoilment while preserving, improving and renewing the quality and usefulness of all our resources. Our deep spiritual confidence that this nation will survive the perils of today, which may well be with us for decades to come, compels us to invest in our nation's future, to consider and meet our obligations to our children and the numberless generations that will follow.

    Ibid.

10 / MOVING AHEAD

You cannot possibly move ahead in this country, we cannot possibly develop our resources, we cannot possibly develop our strength unless we make the best use we can of the land, the water, the minerals, that have been given to us and which have made our country great.

    Campaign address, Saginaw, Mich., Oct. 14, 1960

11 / DENIAL OF HERITAGE

If we continue to ignore the polluting of our streams, the littering of our national forests, we will be denying to ourselves and to our children a heritage which we were the beneficiaries of.

    Campaign address, Valley Forge, Pa., Oct. 29, 1960

Development of Natural Resources

12 / RESOURCE NEEDS

The economic growth of the United States has been favored by an abundant supply of natural resources of almost every sort. But resource needs and supplies are not static. As our needs mount, as past reserves are depleted, and as technological requirements change, we must constantly develop new supplies if growth is not to be inhibited.

    Message to Congress on the economy, Feb. 2, 1961

13 / PROGRAM OF DEVELOPMENT

We will apply to the development of our resources the same scientific talents and energies which we have applied to the development of our national defenses, inquiring into methods of preventing evaporation, of controlling weather, of retaining snowpacks, above all, of converting salt water to fresh water.

> Campaign address, Billings, Mont., Sept. 22, 1960

14 / PUBLIC DEVELOPMENT

In the long run, the public development of natural resources too vast for private capital—and federally encouraged research, especially basic research—are both sources of tremendous economic progress.

> Campaign address, Associated Business Publications Conference, New York City, Oct. 12, 1960

15 / NATIONAL EFFORT REQUIRED

Only a national effort can explore the mysteries of outer space, harvest the products of ocean depths and mobilize the human, natural and material resources of our land.

> Address, 30th anniversary of the Tennessee Valley Authority, Muscle Shoals, Ala., May 18, 1963

Land

16 / EFFICIENT CONSERVATION AND UTILIZATION OF LAND

The scope of agricultural technology promises abundance tomorrow as well as today. For the first time in our history we can confidently predict that our future food and fiber needs can be met with fewer acres of cropland. In spite of a 65,000,000 increase in population by 1980, our farms will be able to produce all we need with 50,000,000 fewer acres than we have in cropland today.

This prospect offers us an opportunity to take advantage of the unused acres for a wide range of recreational, esthetic, and economic purposes. Land use changes are not only important to balanced production, they can also supply the growing demand for outdoor recreational areas and wildlife promotion, for woodlots and forests, and for grazing. We can transfer cropland to grass and trees—and we can place greater emphasis on wildlife and recreation development in the small watershed programs.

Message to Congress on agriculture, Jan. 31, 1962

17 / PRESERVING OUR FORESTS

Our forest lands present the sharpest challenge to our foresight. Trees planted today will not reach the minimum sizes needed for lumber until the year 2000. Most projections of future timber requirements predict a doubling of current consumption within 40 years. At present cutting rates, we are using up our old growth timber in Western stands. Because of the time requirements involved, we must move now to meet anticipated future needs, and improve the productivity of our nearly 500 million acres of commercial forest land.

Message to Congress on natural resources, Feb. 23, 1961

18 / USE OF PUBLIC LANDS

The Federal Government owns nearly 770 million acres of public land, much of it devoted to a variety of essential uses. But equally important are the vacant, unappropriated, and unreserved public domain lands, amounting to some 477 million acres—a vital national reserve that should be devoted to productive use now and maintained for future generations.

Ibid.

Water

19 / WATER RESOURCES

Our nation has been blessed with a bountiful supply of water; but it is not a blessing we can regard with complacency. We now use over 300 billion gallons of water a day, much of it wastefully.

Ibid.

20 / KEY TO NATIONAL DEVELOPMENT

Our nation's progress is reflected in the history of our great river systems. The water that courses through our rivers and streams holds the key to full national development. Uncontrolled, it wipes out homes, lives and dreams, bringing disaster in the form of floods. Controlled, it is an effective artery of transportation, a boon to industrial development, a source of beauty and recreation, and the means of turning arid areas into rich and versatile cropland. In no resource field are conservation principles more applicable. By 1980, it is estimated our national water needs will nearly double; by the end of the century they will triple. But the quality of water which nature supplies will remain almost constant.

Our goal, therefore, is to have sufficient water sufficiently clean in the right place at the right time to serve the range of human and industrial needs. And we must harmonize conflicting objectives. For example, irrigation v. navigation, multiple-purpose reservoirs v. scenic park sites. Comprehensive and integrated planning is the only solution of this problem, requiring cooperative efforts at all levels of government.

Message to Congress on conservation, March 1, 1962

21 / ECONOMIC IMPORTANCE

No State, no region, no nation in the world today can be economically strong without an adequate supply of water. . . . already the water shortage is nationwide in scope.

Campaign address, Billings, Mont., Sept. 22, 1960

22 / FLOODS AND SHORTAGES

Our supply of water is not always consistent with our needs of time and place. Floods one day in one section may be countered in other days or in other sections by the severe water shortages which are now afflicting many eastern urban areas and are particularly critical in the West.

Message to Congress on natural resources, Feb. 23, 1961

23 / WATER POLLUTION

I can imagine nothing more wasteful than to pollute our rivers and permit valuable water to flow to the sea in conditions where other people cannot use it. Our goal must be the fullest utilization of every drop and gallon of water in every river system in America.

Campaign address, Billings, Mont., Sept. 22, 1960

24 / WATER POLLUTION CONTROL

Pollution of our country's rivers and streams has—as a result of our rapid population and industrial growth and change—reached alarming proportions. To meet all needs—domestic, agricultural, industrial, recreational —we shall have to use and reuse the same water, maintaining quality as well as quantity. In many areas of the country we need new sources of supply—but in all areas we must protect the supplies we have. Current corrective efforts are not adequate.

Message to Congress on natural resources, Feb. 23, 1961

25 / MILLIONS AFFECTED BY WATER POLLUTION

We must . . . continue our fight against water pollution because 31,000,000 Americans . . . live in communities where untreated or inadequately treated sewage is being discharged into their rivers and streams.

Address, American Society of Newspaper Editors, Washington, D.C., April 19, 1963

26 / ECONOMIC IMPROVEMENT THROUGH POLLUTION CONTROL

Cleaning up our great rivers would not only increase opportunity for fishermen ten or twenty fold, it would do it in areas where population is concentrated and where those opportunities are most urgently needed.

Campaign statement on recreation, Washington, D.C., Oct. 28, 1960

27 / TO BENEFIT ALL AREAS

Our available water supply must be used to give maximum benefits for all purposes—hydroelectric power, irrigation and reclamation, navigation, recreation, health, home, and industry. If all areas of the country are to enjoy a balanced growth, our Federal reclamation and other water resource programs will have to give increased attention to municipal and industrial water and power supplies as well as irrigation and land redemption.

Message to Congress on natural resources, Feb. 23, 1961

28 / SALINE WATER CONVERSION

No water resources program is of greater long-range importance—for relief not only of our shortages, but for arid nations the world over—than our efforts to find an effective and economical way to convert water from the world's greatest, cheapest natural resources—our oceans—into water fit for consumption in the home and by industry. Such a breakthrough would end bitter struggles between neighbors, states, and nations —and bring new hope for millions who live out their lives in dire shortage of usable water and all its physical and economical blessings, though living on the edge of a great body of water throughout that parched lifetime. This Administration is currently engaged in redoubled efforts to select the most promising approaches to economic desalinization of ocean and brackish waters, and then focus our energies more intensively on those approaches. . . .

I now pledge that, when this know-how is achieved, it will immediately be made available to every nation in the world who wishes it, along with appropriate technical and other assistance for its use. Indeed the United States welcomes now the cooperation of all other nations who wish to join this effort at present.

Ibid.

29 / STAKE IN QUEST FOR ECONOMICAL DESALINIZATION OF SEA WATER

. . . whichever nation wins that race, to develop an economical way of using our seas for plants and human consumption, will have done more to win the friendship of people who live in deserts around great oceans than all the sputniks in outer space.

Campaign address, Billings, Mont., Sept. 22, 1960

30 / OCEAN RESOURCES

The sea around us represents one of our most important but least understood and almost wholly undeveloped areas for extending our resource base. Continental shelves bordering the United States contain roughly 20 percent of our remaining reserves of crude oil and natural gas. The ocean floor contains large and valuable deposits of cobalt, copper, nickel, and manganese. Ocean waters themselves contain a wide variety of dissolved salts and minerals. Salt (and fresh water) fisheries are among our most important but far from fully developed reservoirs of protein foods. At present levels of use, this country alone will need an additional 3 billion pounds of fish and shellfish annually by 1980, and many other countries with large-scale protein deficiency can be greatly helped by more extensive use of marine foodstuffs. But all this will require increased efforts, under Federal leadership, for rehabilitation of depleted stocks of salmon and sardines in the Pacific, groundfish and oysters in the Atlantic, lake trout and other desirable species in the Great Lakes, and many others through biological research, development of methods for passing fish over dams, and control of pollution. This Administration intends to give concerted attention to our whole national effort in the basic and applied research of oceanography.

Message to Congress on natural resources, Feb. 23, 1961

31 / BELOVED OCEAN

I know that all of you share the great affection we have for that ever-changing ocean upon which we so much depend.

> Remarks on reviewing the Coast Guard training bark *Eagle*, Navy Yard Annex, Anacostia River, Aug. 15, 1962

Air

32 / AIR POLLUTION CONTROL

. . . air pollution, [is] a serious hazard to the health of our people that causes an estimated $7.5 billion annually in damage to vegetation, livestock, metals, and other materials. We need an effective Federal air pollution control program now. For although the total supply of air is vast, the atmosphere over our growing metropolitan areas—where more than half the people live—has only limited capacity to dilute and disperse the contaminants now being increasingly discharged from homes, factories, vehicles, and many other sources.

> Message to Congress on natural resources, Feb. 23, 1961

Power

33 / THE KEY

The key to this century is power—power on the farm as well as the factory—power in the country as well as the city.

> Address, Oahe Dam, Oahe, S.D., Aug. 17, 1962

34 / POWER DEVELOPMENT

One of the major challenges in resource conservation lies in the orderly development and efficient utilization of energy resources to meet the nation's electric power needs, needs which double every decade. The goal of this Administration is to insure an abundance of low-cost power for all consumers—urban and rural, industrial and domestic. To achieve this we must use more effectively all sources of fuel, find cheaper ways to harness nuclear energy, develop our hydroelectric potential, utilize presently unused heat produced by nature or as a by-product of industrial processes, and even capture the energy of the tides, where feasible.

> Message to Congress on conservation, March 1, 1962

35 / EXPANSION OF POWER FACILITIES

To keep pace with the growth of our economy and national defense requirements, expansion of this nation's power facilities will require intensive effort by all segments of our power industry. Through 1980, according to present estimates of the Federal Power Commission, total installed capacity should triple if we are to meet our nation's need for essential economic growth. Sustained heavy expansion by all power suppliers—public, cooperative, and private—is clearly needed.

Message to Congress on natural resources, Feb. 23, 1961

36 / PUBLIC AND PRIVATE PARTICIPATION

We look forward to the day when energy will flow whenever and wherever the demand requires through physically integrated supply systems owned and operated by both private and public institutions within our traditional framework of competition.

Address, Oahe Dam, Oahe, S.D., Aug. 17, 1962

37 / COMPETITIVE SHORTSIGHTEDNESS AND WASTE

If the railroads prevent coal slurry pipelines from conveying the resources of our mines—if the mining interests prevent the use of nuclear energy for public and private transmission—if public and private power interests veto each other's progress, or if one region refuses to permit another to share its abundance—then we shall be entering a decade of challenge and crisis with an inexcusable, vulnerable attitude of waste. And the American people will be the losers.

Ibid.

Recreational Facilities

38 / RECREATIONAL NEEDS

America's health, morale, and culture have long benefited from our national parks and forests, and our fish and wildlife opportunities. Yet these facilities and resources are not now adequate to meet the needs of a fast-growing, more mobile population.

Message to Congress on natural resources, Feb. 23, 1961

39 / DEMAND FOR OUTDOOR RECREATION

The demand for outdoor recreation is growing dramatically. Americans are seeking the out of doors as never before—about 90 percent participate annually in some form of outdoor recreation.

> Letter to the President of the Senate, Lyndon B. Johnson, and the Speaker of the House of Representatives, John W. McCormack, on the expansion of outdoor recreation resources, Washington, D.C., Feb. 14, 1963

40 / ADEQUATE RECREATIONAL FACILITIES BASIC TO CONSERVATION

Adequate outdoor recreational facilities are among the basic requirements of a sound national conservation program. The increased leisure time enjoyed by our growing population and the greater mobility made possible by improved highway networks have dramatically increased the nation's need for additional recreational areas. The 341,000,000 visits to Federal land and water areas recorded in 1960 are expected to double by 1970 and to increase fivefold by the end of the century. The need for an aggressive program of recreational development is both real and immediate.

> Message to Congress on conservation, March 1, 1962

41 / RECREATIONAL USES OF LAND AND WATER

Land and water not needed to produce food and fiber should be directed to alternative uses of benefit to the nation.

> Message to Congress on agriculture, Jan. 31, 1962

42 / NEED FOR A LAND ACQUISITION PROGRAM

Our magnificent national parks, monuments, forests, and wildlife refuges were in most cases either donated by States or private citizens or carved out of the public domain, and . . . these sources can no longer be relied upon. The nation needs a land acquisition program to preserve both prime Federal and State areas for outdoor recreation purposes. The growth of our cities, the development of our industry, the expansion of our transportation system—all manifestations of our vigorous and expanding society—preempt irreplaceable lands of natural beauty and unique recreation value. In addition to the enhancement of spiritual, cultural, and physical values resulting from the preservation of these resources, the expenditures for their preservation are sound financial investment. Public acquisition costs can become multiplied and even prohibitive with the passage of time.

> Letter to the President of the Senate, Lyndon B. Johnson, and the Speaker of the House of Representatives, John W. McCormack, on the expansion of outdoor recreation resources, Washington, D.C., Feb. 14, 1963

43 / PROPOSED FEDERAL LAND AND WATER CONSERVATION FUND

The Land and Water Conservation Fund measure I am proposing [transmitted to Congress 2.14.63] will enable the States to play a greater role in our national efforts to improve outdoor recreation opportunities. . . . The Outdoor Recreation Resources Review Commission recommended that the States play the pivotal role in providing for present and future outdoor recreation needs. They face major problems, however, in financing needed outdoor recreation facilities. Accordingly, I am proposing in the Land and Water Conservation Fund a program of grants-in-aid to the States to assist them in their outdoor recreation planning, acquisition and development. The proposed grants-in-aid would be matched by the States and thus serve to stimulate and encourage broad State action.

> *Ibid.*

The Tennessee Valley Authority

44 / TRANSFORMATION

. . . the Tennessee Valley Authority . . . transformed a parched, depressed and flood-ravaged region into a fertile, productive center of industry, science and agriculture.

> Address, Vanderbilt University, Nashville, Tenn., May 18, 1963

45 / THE ACCOMPLISHMENT

No one—no one in Washington and no one in the Tennessee Valley—knew whether this effort could ever overcome the forces of poverty and despair and destruction which had devastated this region for so long. There were many, moreover, who still regarded the whole undertaking with doubt, with scorn or with outright hostility. Some said it couldn't be done. Some said it wouldn't be done. But today, thirty years later, it has been done—and there is still more for TVA to do.

> Address, 30th anniversary of the Tennessee Valley Authority, Muscle Shoals, Ala., May 18, 1963

46 / TOP POWER SYSTEM

TVA, by any objective test, is not only the largest but one of the best managed power systems in the country.

Ibid.

47 / NATIONAL ROLE

As an example of its national roll, I would cite to you the more than 2,000 pilgrims to TVA who come from other lands—the Kings and the Prime Ministers, the students and the technicians—the undecided and the uncommitted who gain here an impression of growth and vitality and concern for human well-being which cannot be matched anywhere else in the world.

Ibid.

48 / SYMBOL OF COOPERATION

TVA . . . stands for cooperation—cooperation between public and private enterprise—between upstream and downstream interests—between those concerned with power and navigation, flood control and recreation —and, above all, cooperation between the Federal Government and the 7 states of this area.

Ibid.

49 / NATIONAL PROBLEM

. . . the conquest of floods and poverty in this valley was not a local or regional problem.

Ibid.

50 / UNIQUE LEGISLATIVE CREATURE

. . . it was only a beginning. For no other Federal Agency has ever tried to combine the power of Government with the flexibility of private enterprise. No other effort had ever been made to fit the patterns of public administration to the comprehensive needs of one valley.

Ibid.

51 / BENEFITS TO STATES BEYOND THE TENNESSEE VALLEY

Flood regulation by the TVA benefits the lower Ohio and Mississippi Valleys as well. Its navigable waterway system has opened up this inland region as a market for 20 states.

Ibid.

52 / SERVES NATIONAL NEEDS

The power lines serving the Atomic Energy Commission at Oak Ridge and the Redstone Arsenal at Huntsville are serving the entire nation.

Ibid.

53 / NEW FRONTIERS FOR TVA

There are those who say that the TVA has finished its job and outlived its challenge. But all of the essential roles of TVA remain, their importance increasing as the importance of this area's atomic energy, military and commercial activities increases. And new opportunities, new frontiers to explore, are opening up every year—including work on the smaller upstream tributaries—reclaiming land scarred by coal strip mining—new types of national recreational areas—and new studies of flood land zoning and planning, to name but a few. In short, the work of TVA will never be over. There will always be new frontiers for it to conquer. For in the minds of men the world over, the initials TVA stand for progress.

Ibid.

15

Space

A New Age: America's Goals

1 / SPACE EXPLORATION

. . . a new age of discovery is opening for the human race . . . an age which may well dwarf the explorations of Columbus, Magellan and Sir Francis Drake.

Address, Democratic Party dinner, Miami Beach, March 10, 1962

2 / TIME FOR LEADERSHIP

It is time . . . for this nation to take a clearly leading role in space achievement, which in many ways may hold the key to our future on earth.

Message to Congress on urgent national needs, May 25, 1961

3 / FREE MEN MUST SHARE

This is not merely a race. Space is open to us now; and our eagerness to share its meaning is not governed by the efforts of others. We go into space because whatever mankind must undertake, free men must fully share.

Ibid.

4 / BASIC OBJECTIVES OF THE SPACE PROGRAM

In the national interest the United States must build the capacity to advance the most modern science and technology to the utmost, and extract from it the wealth of benefits it holds for this country's freedom, economy, professions, education and standard of living.

The defense aspects of this aerospace technology provide the opportunity for performing all such objectives by helping to insure against the possibility that the infinitely promising new dimensions which human ingenuity has opened could be used for economic or military aggression against the free world.

> Annual report to Congress on the National Aeronautics and Space Administration and other government agencies, Jan. 31, 1962

5 / LEADERSHIP'S DEMAND

The exploration of space will go ahead whether we join in it or not, and it is one of the great adventures of all time, and no nation which expects to be the leader of other nations can expect to stay behind in this race for space.

> Address, Rice University, Houston, Sept. 12, 1962

6 / BELKA AND STRELKA

It is, I think, a source of concern to us all that the first dogs carried around in outer space were not named Rover and Fido, but, instead, were named Belka and Strelka.

> Campaign remarks, Muskegon, Mich., Sept. 5, 1960

7 / AMERICA'S TRADITION OF LEADERSHIP

Those who came before us made certain that this country rode the first waves of the industrial revolution, the first waves of modern invention and the first wave of nuclear power. And this generation does not intend to founder in the backwash of the coming age of space. We mean to be a part of it—we mean to lead it.

> Address, Rice University, Houston, Sept. 12, 1962

8 / FOR THE BENEFIT OF MANKIND

Our leadership in science and industry, our hopes for peace and security, our obligations to ourselves as well as others—all require us to make this effort to solve these mysteries, to solve them for the good of all men and to become the world's leading spacefaring nation. We set sail on this new sea because there is new knowledge to be gained and new rights to be won and they must be won and used for the progress of all people. For space science like nuclear science and all technology has no conscience of its own. Whether it will become a force for good or ill depends on man, and only if the United States occupies a position of pre-eminence can we help decide whether this new ocean will be a sea of peace or a new terrifying theatre of war.

I do not say that we should or will go unprotected against the hostile misuse of space any more than we go unprotected against the hostile use of land or sea. But I do say that space can be explored and mastered without feeding the fires of war, without repeating the mistakes that man has made in extending his writ around this globe of ours.

Ibid.

9 / TOSSED CAP

This nation has tossed its cap across the wall of space, and we have no choice but to follow it.

Remarks at dedication of the Aero-Space Medical Health Center, Brooks Air Force Base, Tex., Nov. 21, 1963

Accomplishments and Progress of
the Space Program

10 / THE NEW OCEAN

I know that I express the great happiness and thanksgiving of all of us that Colonel Glenn has completed his trip, and I know that this is particularly felt by Mrs. Glenn and his two children.

A few days ago Colonel Glenn came to the White House and visited me, and he is—as are the other astronauts—the kind of American of whom we are most proud.

Some years ago, as a Marine pilot, he raced the sun across this country—and lost. And today he won.

I also want to say a word for all those who participated with Colonel Glenn in Canaveral. They faced many disappointments and delays—the burdens upon them were great—but they kept their heads and they made a judgment, and I think their judgment has been vindicated.

We have a long way to go in this space race. We started late. But this is the new ocean, and I believe the United States must sail on it and be in a position second to none.

Some months ago I said that I hoped every American would serve his country. Today Colonel Glenn served his, and we all express our thanks to him.

Statement on Col. John H. Glenn, Jr.'s orbital space flight, Washington, D.C., Feb. 20, 1962

11 / THE BEST COMPUTER

I think one of the things which warmed us the most during this flight was the realization that however extraordinary computers may be . . . man is still the most extraordinary computer of all. His judgment, his nerve and the lessons he can learn from experience still make him unique and, therefore, make manned flight necessary.

> Remarks at White House lawn ceremony honoring Maj. Leroy Gordon Cooper, Jr., for 22-orbit space flight (May 15–16), May 21, 1963

12 / THE YEAR 1962 IN UNITED STATES SPACE HISTORY

The year 1962 was a period of acceleration, accomplishment, and relative progress for the United States in its space leadership drive. In both number and complexity of space projects, the past year was the most successful in our brief but active space history. The benefits of our peaceful space program, in both its civilian and military aspects, are becoming increasingly evident. Not only have the horizons of scientific knowledge been lifted, but the resulting international cooperation and worldwide dissemination of knowledge and understanding have strengthened the world image of this country as a force for peace and freedom. The economic benefits of our national space program are also revealing themselves at an increasing rate. These growing space successes have required the support of increasing budgets.

> Message to Congress on space program, Jan. 28, 1963

Mankind's Opportunity for
Peaceful Cooperation

13 / INTERNATIONAL COOPERATION POSSIBLE

There is no strife, no prejudice, no national conflict in outer space as yet. Its hazards are hostile to us all. Its conquest deserves the best of all mankind and its opportunity for peaceful cooperation may never come again.

> Address, Rice University, Houston, Sept. 12, 1962

14 / UNIVERSAL OWNERSHIP

The ocean, the atmosphere and outer space belong not to one nation or to one ideology but to all mankind.

> Address, centennial meeting of the National Academy of Sciences, Washington, D.C., Oct. 22, 1963

15 / UNIVERSAL EFFORT

We believe that when men reach beyond this planet, they should leave
their national differences behind them.

> News conference, Washington, D.C., Feb. 21, 1962

16 / GAINS FOR PEACE THROUGH POSSIBLE SOVIET-AMERICAN SPACE
   PROJECTS

A cooperative Soviet-American effort in space science and exploration
would emphasize the interests that must unite us rather than those that
always divide us. It offers us an area in which the stale and sterile dogmas
of the "cold war" could be literally a quarter of a million miles behind.
And it would remind us on both sides that knowledge, not hate, is the
passkey to the future—that knowledge transcends national antagonisms
—that it is the possession, not of a single class or of a single nation or a
single ideology, but of all mankind.

> Address, Berkeley Division of the University of California, March 23, 1962

17 / PROPOSAL OF U.S.–SOVIET COOPERATION IN SPACE EXPLORATION

The tasks are so challenging, the cost so great, and the risks to the brave
men who engage in space exploration so grave, that we must in all good
conscience try every possibility of sharing these tasks and costs and of
minimizing these risks.

> Letter to Premier Nikita Khrushchev on space cooperation, Washington, D.C.,
> March 17, 1962

18 / ROOM FOR NEW COOPERATION

In a field where the United States and the Soviet Union have a special
capacity—in the field of space—there is room for new cooperation, for
further joint efforts in the regulation and exploration of space. I include
among these possibilities a joint expedition to the moon.

> Address, U.N. General Assembly, Sept. 20, 1963

19 / PEACEFUL USE OF SPACE

As we extend the rule of law on earth, so must we also extend it to man's
new domain: Outer space.

All of us salute the brave cosmonauts of the Soviet Union. The new
horizons of outer space must not be riven by the old bitter concepts of

imperialism and sovereign claims. The old reaches of the universe must not become the new arena of an even colder war. To this end, we shall urge proposals extending the United Nations Charter to the limits of man's exploration in the universe, reserving outer space for peaceful use, prohibiting weapons of mass destruction in space or on celestial bodies, and opening the mysteries and benefits of space to every nation.

Address, U.N. General Assembly, Sept. 25, 1961

16

Freedom's Road

Facing the New Frontier

1 / THE NEW FRONTIER

The pioneers of old gave up their safety, their comfort and sometimes their lives to build a new world here in the West. They were not the captives of their own doubts, the prisoners of their own price tags. Their motto was not "every man for himself"—but "all for the common cause." They were determined to make that new world strong and free, to overcome its hazards and its hardships, to conquer the enemies that threatened from without and within.

   Today some would say that those struggles are all over—that all the horizons have been explored—that all the battles have been won—that there is no longer an American frontier. But I trust that no one in this vast assemblage will agree with those sentiments. For the problems are not all solved and the battles are not all won—and we stand today on the edge of a new frontier—the frontier of the 1960's—a frontier of unknown opportunities and perils—a frontier of unfulfilled hopes and threats.

Acceptance speech, Democratic National Convention, Los Angeles, July 15, 1960

2 / "A SET OF CHALLENGES"

The New Frontier of which I speak is not a set of promises—it is a set of challenges. It sums up not what I intend to offer the American people, but what I intend to ask of them. It appeals to their pride, not their pocketbook—it holds out the promise of more sacrifice instead of more security. But I tell you the New Frontier is here, whether we seek it or not. Beyond that frontier are uncharted seas of science and space, unsolved problems of peace and war, unconquered pockets of ignorance and prejudice, unanswered questions of poverty and surplus.

Ibid.

3 / BID FOR NEW PIONEERS

It would be easier to shrink back from that frontier, to look to the safe mediocrity of the past, to be lulled by good intentions and high rhetoric. . . . But I believe the times demand invention, innovation, imagination, decision. I am asking each of you to be new pioneers on that New Frontier. My call is to the young in heart, regardless of age—to the stout in spirit, regardless of party—to all who respond to the scriptural call: "Be strong and of good courage; be not afraid, neither be thou dismayed."

Ibid.

4 / AVOIDING SELF-DECEPTION

I see no peril, no burden that this country cannot sail through, unless we attempt to fool ourselves that these are easy, gentle, and prosperous times, without responsibility, without burden.

Campaign remarks, Norristown, Pa., Oct. 29, 1960

5 / NATIONAL FIBER

We . . . have no greater asset than the willingness of a free and determined people, through its elected officials, to face all problems frankly and meet all dangers free from panic or fear.

State of the Union Message, Jan. 30, 1961

6 / CALL TO SERVICE

Since this country was founded, each generation of Americans has been summoned to give testimony to its national loyalty. The graves of young Americans who answered the call to service are found around the globe.

Now the trumpet summons us again—not as a call to bear arms, though arms we need; not as a call to battle, though embattled we are; but a call to bear the burden of a long twilight struggle, year in, and year out, "rejoicing in hope, patient in tribulation"—a struggle against the common enemies of man: tyranny, poverty, disease, and war itself.

Can we forge against these enemies a grand and global alliance, North and South, East and West, that can assure a more fruitful life for all mankind?

Inaugural address, Jan. 20, 1961

7 / CALL FOR NEW REVOLUTIONARIES

I have said on many occasions . . . that we stand on the edge of the new frontier, a frontier that will demand of all of us, wherever we may live, in the White House or individual homes, the same qualities of courage and conviction in 1960, for we are going to move, in the next decade, into the most challenging, changing, revolutionary policy, and hazardous decade in the long years of this country, and perhaps in the long history of freedom.

Campaign address, Valley Forge, Pa., Oct. 29, 1960

8 / TURNING POINT

Nineteen hundred and sixty, whether we wish it or not, whether there were an election or not, is a turning point in our history. Either we move with new leadership, new programs, and a new spirit of education, or we stand still and therefore fall back. This is the call of the new frontier.

Campaign address, Anchorage, Alaska, Sept. 3, 1960

9 / COMPLACENCY

We cannot be satisfied with things as they are. We cannot be satisfied to drift, to rest on our oars, to glide over a sea whose depths are shaken by subterranean upheavals.

Campaign address, Syracuse, N.Y., Sept. 29, 1960

10 / ONWARD!

I believe it's important that this country sail, and not lie still in the harbor.

Address to the nation on the economy, Washington, D.C., Aug. 13, 1962

11 / COMMITMENT TO AMERICA'S GOALS

The untapped energies of the American people which are more powerful than the atom itself must once again be committed to great national objectives.

Campaign address, Anchorage, Alaska, Sept. 3, 1960

12 / SELF-SACRIFICE

Ask not what your country can do for you: Ask what you can do for your country.

> Inaugural address, Jan. 20, 1961

13 / OPPORTUNITIES

The Chinese word "crisis" is composed of two characters, one signifying danger and the other signifying opportunity. . . . the new frontiers of 1960's will bring us both danger and opportunities. Our task is to overcome the dangers in order to see the opportunities.

> Campaign address, Valley Forge, Pa., Oct. 29, 1960

14 / TIME OF MATURITY

This is a time of national maturity and understanding and willingness to face issues as they are, not as we would like them to be. It is a test of our ability to be far-seeing and calm, as well as resolute, to keep an eye on both our dangers and our opportunities, and not to be diverted by momentary gains or setbacks, or pressures. . . . We must distinguish the real from the illusory, the long range from the temporary, the significant from the petty. But if we can be purposeful, if we can do our duty undeterred by fanatics or frenzy at home or abroad, then surely peace and freedom can prevail. We shall be neither Red nor dead, but alive and free and worthy of the traditions and responsibilities of . . . the United States of America.

> Address, University of North Carolina, Chapel Hill, Oct. 12, 1961

15 / MEETING THE RESPONSIBILITIES OF OUR TIME

To meet these urgent responsibilities will take determination, and dedication, and hard work. But I believe that America is ready to move from self-indulgence to self-denial. It will take will and effort. But I believe that America is ready to work. It will take vision and boldness. But I believe that America is still bold.

> Address, Franklin D. Roosevelt memorial program on 25th anniversary of signing of Social Security Act, Hyde Park, N.Y., Aug. 14, 1960

16 / EVERY GENERATION'S OBLIGATION

Every generation of Americans must be expected in their time to do their part to maintain freedom for their country and freedom for those associated with it. There is no final victory, but rather all Americans must be always prepared to play their proper part in a difficult and dangerous world.

Address at dedication of war memorial in Battery Park, New York City, May 23, 1963

17 / FOR POSTERITY

Let us all, whether we are public officials or private citizens, Northerners or Southerners, farmers or city dwellers . . . resolve that we, in our time, will build a better nation for "generations yet unborn."

Address, 30th anniversary of the Tennessee Valley Authority, Muscle Shoals, Ala., May 18, 1963

18 / AMERICA'S PROMISE

I believe . . . in the United States of America, in the promise that it contains and has contained throughout our history of producing a society so abundant and creative and so free and responsible that it can not only fulfill the aspirations of its citizens, but serve equally well as a beacon for all mankind.

Acceptance speech, Liberal Party Convention, New York City, Sept. 14, 1960

19 / VISION OF HOPE

I look forward to a great future for America—a future in which our country will match its military strength with our moral restraint, its wealth with our wisdom, its power with our purpose.

I look forward to an America which will not be afraid of grace and beauty, which will protect the beauty of our natural environment, which will preserve the great old American houses and squares and parks of our national past and which will build handsome and balanced cities for our future.

I look forward to an America which will reward achievement in the arts as we reward achievement in business or statecraft.

I look forward to an America which will steadily raise the standards of artistic accomplishment and which will steadily enlarge cultural opportunities for all of our citizens.

And I look forward to an America which commands respect throughout the world not only for its strength but for its civilization as well.

And I look forward to a world which will be safe not only for democracy and diversity but also for personal distinction.

Address, Amherst College, Mass., Oct. 26, 1963

20 / GOOD CONSCIENCE

With a good conscience our only sure reward, with history the final judge of our deeds, let us go forth to lead the land we love, asking His blessing and His help, but knowing that here on earth God's work must truly be our own.

> Inaugural address, Jan. 20, 1961

Brotherhood

21 / UNITY FROM DIVERSITY

Many a great nation has been torn by religious feuds and holy wars—but never the United States of America. For here diversity has led to unity— liberty has led to strength.

> Campaign address, Mormon Tabernacle, Salt Lake City, Sept. 23, 1960

22 / MUTUAL RESPECT

Our nation has been uniquely blessed in the rich and creative diversity of its religious traditions. Each of the major faiths has added brilliantly to the ample spiritual treasures of our country. Despite deeply held convictions, which each creed has about its particular sacred beliefs, we can all, as Americans, join in saying that our very variety has given the world a matchless illustration of the truth that different religious groups can live peacefully and productively together in an atmosphere of mutual respect and understanding.

> Statement on the Jewish High Holy Days, Washington, D.C., Aug. 29, 1960

23 / HARVEST OF FREEDOM

The harvest of freedom in America sprang from the search for religious liberty. To these shores came men and women of all races and all faiths who had tasted the bitter fruits of bigotry and hungered for the bread of freedom.

> Letter to Conference of the National Conference of Christians and Jews, Washington, D.C., Oct. 10, 1960

24 / AT THE ALAMO

Side by side with Bowie and Crockett died McCafferty and Bailey and Carey—but no one knows whether they were Catholics or not. For there was no religious test at the Alamo.

> Campaign address, Greater Houston Ministerial Association, Sept. 12, 1960

25 / SUPREMACY OF MORAL LAW

I have never felt that we should attempt to use the great impulse toward God and religion, which all people feel, as an element in the cold war struggle. Rather, it is not an arm, but the essence of the issue—not in the organization of the economy so much—as the supremacy of the moral law and therefore the right of the individual, his right, to be protected by the state and not be at the mercy of the state.

> Remarks, 46th Biennial General Assembly of the Union of American Hebrew Congregations, Washington, D.C., Nov. 13, 1961

26 / MORAL LEADERSHIP

Our Founding Fathers rose to heights of moral leadership in the world because they understood their own frailties and were humble in the face of man's capacities for goodness and greatness.

> Statement on the Jewish High Holy Days, Washington, D.C., Aug. 29, 1960

27 / SPIRIT OF TOLERANCE

In a world where society is becoming even more close knit—where we rub elbows with our fellows—it is not enough that we have "a government which gives no sanction to bigotry and no assistance to persecution." It is incumbent upon all of us to encourage a spirit of tolerance, not only from Government but from one group within the community toward another. Tolerance implies no lack of commitment to one's own beliefs. Rather, it condemns the oppression or persecution of others.

> Letter to Conference of the National Conference of Christians and Jews, Washington, D.C., Oct. 10, 1960

28 / ACHIEVING TOLERANCE

In achieving this spirit of tolerance throughout the community, the moral leadership of every person and every Government official, including the Chief Executive, must play an important part. It is neither enough to depend upon others to show the way, nor sufficient to allow leadership to rest upon a dedicated few. The moral commitment must be a part of our basic beliefs and our instinctive actions.

> *Ibid.*

29 / FAITH IN FELLOW MAN

Let patriotism be reflected in the creation of confidence rather than crusades of suspicion.

> Address, Democratic Party dinner, Los Angeles, Nov. 18, 1961

30 / "FAITH IN MAN'S ABILITY"

I believe in human dignity as the source of national purpose, in human liberty as the source of national action, and the human heart as the source of national compassion, and in the human mind as the source of our invention and our ideas. It is, I believe, this faith in our fellow citizens as individuals and as people that lies at the heart of the liberal faith, for liberalism is not so much a party creed or a set of fixed platform promises as it is an attitude of mind and heart, a faith in man's ability through the experiences of his reason and judgment to increase for himself and his fellow men the amount of justice and freedom and brotherhood which all human life deserves.

Acceptance speech, Liberal Party Convention, New York City, Sept. 14, 1960

31 / NONSECTARIAN PROBLEMS

War and hunger and ignorance and despair know no religious barriers.

Campaign address, Greater Houston Ministerial Association, Sept. 12, 1960

32 / ESSENCE OF BROTHERHOOD

How may we create a more perfect world community and expand the limits of our present capacity to help our fellow men?

Statement on the Jewish High Holy Days, Washington, D.C., Aug. 29, 1960

33 / MANKIND'S INDIVISIBILITY

The supreme reality of our time is our indivisibility as children of God and the common vulnerability of this planet.

Address to Irish Parliament, Dublin, June 28, 1963

Insights

34 / HERITAGE OF FREEDOM

We dare not forget today that we are the heirs of that first revolution.

Inaugural address, Jan. 20, 1961

35 / LIBERTY'S SENTINEL

The enemy is lean and hungry and the United States is the only strong sentinel at the gate.

Campaign address, Sheraton Park Hotel, Washington, D.C., Sept. 20, 1960

36 / IMMIGRANTS

All Americans are immigrants. Some have come in more recent years than others.

Campaign remarks, Overseas Press Club, New York City, Aug. 5, 1960

37 / ORIGINS

Most of us are descended from that segment of the American population which was once called an immigrant minority. Today, along with our children and grandchildren, we do not feel minor. We feel proud of our origins and we are not second to any group in our sense of national purpose.

Acceptance speech, Liberal Party Convention, New York City, Sept. 14, 1960

38 / SURVIVAL

We believe that our society is the best, but that does not mean that it automatically survives.

Campaign remarks, University of Southern California, Los Angeles, Nov. 1, 1960

39 / MAINTAINING OUR STRENGTH

We are a great and strong country—perhaps the greatest and strongest in the history of the world. But greatness and strength are not our natural rights. They are not gifts which are automatically ours forever. It took toil and courage and determination to build this country—and it will take those same qualities if we are to maintain it. For, although a country may stand still, history never stands still.

Campaign address, Raleigh, N.C., Sept. 17, 1960

40 / SELF-RESTRAINT

Liberty calls for certain qualities of self-restraint and character which go with self-government.

Campaign address, Shrine Auditorium, Los Angeles, Sept. 9, 1960

41 / LIMITS TO FREEDOM IN A DEMOCRACY

Every time a regulation is promulgated, a custom is accepted, or an agreement is reached, the complete freedom that exists under a state of anarchy is circumscribed to some degree. But this is a fundamental aspect of civilization. Men agree among themselves to limit their unrestricted "freedom" in some field in order to achieve some other goal that is highly valued. Thus, we impose traffic regulations over the behavior of automobile drivers to help realize the goal of staying alive, and we impose educational regulations on families and children because we believe that literacy is essential to the functioning of modern society.

> Campaign statement: "Agricultural Policy for the New Frontier," Washington, D.C., Oct. 9, 1960

42 / POLITICAL SERVICE

I think we serve this country, and our party serves this country, when we tell the truth, when we present the facts, honestly and clearly, and give the American people an opportunity to make their judgment.

> Campaign remarks, Paducah, Ky., Oct. 8, 1960

43 / ASTONISHING PROFESSION

Politics is an astonishing profession. It has permitted me to go from being an obscure lieutenant under General MacArthur to Commander in Chief in fourteen years.

> Address, National Football Foundation dinner, New York City, Dec. 5, 1961

44 / LOCAL EFFORT

I do not believe that Washington should do for the people what they can do for themselves through local and private effort.

> Campaign address, Associated Business Publications Conference, New York City, Oct. 12, 1960

45 / VOLUNTARY EFFORT

I do not favor state compulsion when voluntary individual effort can do the job and do it well.

> Acceptance speech, Liberal Party Convention, New York City, Sept. 14, 1960

46 / THE PEOPLE'S NEED

The Federal Government is the people and the budget is a reflection of their need.

> Address, American Society of Newspaper Editors, Washington, D.C., April 19, 1963

47 / GOVERNMENT SPENDING TEST

The true test is: Are we spending the least amount that is consistent with our necessary national goals?

  Address to the nation on the economy, Washington, D.C., Aug. 13, 1962

48 / INFORMATION AND SURVIVAL OF FREEDOM

The whole history of the world, from the struggle of the Athenians against the Macedonians, to the experience of the British before World War II, in their competition with the Nazis, all show that for a free society to survive, to successfully compete, the leaders have to tell the truth. They have to be informed. They have to share their information with the people.

  Campaign remarks, University of Southern California, Los Angeles, Nov. 1, 1960

49 / PRIMARY FUNCTION OF OUR FREE PRESS

Without debate, without criticism, no Administration and no country can succeed—and no republic can survive. . . . that is why our press was protected by the First Amendment—the only business in America specifically protected by the Constitution—not primarily to amuse and entertain, not to emphasize the trivial and the sentimental, not to simply "give the public what it wants"—but to inform, to arouse, to reflect, to state our dangers and our opportunities, to indicate our crises and our choices, to lead, mold, educate and sometimes even anger public opinion.

  Address, American Newspaper Publishers Association, New York City, April 27, 1961

50 / FREE PRESS INTEGRITY TEST: APPLICABLE TO ALL GROUPS

Every newspaper now asks itself, with respect to every story: "Is it news?" All I suggest is that you add the question: "Is it in the interest of the national security?" And I hope that every group in America—unions and businessmen and public officials at every level—will ask the same question of their endeavors, and subject their actions to the same exacting test.

  Ibid.

51 / THE PEOPLE'S JUDGMENT

We hold the view that the people make the best judgment in the long run.

  Campaign remarks, rally, Greensboro, N.C., Sept. 17, 1960

52 / TIME OF NATIONAL DECISION

A political campaign, I think, should be more than just a contest between two men or two political parties. In a very real sense, it should be a time of decision for the nation.

> Campaign remarks, Pat Clancy Dinner, Astor Hotel, New York City, Oct. 20, 1960

53 / DAILY CHORE

Democracy must be a daily way of life.

> Address at dinner given by President Antonio Segni of Italy, Rome, July 1, 1963

54 / "PURSUIT OF HAPPINESS"

The writers of the Declaration of Independence did not promise us happiness—they promised only the "pursuit of happiness"—and by this they meant fulfillment as a nation and as human beings. It is this pursuit —this endless questing—which we must now resume. There are new problems, new dangers, new horizons—and we have rested long enough. The world is changing—the perils are deepening—the irresistible march of history moves forward. We must now take the leadership in that great march—or be forever left behind.

> Address, Franklin D. Roosevelt memorial program on 25th anniversary of signing of Social Security Act, Hyde Park, N.Y., Aug. 14, 1960

55 / SIMPLE TIMES GONE

The world is full of contradictions and confusion, and our policy seems to have lost the black and white clarity of simpler times when we remembered the Maine and went to war.

> Address, Mormon Tabernacle, Salt Lake City, Sept. 26, 1963

56 / IRREVERSIBLE CHANGE

We cannot return to the day of the sailing schooner or the covered wagon, even if we wished. And if this nation is to survive and succeed in the real world of today, we must acknowledge the realities of the world.
> *Ibid.*

57 / CONFRONTING REALITY

As every past generation has had to disenthrall itself from an inheritance of truisms and stereotypes, so in our time we must move on from the reassuring repetition of stale phrases to a new, difficult but essential confrontation with reality. For the great enemy of the truth is very often not the lie—deliberate, contrived and dishonest—but the myth—persistent, persuasive and unrealistic. Too often we hold fast to the clichés of our forebears. We enjoy the comfort of opinion without the discomfort of thought . . . we cannot understand and attack our contemporary problems in 1962 if we are bound by traditional labels and worn-out slogans of an earlier era.

    Commencement address, Yale University, New Haven, June 11, 1962

58 / UNENDING TASK

Democracy is never a final achievement. It is a call to untiring effort, to continual sacrifice and to the willingness, if necessary, to die in its defense.

    Address at El Bosque housing project, San José, Costa Rica, March 19, 1963

59 / DEMOCRACY'S GOAL

The ideal of full employment, in the large sense that each individual shall become all that he is capable of becoming, and shall contribute fully to the well-being of the nation even as he fully shares in that well-being, is at the heart of our democratic belief.

    Manpower report to Congress, March 11, 1963

60 / EQUALITY

There is no place for second-class citizenship in America.

    Campaign statement to Chinese-American citizens, Hyannis, Mass., Aug. 6, 1960

61 / AID FOR AMERICAN INDIANS

Indians have heard fine words and promises long enough. . . . In pledging assistance to American Indians we are offering them new opportunities not only as Americans of Indian descent, but as American citizens who, through no fault of their own, have not had these opportunities until now.

    Campaign letter to Oliver La Farge, President, Association of American Indian Affairs, Washington, D.C., Oct. 28, 1960

62 / HERE ON EARTH

I am concerned with what is on the other side of the moon, but I am also concerned . . . with the condition or life of the man or woman on the other side of the street.

    Campaign address, National Conference on Constitutional Rights and American Freedom, New York City, Oct. 12, 1960

63 / MEASURE OF RESPONSIBILITY

All Americans must be responsible citizens—but some must be more responsible than others, by virtue of their public or their private position, their role in the family or community, their prospects for the future or their legacy from the past. Increased responsibility goes with increased ability—for of those to whom much is given, much is required.

Address, Vanderbilt University, Nashville, Tenn., May 18, 1963

64 / A SLIPPAGE

There has . . . been a change—a slippage—in our intellectual and moral strength. . . . A dry rot . . . is seeping into every corner of America —in the payola mentality, the expense account way of life, the confusion between what is legal and what is right. Too many Americans have lost their way, their will and their sense of historic purpose.

Acceptance speech, Democratic National Convention, Los Angeles, July 15, 1960

65 / EXPENSE-ACCOUNT LIVING

Expense-account living has become a byword in the American scene . . . the time has come when our tax laws should cease their encouragement of luxury spending as a charge on the Federal treasury. The slogan—"It's deductible"—should pass from our scene.

Message to Congress on taxes, April 20, 1961

66 / MORALITY LAGGING

Morality in private business has not been sufficiently spurred by morality in public business.

State of the Union Message, Jan. 30, 1961

67 / SOUL SEARCHING

Setting aside a specific season of the year for candid soul searching and for a hard look at the gap between what we aspire to achieve and our own meager attainments is a spiritually fruitful device.

Statement on the Jewish High Holy Days, Washington, D.C., Aug. 29, 1960

68 / VISION

We should be blind neither to our basic strength nor to our basic problems.

Address, National Association of Manufacturers, New York City, Dec. 6, 1961

69 / NATIONAL SELF-INTEREST

We must recognize that every nation determines its policies in terms of its own interests.

Address, Mormon Tabernacle, Salt Lake City, Sept. 26, 1963

70 / THE LONG VIEW

I sometimes think we are too much impressed by the clamor of daily events. The newspaper headlines and the television screens give us a short view. They so flood us with the stop-press detail of daily stories that we lose sight of . . . the great movements of history. Yet it is the profound tendencies of history, and not the passing excitements, that will shape our future.

Address, Berkeley Division of the University of California, March 23, 1962

71 / NATIONAL PRESTIGE

Prestige is not popularity. Prestige is the image which you give of a vital society which persuades other people to follow our leadership.

Campaign remarks, Elgin, Ill., Oct. 25, 1960

72 / FOREIGN RELATIONS

The knowledge of foreign languages, the knowledge of foreign cultures, the knowledge of foreign history, is really the most important asset that we, as a nation, have in our relations with countries abroad.

Campaign remarks, Overseas Press Club, New York City, Aug. 5, 1960

73 / BUSINESS OPPORTUNITIES ABROAD

. . . for almost any American business, life can begin anew at the ocean's edge.

Remarks, White House Conference on Export Expansion, Sept. 17, 1963

74 / AMERICAN ESTEEM FOR THE RUSSIAN PEOPLE

As Americans, we find Communism profoundly repugnant as a negation of personal freedom and dignity. But we can still hail the Russian people for their many achievements—in science and space, in economic and industrial growth, in culture and in acts of courage.

Commencement address, American University, Washington, D.C., June 10, 1963

75 / NATIONAL INITIATIVE

Our goal is to influence history instead of merely observing it.

> Campaign address, Democratic Women's luncheon, New York City, Sept. 14, 1960

76 / NATIONAL ETHIC

A nation reveals itself not only by the men it produces but also by the men it honors, the men it remembers.

> Address, Amherst College, Mass., Oct. 26, 1963

77 / THE QUESTIONING MIND

The men who create power make an indispensable contribution to the nation's greatness. But the men who question power make a contribution just as indispensable, especially when that questioning is disinterested. For they determine whether we use power or power uses us.

> *Ibid.*

78 / ART IN DEMOCRACY

In free society art is not a weapon and it does not belong to the sphere of polemics and ideology. Artists are not engineers of the soul. It may be different elsewhere. But democratic society—in it—the highest duty of the writer, the composer, the artist is to remain true to himself and to let the chips fall where they may.

> *Ibid.*

79 / DISCIPLINE

I know that there is some feeling by Americans that the arts are developed in solitude, that they are developed by inspiration and by sudden fits of genius. But the fact of the matter is that success comes in music or in the arts like success comes in every other form of human endeavor—by hard work, by discipline, over a long period of time.

> Remarks at a youth concert, White House lawn, Aug. 6, 1962

80 / INEQUITY

There is always inequity in life. Some men are killed in war and some men are wounded, and some men never leave the country, and some are stationed in the Antarctic and some are stationed in San Francisco. It's very hard in military or in personal life to assure complete equality. Life is unfair.

> Remarks on the plaints of army reservists recalled to duty, news conference, Washington, D.C., March 21, 1962

81 / PARENTAL RESPONSIBILITY

We are very much concerned with that area. . . . But this is a matter which goes to the responsibility of the private citizen. The Federal Government cannot protect the standards of young boys or girls—the parents have to do it, in the first place. We can only play a very supplemental role and a marginal role. . . . It rests with the families involved—with the parents involved.

> Statement on protecting the young from the effect of crime and violence in moving pictures and in television and radio programs, news conference, Washington, D.C., Feb. 1, 1961

82 / CORPORAL PUNISHMENT OF SCHOOL CHILDREN OPPOSED

I think when we talk about corporal punishment, we have to think about our own children. We are rather reluctant to see other people administering punishment to our own children. Because we are reluctant, it puts a special obligation on us to maintain order and to send children out from our homes who accept the idea of discipline. So I would not be for corporal punishment in the school, but I would be for very strong discipline at home so that we don't place an unfair burden on our teachers.

> News conference, Washington, D.C., May 22, 1963

83 / LEISURE TIME

With the coming of automation, the expansion of the labor force, the extension of the lifelines of each individual, the speed of modern communication and transportation, all contribute to the amount of time that each American will have for himself and his family. . . . If we permit our lives individually to decline so that leisure time becomes a burden rather than an opportunity, quite obviously we have lost more than we have gained.

> Campaign address, Valley Forge, Pa., Oct. 29, 1960

84 / IMPORTANCE OF OUR HIGHWAY SYSTEM

Our highway system is important because of our needs of defense, safety, and economic growth. In case of defense emergency, a good system of highways would be necessary for quick movement of goods and munitions. Meanwhile, some 40,000 people a year lose their lives in automobile accidents, partially because of inadequate highways, and we must act to reduce this loss of life. In addition, we must have a highway system adequate for our needs if the United States is to have a strong and expanding economy. Poor highways increase the cost of transportation, and all Americans benefit from better roads.

> Campaign statement answering question in written interview, *Highway Highlights* (Sept.–Oct. 1960 issue)

85 / HIGHWAY SAFETY

Better, more modern highways—with less congestion, fewer dangerous curves and intersections, more careful grades and all the rest—mean greater highway safety. It has been estimated that more fatalities will be suffered in traffic accidents between now and 1975, when the new system is fully operative, than were suffered by American troops in every conflict from the Civil War through Korea.

> Message to Congress on the Federal highway program, Feb. 28, 1961

Shafts of Light and Wisdom

86 / QUEST FOR LIGHT

We are not here to curse the darkness, but to light the candle that can guide us through that darkness to a safe and sane future.

> Acceptance speech, Democratic National Convention, Los Angeles, July 15, 1960

87 / THE ONE CERTAINTY

Every area of trouble gives out a ray of hope, and the one unchangeable certainty is that nothing is certain or unchangeable.

> State of the Union Message, Jan. 11, 1962

88 / EACH GENERATION'S TASK

It is the task of every generation to build a road for the next generation.

> Address, ILGWU cooperative houses dedication, New York City, May 19, 1962

89 / QUICK-CHANGING SCENE

Today there can be no status quo.

> Acceptance speech, Democratic National Convention, Los Angeles, July 15, 1960

90 / CHANGE

Change is the law of life. And those who look only to the past or the present are certain to miss the future.

Address, Paulskirche, Frankfurt, West Germany, June 25, 1963

91 / DISSENT

. . . we greet healthy controversy as the hallmark of healthy change.

State of the Union Message, Jan. 30, 1961

92 / HISTORY'S LESSONS

The only significance of analyzing the past is that it does give us some key to the future.

Campaign address, Pocatello, Idaho, Sept. 6, 1960

93 / PERSPECTIVE

We celebrate the past to awaken the future.

Address, Franklin D. Roosevelt memorial program on 25th anniversary of signing of Social Security Act, Hyde Park, N.Y., Aug. 14, 1960

94 / ENTERPRISE

Things do not happen. They are made to happen.

Ceremony at site of projected San Luis Dam, Los Banos, Calif., Aug. 18, 1962

95 / TIME

We must use time as a tool, not as a couch.

Address, National Association of Manufacturers, New York City, Dec. 6, 1961

96 / STRENGTH

Words are not a substitute for strength.

Campaign address, American Legion Convention, Miami Beach, Oct. 18, 1960

97 / CIVILITY AND SINCERITY

Civility is not a sign of weakness, and sincerity is always subject to proof.

Inaugural address, Jan. 20, 1961

98 / LEADERSHIP AND LEARNING

Leadership and learning are indispensable to each other.

Text of undelivered Dallas address, Nov. 22, 1963

99 / INTERNATIONAL COLLABORATION

No one can doubt that cooperation in the pursuit of knowledge must lead to the freedom of the mind and freedom of the soul.

Address, Berkeley Division of the University of California, March 23, 1962

100 / PURPOSE

Effort and courage are not enough without purpose and direction.

Campaign address, Raleigh, N.C., Sept. 17, 1960

101 / JUSTICE

The achievement of justice is an endless process.

Address at dinner given by President Antonio Segni of Italy, Rome, July 1, 1963

102 / BLIGHT IN "RANDOM VILLAGE"

Neither injustice nor crime nor disease nor slums can be confined to one group in the village.

Address, American Society of Newspaper Editors, Washington, D.C., April 19, 1963

103 / ART PROCLAIMS TRUTH

Art establishes the basic human truths which must serve as the touchstones of our judgment.

Address, Amherst College, Mass., Oct. 26, 1963

104 / FREEDOM AND ART

You have to be a free man to be a great artist.

Remarks, dedication of marker at grave of Ignace Jan Paderewski, Arlington, Va., May 9, 1963

105 / THE USES OF POETRY

When power leads man toward arrogance, poetry reminds him of his limitations. When power narrows the areas of man's concern, poetry reminds him of the richness and diversity of his existence. When power corrupts, poetry cleanses.

Address, Amherst College, Mass., Oct. 26, 1963

Index

Note: Numbers in index refer to chapter number and item number, not to page number.

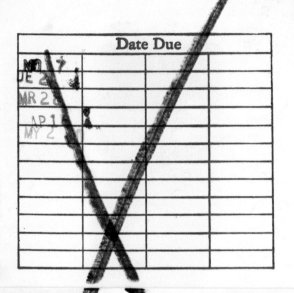